Women Writing About Men

Women Writing About Men

Jane Miller

Pantheon Books
New York

All rights reserved under International and Pan-American
Copyright Conventions. First published in the United States by
Pantheon Books, a division of Random House, Inc.,
New York. Originally published in Great Britain by
Virago Press, Limited, London

Library of Congress Cataloging-in-Publication Data
Miller, Jane, 1932–
    Women writing about men.

    Bibliography: p.
    Includes index.
        1. English fiction – Women authors – history
    and criticism.   2. Men in literature.
    3. American fiction – Women as authors –
    History and criticism.   4. Women – Books and
    reading.   I. Title.
    PR830.M45M55   1986   823'.008'09287
    85-25907
    ISBN 0-394-74425-X

Manufactured in Great Britain.
First American Edition.

Contents

Introduction 1

1 Men in their Wisdom 11

2 Fathers and Gentlemen 46

3 Brothers 77

4 Sons 103

5 Heroes 134

6 Another Story 163

7 Resisting the Bullies 195

8 Women's Men 227

Notes 265

The Writers and their Works 291

Selected Bibliography 295

Index 305

In memory of Tony White

Acknowledgements

A term's leave from the University of London Institute of Education made it possible to complete this book, and I want to thank my colleagues for letting me have it and for their support. I also want to thank Tony Burgess and students on the MA course for their encouragement and tolerance in hearing me out on the subject of this book. Too many people have had their ears bent by me during the last few years. I cannot list them all, though I do thank them. Amongst those on whose friendship, company and conversation I have depended are Shyama Iyer, Jean Jones, Christian McEwen, Rachel Miller, Jonathan Miller, Gemma Moss, Naomi Roberts, Harold Rosen, Carolyn Steedman, Mary Taubman, Emma Tennant and Halim Thomas. I have also to record a whole lifetime of gratitude to my parents, Ruth and Bob Collet. I expect Georgia, Sam, Daniel and Karl Miller will find themselves somewhere in the book. They will bring their well-developed critical senses to bear on that presence as they have on so much else. This book is for them. It could not have been written without their affection, loyalty and scepticism. I owe a special debt to my editor, Ursula Owen, for her faith in the project and her patience. From my daughter Georgia I have received twenty-one years of wit and understanding and, more recently and importantly, help with proof-reading. Thanks finally to Sharon Gratton and Christina Pulle for always being calm, efficient and friendly.

Earlier versions of the sections on Alexandra Kollontai, on Dorothy Richardson and on Christina Stead first appeared in the *London Review of Books*. I would like to thank that paper's editors for permission to use some of that material.

Thanks as well to Alice Walker and The Women's Press for permission to quote from *The Color Purple*, and to Geoffrey Thurley's Oasis Books for permission to quote from his translation of a poem by Anna Akhmatova in *White Flock*.

Introduction

Women have been excluded by the vagaries of the communal 'we' which can seem to include them. If they lurk, as they do, within 'human beings' or even 'men', it is as men's daughters and wives and mothers and sisters, or even, deceptively, as people just like men, as good as men. It is the sharing – however unequally and ambiguously – of culture and language and values which has made a women's 'we' so hard to assert. Women who dare to do so, to claim particular experiences, dilemmas, qualities or vision as peculiar to, even common to, women, have needed to contend with their own objections as well as with men's. Labelled and tucked into men's defining inclusions of them, women are hard put to know where they begin and end. They will have learned their own wariness of arguments and generalisations mounted on the personal and the idiosyncratic. Yet a bypassing of their own inhibitions in this respect is enjoined on them by the character of their relation to men and to men's culture. They have had to return to their personal knowledge in order to explain what it is that they recognise in other women's lives and why that recognition is important. Recognition is the beginning of an understanding of women's relations with men and of the effect on women's identity of their participation in a male and dominantly heterosexual culture.

This is a book about novels by women and about the men in them. It is also a book about women reading and the sense they may come to make of other women's accounts of the world. Its focus is the novel as a form which women writers have used to question and challenge men's appropriation of women's experience. Its organisation and its themes follow and attempt to enact my own history as a woman and as a reader through novels written by women from the early nineteenth century to the present day. I shall get closer to my starting point with an example from my own reading. It is one which characterises an aspect of my realisation that I was simultaneously included and excluded by men as a reader of literature. I first read T. S. Eliot's *Journey of the Magi* at school. Four lines of it have remained with me.

At the end we preferred to travel all night,
Sleeping in snatches,
With the voices singing in our ears, saying
That this was all folly.

I have thought of those voices of Eliot's 'singing in our ears' as men's voices, and as the kind of men's voices which women have learned to impersonate and to hear as uneasily duplicated and echoed by the sounds of their own. I also know myself to be excluded from the poem's 'we', even as I accept the invitation of the poem and of its narrator to understand his story as a human one, to which I have access. A central theme of this book will be that women readers are so used to confusions of that kind and to the androgyny they encourage and depend on that they may read women's writing in the same way and fail to see that women have necessarily written out of that very ambiguity.

Novels are stories, and stories are organised to avoid the response 'So what?' If they are not replete with beginnings and complications, with resolutions and endings and values and a time sequence, we know that we are being played with, even tested. A culture is its stories, and it is always significant that some people tell stories and other people listen to them. The challenge for women who have told stories and written novels has revolved around their right to assert as a story and as an adventure events, and the living of them, which the culture allows for and yet excludes from being representatively human. So long as the ending, the completion, of a woman's story is marriage to a man, a woman's adventure will not be a man's adventure. Its time scale will be different, for a woman's adventure will occupy only a small strip of her life, when she is very young. It will test her and put her through her paces; but the proceedings, like the outcome, will be circumscribed by the conventions of the society she inhabits, which will figure in her adventure as protagonists bent above all on controlling what she can tell and how.

I shall want to suggest that most women's novels are engaged at some level in extricating their authors as well as their heroines from charges of abnormality. If marriage is the 'normal' ending to a woman's adventure and the necessary completion of a woman's existence, circumstances which deflect a woman from or deny her that outcome, deservedly or not, may be read as unfortunate if not perverse. That characterisation is too simple, of course, for writers from Maria Edgeworth onwards have found ways to divert that trajectory and even to propose alternative time scales and alternative endings. But they have often done so allusively, obliquely and with circumspection. If events leading to a marriage constitute the form of the novel about women, that form determines the heroine's future as well as the terms and the terrain of her scope for heroic or admirable behaviour. What a heroine can know of her future must be winnowed out of her experience to date, and that will throw her back to models of men, of marriage and of family life drawn from her childhood. The prospects of marriage to a man are prefigured by her childhood roles, and many of her adult relationships with men will carry aspects of those earlier relations – as a daughter or a sister of men, or from memories of a mother who was also, perhaps, a mother of sons – and may resemble them.

The men in women's novels are not just men, but men seen from a woman's perspective. That is an essential perspective – and it is often ignored or misunderstood – because it can supply us with an outsider's vision of a culture. My book will be a disappointment, I expect, for anyone hoping for a gallery neatly hung with the portraits women have painted of men. I have wanted to show that men are to be found in women's novels as they are to be found in women's heads and histories: equivocally. They arc ourselves, our protectors, our representatives and our opponents.

For in controlling our needs and our natures and our vision they become deaf to our stories the more finely tuned we become to theirs. Theirs, but also ours, are 'the voices singing in our ears', and I have not wanted to expel them, beguiling and misleading though they have often been. They will be heard singing here, as readers and as relatives, as critics and as theorists, as novelists and as standard bearers of all that is true and excellent and withheld. They are also men as women have seen and known and articulated them within fictions which both match and collide with the fictions of men. No more than other women do those women who have written novels speak for all women. It may be, though, that women who read and write a good deal have heard men's voices more insistently than other women, and have had to improvise all the more ringingly and decisively the descants which might – for a time at least – drown them out.

The book has several somewhat wavering chronologies to it, but it does not go quite as the crow flies. If I begin with Jane Austen and end in the 1980s that is only part of the story. For I have wanted to set my own development as a reader alongside changes in women's novels over the last two hundred years. The inter-weaving of those two histories may well be thought to have landed me with some arbitrary choices of novels and even more arbitrary approaches to them.

I begin with questions. They are questions which, as a woman and as a reader, I have gradually come to see as essential, if tentative, starting points for an understanding of the relation of women writers and readers to the traditions of the novel and to critical discourse about novels. The questions which emerge from what I want to characterise as a learned androgyny are about that androgyny and about how women writers and readers have dealt with their sense of being impersonators, outsiders masquerading as insiders. I make analogies between that experience and bilingualism and immigration, in order to explore both the strengths of women's perspectives and the source and nature of particular fears in women writers. They are fears about writing, about love, about ignorance and about morality. Women's dependence on men can isolate them from each other, and that isolation has bred distrust of their own judgement and authority.

Women who have moved, individually and collectively, towards what they would want to see as feminist understandings of sexual and social relations have needed to start then, as I have suggested, from what they know in their own lives. That personal knowledge is potentially political knowledge, though it may be pre-political in the sense of being untheorised and ungeneralised, embedded still in women's peculiar isolation. I have wanted, as I moved from readings of Jane Austen to readings of some contemporary novelists, to represent that shift as multi-dimensional for both readers and writers. There is, first, the shift from accommodations and angers produced by the narrow perspectives available to women of a particular class and place and time to analyses of sexual relations, as sites of oppression and conflict within social arrangements founded on class and race antagonisms. There is then the shift lived by individual women, and by individual women readers, away from doubleness, ambivalence, uneasiness about an identity defined by what it is not and always in some sort of relation to what it is not, towards more confident assertions. Another version of that shift is from the preoccupations of novelists like Jane Austen, the Brontës and George Eliot with the sexual inequities of family life to a concern with the sources and the implications of those inequities. There is, finally, a shift from an uncomfortable acceptance of the novel form as an apt mode of expression for a woman's vision to the beginnings of resistance to and a critique of narrative itself as embodying assumptions which are inimical to women's language and experience.

So, from a first chapter of questions, speculation and hypotheses issuing from what I have, uncandidly, called pre-political experience, I move to novels in which women have tackled the prospect of marriage to a man in terms of what a woman could know about men. Chapter 2 deals with Jane Austen's treatment of fathers – gentlemen and figures of authority in her novels – who present her heroines with ambiguous models of male worth and ambiguous messages about the prospects of happiness in marriage and the relation of women to the class of their fathers and their husbands. I grew up without brothers and with a strong sense that I was not alone in looking, probably in vain, for a brother as the only possible mate. It is for that reason that I have discussed this theme in Chapter 3 in terms of the phantom or surrogate brother in the novels of the Brontës rather than through a novel like George Eliot's *The Mill on the Floss*, where a real brother–sister relationship occupies the centre of the story. Women have not often written about the relation of a mother to her son, perhaps because that stands for the most painful clash between a culture's stories about a woman and her own stories about herself. In Chapter 4, I have looked at the way Rebecca West and George Eliot tackled the subject.

These chapters on fathers and brothers and sons could be said to present limiting cases, in the sense that all three themes are to be found in many other women's novels, and Jane Austen, the Brontës and George Eliot could easily be approached through alternative relationships between women and men. There were several reasons for beginning in this way. One is that authority, doubleness and creativity are central ideas of the work of, respectively, Jane Austen, the Brontës and George Eliot, and those ideas are partly carried by the presence in the novels of fathers and brothers and sons. Another reason is that these are all writers I have returned to at different stages of my life, when I have cast myself in my reading as a daughter, a sister, a wife or a mother.

By Chapter 5, which is about the discrepancy between men's heroes and women's heroes, I have become less guarded as a reader and less covert in my plans to develop a feminist theory of reading and of writing which is both political and necessarily and wilfully eclectic. As I return to some of the same authors and look at some new ones, marriage has by now dissolved as a consummation with equivalent meanings for men and for women, and romance and pornography come to be seen as gendered fantasies about power. In Chapter 6, I return to the novel as a form, to narrative and to Dorothy Richardson's novel about the possibilities of a new voice and a new logic to match the bisexuality of women's experience. In Chapter 7, I follow five twentieth-century novelists and chart the development from a feminist anger cited still within the injustices of family life to a politics which sees sexual relations on a continuum with other forms of mutilating oppression. In the last chapter I take up this theme in relation to several American writers who are Black or working-class or, as in the case of Maxine Hong Kingston, members of a racial minority. They are writers who are able to make essential links between class and race oppression and the oppression of women, and they allow me to try for a tentative synthesis of recent feminist theorising about women's relations with men.

A last autobiographical note. As a teacher, my concern during the last ten years or so has been with the experiences of bilingual children in school and with the place of literature in the curriculum. Those might well be thought to be 'educational issues' of quite a specialised kind. Yet this book has grown out of those concerns and out of the questions they pose. The questions are about culture, about language and about how we have all learned to read literature. Children are not invited to become readers by stories which neglect their lives and their knowledge. Emerson must have meant something like that when he wrote about his reading of history: 'The fact narrated must correspond to something in me to be credible or intelligible.'[1] We do not find ourselves in books, but we do expect to be able to make our way in them as experienced storytellers of our own lives. What kinds of effort of thinking and feeling are we requiring of children when we ask them to read? I have come to feel implicated in that question, and not just as a teacher. For women's relation to culture, to reading, and indeed to education, poses a similar question.

Men have invited us into their stories, their literature and into their ways of reading it. Many of us have accepted the invitation. Yet once in, gratitude can turn to dismay. For the invitation has often turned out to be a demonstration of our exclusion from stories and from understandings of them. Because some women have done it all *as if* they were men, even *as well as* men, the problem has been shelved. Yet for many of us there could be the unnerving and even debilitating discovery of ourselves as out-siders, as immigrants or dependants, or, at best, as a kind of bargain or 'free gift'. I shall want to argue, however, that a recognition of that exclusion has not been disabling. Far from it. Seeing it for what it is has felt for some of us like a miraculous rescue, performed in the nick of time.

That rescue was performed for me about fifteen years ago when I first read Dorothy Richardson, having come across one volume of her work on the shelf marked 'Travel' in an extremely small library in Scotland. *Pilgrimage* has been very important to me. Never before had I been so interested by anything I had read. Yet I was also often maddened by it and by its author, beadily aware that she could sometimes be boring and 'bad'. I found that I needed to ponder the interest I had in her and to consider why I could read this utterly divided writer with such utterly divided feelings about her. Knowing her, as by now I feel I do, I would expect her rather tetchily to reprove me for the simple-minded way in which I learned to be a feminist from reading her novels. For she was never simple-minded or single-minded or ready to deliver herself of easy solutions. She explored and she registered dividedness; and from her I learned to recognise my own dividedness and to discover it in other writers. For dividedness is one of the things women have in common; that and not being men. Moreover, they have felt that dividedness and expressed it in terms of their relation to men. Poets and novelists have said it better than I can. Angela Carter, for instance, in that conjuring trick of a novel, *The Passion of New Eve*, makes her hero-turned-heroine say it like this:

This intensive study of feminine manners, as well as my everyday work about the homestead, kept me in a state of permanent exhaustion. I was tense and preoccupied; although I was a woman, I was now also passing for a woman, but then, many women born spend their whole lives in just such imitations.[2]

Adrienne Rich gives another version of that dividedness, more plaintively perhaps, but also in a way which many women are bound to recognise:

The phantom of the man-who-would-understand,
the lost brother, the twin –

for him did we leave our mothers,
deny our sisters, over and over?[3]

Virginia Woolf knew all too well that she was wrong when she went to the British Museum to look up everything that men had written about women and then found that

Women do not write books about men – a fact that I could not help welcoming with relief, for if I had first to read all that men have written about women, then all that women have written about men, the aloe that flowers once in a hundred years would flower twice before I could set pen to paper.[4]

She was wrong, as she knew, because women have always written about men, but they have needed to be extremely circumspect about doing so. To read as a woman is to confront that circumspection as a mode of being and a kind of language, which can be powerfully subversive and potentially revolutionary.

In considering how women have written about men I have needed to allude, often too glancingly, to debates within the women's movement and, more particularly, within feminist discussion of literary criticism and literary theory. In some cases the notes at the end of the book will give, as well as sources, more detail about these arguments. The notes represent at least, as does the bibliography, the background reading which has been essential to me and which may be useful to readers.

I

Men in their Wisdom

Women always know their questions are insincere, a treachery towards their silent knowledge.

Dorothy Richardson[1]

I shall start with questions, some of them insincere, most of them treacherous and too many of them unanswerable. They will be questions about reading and about writing and questions about women and about men. They will issue, as women's questions must, from the doubleness of my own experience – what I have come to think of as a learned androgyny – and though they will be innocently posed they will also be the questions of an imposter, a practised liar, schooled to a double vision and bilingualism. I shall look for answers to my questions in the novels women have written during the last two hundred years, and because I am necessarily disingenuous I shall ask how women have written about men. Most feminist discussion of women's novels has concentrated on the women in them, and it is not surprising that in doing so it has needed to focus on a good deal of silence and subterfuge in its search for the material of female experience there. Can women know whether other women even experience their lives *as women's lives* when the very questions they ask echo double-voiced and two-faced out of all those stories told about women which are not quite the ones they tell about themselves. Even to ask what women are, to wonder whether they are more or less or different from men's views of them, can hurtle us into that language of polarities which has for so long prevented women from penetrating their own confusions. For instance, can a woman be innocently a woman as she reads, or as she writes?

Imagine. A young mother is suckling her son. As he wriggles from her into sudden, heavy sleep, milk spurts from her breast and on to the pages of Volume VII of Proust's *A la Recherche du Temps Perdu*. She dabs the book with a muslin napkin, buttons herself, reads on, while her son sleeps. She is an obedient woman, a mother, a cleaner, an androgynous reader. When her son is older and has learned rhythmically to beat his custard-cream biscuit on the tray of his high chair, she steals moments to follow Saint-Loup with his regiment or the Baron de Charlus sidling past the concierge.

That story is my story. It is the story of a woman who has learned from stories how to be a mother as well as how to be a reader. It is also the beginning of the story of this book, for the woman who read Proust as she fed her son could also, and effortlessly, transform herself into the drummer boy of Saint Loup's regiment, a catamite for the Baron or even the concierge. She knew her place. This chapter will explore that place as novelists and critics have described it. It will deal in duplicity and circumspection and it will attempt to map the terrain on which women's fictions overlap with their lives.

   Of course, I too want to hear what women writers have been telling us about women. I am almost certain, though, that it will be easier to know what this is if we first attend to what they have distinguished as male. That will not be simple either, for it will seem at times like the whole world, or at least everything that is significant and serious in it. Even the language we use to think about ourselves can feel borrowed from men and explosive. We inch ourselves more warily still into the language of novels and the language for writing about them. Courage. We are, after all, bilingual. We might remember how Kafka described his sense of writers like himself moving into German, the language of the powerful, 'boisterously or secretively or even masochistically appropriating foreign capital that they had not earned but, having hurriedly seized it, stolen'.[2]

   Men's presence in women's novels reflects and challenges their presence in women's lives and heads. They are there, of course, as brothers and lovers, as husbands and fathers, occasionally even as sons. They are there as priests and teachers and masters and doctors and artists and employers and seducers. Sometimes they are there as God. They are there to allow women to be women and as dispensers and withholders of approval and money and motherhood itself. If women have not always found it easy to write about them that is because men are also quite often not there. Indeed, for much of women's history men were not there when they were doing the serious and significant things for which women could not but defer to them. All that learning and fighting and hunting and judging and governing has usually gone on when men were somewhere else. So that it has not just been difficult for women to write about men, but risky. They could get it wrong, and women have reason to dread the penalties for getting such things wrong.

Men have not, though, been present in women's novels simply as characters, in tweeds or surplices, in loin-cloths or epaulettes. They have been there, palpably, as novelists, as critics and as readers. For if, as Virginia Woolf wrote, 'we think back through our mothers if we are women',[3] a woman writer unavoidably, as Elaine Showalter puts it, 'thinks back through her fathers as well.'[4] Here, for instance, is Conrad, unavoidably present in Dorothy Richardson's novel *Pilgrimage*, as one of the 'fathers' she must confront in creating what I shall want to suggest is the first explicitly feminist novel:

Even God would enjoy reading *Typhoon*. Then *that* is 'great fiction'? 'Creation'? Why these falsifying words, making writers look cut off and mysterious? *Imagination.* What is imagination? It always seems insulting, belittling, both to the writer and to life. He looked and listened with his whole self – perhaps he is a small pale invalid – and then came 'stalked about gigantically' . . . not made, nor created, nor begotten, but *proceeding* . . . and working his salvation. That is what matters to him. In the day of judgment, though he is a writer, he will be absolved. Those he has redeemed will be there to shout for him. But he will still have to go to purgatory; or be born again as a woman. *Why* come forward suddenly, in the midst of a story, to say they live far from reality? A sudden smooth complacent male voice, making your attention rock between the live text and the picture of a supercilious lounging form, slippers, a pipe, other men sitting round, and then the phrase so smooth and good that it almost compels belief. Why cannot men exist without thinking themselves all there is?[5]

We will hear more of that bafflement and rage as women read themselves into men's stories and withdraw, disappointed to find themselves excluded from them or traduced within them. They will recognise that invitation to join with men in the excitements of literature as the beguiling treacheries of fathers and of brothers.

Men are present in women's novels as their inspiration, as favoured rivals and as makers and sons of the tradition. They are there as the tellers and the heroes of all the great human adventures, of Oedipus, of Ulysses, of King Lear. Women will sometimes have been consoled, because if the great human adventures are men's adventures they are also tragic ones and full of effort. Yet to read as a cheerfully accurate and modest disclaimer about her work Jane Austen's famous little bit of ivory (two inches wide), on which she works 'with so fine a Brush, as produces little effect after much labour',[6] is to ignore her bitterness that so much labour must necessarily be spent on the exiguous and only life she knew. Behind that remark are the traditions of narrative: the quests, the challenges and changes, the achievements, the intrusions and the resolutions: 'The big Bow-Wow strain I can do myself like any now going,'[7] as Scott put it. Women are often there in men's adventures, as milestones, booty, civilising comforts and rewards. Yet in Jane Austen's *Northanger Abbey*, Catherine Morland's life's adventure occupies the months between her seventeenth and eighteenth birthdays. When women have wanted to enter stories as themselves they have needed to change and to resist the very terms of adventure, to subvert its expectations of achievement and of moral growth, even of heroism. They have needed to assert new time scales, mark out new terrains, match their own heroines to men's.

Women carry men in themselves, as sons, as values, as judges. They have learned to impersonate men in most of their manifestations, if not all, and they have even had painfully to imagine sons at that moment when young men escape from the only woman who has any power over them in order to try out their power over other women. Lady Murasaki wrote *The Tale of Genji* at the beginning of the eleventh century in Japan. Here is part of a long conversation in which two teenage boys, Prince Genji and his friend, consider their experience of women so far and what they need to beware of:

'No, let us not worry too much about rank and beauty. Let us be satisfied if a woman is not too demanding and eccentric. It is best to settle on a quiet, steady girl. If she proves to have an unusual talent and discrimination – well, count them an unexpected premium. Do not, on the other hand, worry too much about remedying her defects. If she seems steady and not given to tantrums, then the charms will emerge of their own accord.

'There are those who display a womanly reticence to the world, as if they had never heard of complaining. They seem utterly calm. And then when their thoughts are too much for them they leave behind the most horrendous notes, the most flamboyant poems, the sort of keepsakes certain to call up dreadful memories, and off they go into the mountains or to some remote seashore. When I was a child I would hear the women reading romantic stories, and I would join them in their sniffling and think it all very sad, all very profound and moving. Now I am afraid that it suggests certain pretenses.'[8]

Maria Edgeworth's first novel for adults, *Castle Rackrent*, is a story told by 'an illiterate old steward', Quirk, about men reduced to bestiality through, it might be said, their contemptuous treatment of women. Charlotte Brontë's first novel, *The Professor*, has William Crimsworth telling his own story. Manly tricks with his lapels, his often announced scorn for womanly behaviour and his capacity to meet it 'stony cold and hard' may well merit charges of bad acting. There is no question that *Villette*, which tells a similar story from a woman's point of view, is a far better novel. Yet that awkward male mimicking illuminates some of the questions Charlotte Brontë makes her heroine ask about men in the later novel.

It would certainly not be true to suggest, however, that male impersonation adequately describes what women have been up to when they created men in their novels. They have sometimes needed men in their books in order to contemplate women through men's eyes. They have also wanted and needed to know what men know, to live as men live, to set their own destinies and development hypothetically within male bodies and lives. George Eliot lives at least as much through Daniel Deronda as through Gwendolen Harleth; and F. W. H. Myers tells the story of a visitor asking G. H. Lewes, with whom George Eliot lived, whether Casaubon in *Middlemarch* was based on him. Lewes laughingly denied that he was, and the visitor turned to George Eliot as, 'with a humorous solemnity, which was quite in earnest, nevertheless, she pointed to her own heart'.[9]

Women have usually taken their role as 'the other half' quite literally, so that they have doubted their own vision as too narrow, thought their own knowledge ignorance, veered from their own judgement as distorted. When Ronald Blythe blithely remarks that 'He (the reader) sees everything with Emma's eyes but has to judge it by Mr Knightley's standards'[10] he is saying no more than many, if not most, women novelists were implying. Consider simply the problem for women who write novels of making their heroines serious artists. Many have taste and some have talent. Helen Graham in *The Tenant of Wildfell Hall* actually sells her paintings, and Mirah Lapidoth in *Daniel Deronda* sings for a living. Yet for most of the time, women who have written novels have transposed their own talent and learning and wisdom to men, while creating women who must learn to be satisfied, modestly and unenviously, to bask in their warmth. Constrained both by a need to make their heroines appeal to men and by a desire to understand, or seem to understand, men's eccentric tastes in women, they have often needed to deny the realities they know: dedication and hard work, loneliness and childlessness.

It would be wrong to expect women's attitudes to gender to be realised simply through the actions and the relationships of male and female characters in their novels. Gender, anyway, has symbolic meanings as well as material and historical ones. Those symbolic meanings, which lurk as a rule within oppositions and dichotomies, are not always equivalent to the 'women's concerns, or concerns about women'[11] which a novel may enact. Gender will, as it were, be argued out within individuals, male and female, as well as between them, just as the interplay between realism and romance or fairy tale in a novelist like Jane Austen will overlap with, but never straightforwardly reflect, the conflict for women between men's life possibilities and their own. I shall want to show, for instance, that romantic love can be for women novelists more than a beguiling game. It can also become a weapon for short-circuiting the inexorable male destiny.

I have said that women are bilingual, and I shall return to this. All women who read and write, and that certainly includes women who read and write about literature, have learned to do those things as if they were men. It should also be said that the traditions of written discourse have always (and with varying degrees of deliberateness) excluded most of the human race, and that for all those demanding entry to the terrain a new and second language must be learned. Bilingualism can be an asset (as I have argued elsewhere[12] and will want to reaffirm here), but its acquisition involves splits and instabilities, impersonation, a stepping out of yourself. We can expect double vision and shifting ground in the novels of women. We shall need to hold to notions of dividedness, even as we consider the more straightforward ways in which women have written about men.

In the eighteenth and early nineteenth centuries the difficulty for women lay not simply in their exclusion from those institutions which supported, disseminated and judged literature: education, publishing and criticism; nor in their exclusion from those written forms which buttressed the establishment of professionalism for writers, whether of sermons or scholarship, history or philosophy, science or plays or poetry. Graver impediments were the limitations on women's social experience and those male perceptions of their powers and place, which women were usually obliged to concede. Had they, indeed, anything to write about? And if they had, could they meet male standards in doing so?

The novel was a latecomer and has been seen as a response to and a reflection of the rise of the bourgeoisie in the eighteenth century, to changes in family life and in women's lives. At an early stage women entered the lists as novelists as well as heroines and readers, and before long there were even a few women publishers and editors.[13] Still denied higher education, entry into the professions and involvement in public life, the novel was a way for a few women to make money and was potentially a form which might contain their sense of the world they inhabited. For most of those few, however, it meant the storming of a male citadel, and they often wore men's clothes and used men's names to do so. They were also careful to avoid charges of unfeminine 'coarseness' or to expose themselves as ignorant of men's lives. The novel could seem a welcoming genre for women writers, a capacious invitation to explore family life and everyday minutiae from a woman's point of view. Yet few of the writers I shall be discussing ignored the dangers of that invitation, with its assumptions of women's place and the finality of marriage and childbirth for them. The novel had to be stormed too, made to yield up its infinite disguises, its tricky realisms, its undisclosed intentions.

Women who invade male territory may feel exhilaration. They are also afraid. Disguised perfunctorily as men, they find themselves, colonials or provincials in the metropolis, confronted by their own lives and natures, their desires and bodies, as they have been defined and described by men. If women cannot justly be regarded as conspiring with men's oppression of them, they have certainly not found it easy to tackle men's determinations of them in quite the same language that men have used to colonise them. Dependence, like a colony, is maintained through fear; and fear is a state of being and a central theme in women's novels, which has rarely been confronted for what it is, by men or women readers. For that fear causes fear and occasions blame. It has even been seen as a conciliatory or dismissive gesture made by strong women who write novels on behalf of their weaker sisters.[14] More recently, scrutiny of the centrality of fear in women's novels has been blinkered by subsuming it into a fear which all women must have of men, as perpetrators of rape and violence against them.

One way of looking at women's fear is as an immigrant's fear, the disorientation of anyone who leaves the place where they were born, its people and its language, to enter a foreign country alone. The roots of the self-sufficiency and courage which might impel a young man to leave Bangladesh for London must be severed, the sources of the strength he gathered to demand a new life and learn a new language cut off. That man's bedrock of expectations about the world, effortlessly garnered in childhood, is allowed to seem worthless even as a provisional model for learning to understand a new one, and mastering a new one appears to entail the abandoning or even the desecration of the old.[15] An exhilarated discovering of power must strenuously resist its undermining by feelings of loss, damage and danger. Without conscious and vigilant resistance the immigrant is particularly prey to the myths and pieties of the host community.

There is a sense in which women are immigrants for most of their lives. As they move towards maturity they leave their mothers, those containers and deliverers of double messages, who have more or less prepared them for the realities of their grown-up lives, and enter a world in which men will allow them to be women. Women, of course, have been prepared for that, have learned at least something about what they are not. Their mothers will have taught them to trust themselves to men whom they must also distrust. That moment is, in most literature about women, their adventure, the brief period when the practical and moral choices they make will determine their futures and register their human calibre. It is not a man's adventure. Yet women have listened to the legends and the stories which measure human achievement quite differently. They have felt very much as Jane Austen must have felt when she wrote: 'I have read the Corsair, mended my petticoat, & have nothing else to do.'[16]

In their magnificent exposure of the themes and the imagery of nineteenth-century women writers, Sandra Gilbert and Susan Gubar want us to understand that 'the one plot that seems to be concealed in most of the nineteenth-century literature by women . . . is in some sense a story of the woman writer's quest for her own story; it is the story, in other words, of the woman's quest for self-definition.'[17] In undertaking to explore that adventure, however, women have needed to insert themselves into a discourse, a language, a story, which they have learned from men and which has given them clear instructions about who they are. 'The greater part of what women write about women is mere sycophancy to men', wrote John Stuart Mill, out of his terrible benevolence, and 'All women who write are pupils of the great male writers.'[18] The lessons women learn from those great writers involve them in doubt and doubleness, in translation and rewriting. They learn that they are muses and not writers, heroines and not heroes, sought but not seekers. They will learn that women can be powerful, as angels or as witches, but they will not learn from men how to speak out of such power.

Let us pause to consider androgyny and the possibility that women have been schooled in androgyny. Any such notion must be permeable, for they have also been schooled to be women and to be women for men. They must avoid mannishness and monstrousness, they must keep their cool. Yet women readers who have unlearned their androgyny, or have at least started on the process, become attuned to the expression of danger and of fear in women writers. They learn to recognise fear about writing as a fear about love. Daniel Deronda's mother has defied her father and his Judaism to become a great artist. She has been torn by a conflict between her determination that she is an artist and her knowledge that in being one she has lost her father's love and probably her son's too. 'Every woman,' she tells her son, 'is supposed to have the same set of motives, or else to be a monster. I am not a monster, but I have not felt exactly what other women feel – or say they feel, for fear of being thought unlike others.'[19] That was George Eliot's dilemma. She did not as a rule express it in terms of art or motherhood. Gwendolen Harleth is not an artist, yet there is a sense in which her dilemma is the same. She recognises that she is a woman who must use her beauty to live a life which might be better than her mother's, happier. 'I will not be told that I am what women always are',[20] she declares at the triumphant peak of her adventure, when she is beginning to glimpse the dangers of trusting to men's interest in possessing her for her beauty and courage. She has temporarily forgotten her first public display of apparently irrational terror:

She wondered at herself in these occasional experiences, which seemed like a brief remembered madness, an unexplained exception from her normal life; and in this instance she felt a peculiar vexation that her helpless fear had shown itself, not, as usual, in solitude, but in well-lit company. Her ideal was to be daring in speech and reckless in braving dangers, both moral and physical; and though her practice fell far behind her ideal, this shortcoming seemed to be due to the pettiness of circumstances, the narrow theatre which life offers to a girl of twenty, who cannot conceive herself as anything else than a lady, or as in any position which would lack the tribute of respect. She had no permanent consciousness of other fetters, or of more spiritual restraints, having always disliked whatever was presented to her under the name of religion, in the same way that some people dislike arithmetic and accounts: it had raised no other emotion in her, no alarm, no longing; so that the question whether she believed it had not occurred to her, any more than it had occurred to her to inquire into the conditions of colonial property and banking, on which, as she had had many opportunities of knowing, the family fortune was dependent. All these facts about herself she would have been ready to admit, and even, more or less indirectly, to state. What she unwillingly recognised, and would have been glad for others to be unaware of, was that liability of hers to fits of spiritual dread, though this fountain of awe within her had not found its way into connection with the religion taught her or with any human relations. She was ashamed and frightened, as at what might happen again, in remembering her tremor on suddenly feeling herself alone, when, for example, she was walking without companionship and there came some rapid change in the light. Solitude in any wide scene impressed her with an undefined feeling of immeasurable existence aloof from her, in the midst of which she was helplessly incapable of asserting herself.[21]

At the height of her youth and self-confidence Gwendolen is still chiefly concerned to hide her terror rather than listen to it. It may be seen as a subconscious fear of sex and of men. George Eliot associates that terror with Gwendolen's averting her eyes from money and banking, from religion and morality. She makes fear a matter of solitude and agoraphobia, of dislocation and an incapacity to connect her own experience with other people's. Later, Gwendolen will discover that this terror is the theme, the parameter and the very ether of her adventure, and it will be compounded by the damage she has done to her mother, to her sisters, to her husband's mistress. In casting herself out of a woman's world she has lost love and she has made herself utterly alone in a man's world. It is no wonder that she looks for love and rescue to the epicene Daniel Deronda. That too is part of a pattern in women's novels. If for some of the time women writers bestow men's heroes on their heroines, they just as often present women who look for love from a man like Daniel Deronda, who has the 'deepest interest in the fates of women', or a man like Mr Rochester, who can see in Jane Eyre his 'equal', even 'his likeness'.

What is it to unlearn androgyny? What is it, indeed, to insist that George Eliot has to be read as a woman writing, even while admitting that she herself must have wanted and expected to be read as a man by men? It is likely, anyway, that great imaginative artists of both sexes have sometimes written out of fundamental dualities and contradictions in their lives, which they could embody and explore in their work. For the rest of us it is harder. Let me give an example. When I first read F. R. Leavis on George Eliot in *The Great Tradition* more than twenty-five years ago I do not believe that I was impressed in any way by the fact that he had included two women writers in his small canon of 'great' novelists:

two women and two immigrants, in fact. I may have been like many others of his readers in wanting to argue with his exclusions and his inclusions, and even with his emphatic assurance that such sorting out was the principal job of the critic. I certainly wanted to argue with his plans for amputating Daniel Deronda from a novel which would henceforth be known as *Gwendolen Harleth*. Now I find myself having to make sense of four remarks (and there are many more like them) in the essay[22] and, of course, having to confront the reasons for my failure to dispute them twenty-five years ago.

The first starts from a discussion of *Silas Marner*:

It is indeed remarkable that a woman should have been able to present so convincingly an exclusively masculine *milieu*. It is the more remarkable when we recall the deplorable Bob Jakin of *The Mill on the Floss*, who is so obviously and embarrassingly a feminine product.

The second is about *Middlemarch*:

The honours go easily to Mary, who, her antithesis, may be said to offset her in the representation of her sex; for Mary is equally real. She is equally a woman's creation too, and equally feminine; but femininity in her is wholly admirable . . . she might be said to represent George Eliot's ideal of femininity – she certainly represents a great deal of George Eliot's own characteristic strength.

The third and fourth passages come from the section of the essay dealing with *Daniel Deronda*:

(for the relation between the Victorian intellectual and the very feminine woman in her is not the simple antithesis her critics seem commonly to suppose)

and

The kind of satisfaction she finds in imagining her hero, Deronda (if he can be said to be imagined), doesn't need analysis. He, decidedly, is a woman's creation.

The first sentence of the first passage might, just, on its own, be taken to suggest that it was remarkable that a woman could describe a masculine *milieu* at all, since she probably knew very little about them. Such a generous reading is undermined by the second sentence, where Bob Jakin, a rustic Just William, is 'embarrassingly a feminine product'. There is no excuse here for George Eliot and none for Leavis either. There was no reason why George Eliot should have particular difficulties with boys or men of this kind. Her failure is an embarrassing one because it reveals her weakness, which is feminine, and is remarkable because she could, remarkably, sometimes pull off male creations.

The second passage has this double-edged quality too. Femininity is allied to strength and to George Eliot's strength. She may even, as a woman, have advantages in writing about women. When, however, it comes to adjudicating between the right sort of woman and the wrong sort George Eliot becomes a man for Leavis, someone who is capable of a detachment from her own identity as a woman. She has enough of a woman and enough of a man in her to distinguish between admirable and unadmirable femininity (and the 'but' alerts us to that being a more usual phenomenon), indeed to have an 'ideal of femininity', much as Leavis himself might have had an 'ideal of masculinity'!

Leavis may seem to be in the clear in the third passage. His denial of any 'simple' antithesis in George Eliot between the Victorian intellectual and the very feminine woman in her is disarming. We will not, of course, have any difficulty in agreeing as to what a *very* feminine woman would be, since, by implication, it will not ordinarily include being a Victorian intellectual. Since it is anyway not a 'simple' antithesis it is probably just a complex antithesis, not worth going into, though it is exactly the kind of antithesis George Eliot lived with and wrote about.

The fourth passage needs little unpicking either. Its assumption that Daniel Deronda was a disastrous creation is one I shall want to consider later. The conviction that that disastrousness could only have been perpetrated by a woman makes all clear: when George Eliot is good she is as good as a man and occasionally better for being an exceptional man, i.e. a woman. When she is bad it is because she is a woman. Her badness is easily detectable by men because it is peculiarly apparent when she is writing about men. Remarkably, however, that is not always the case.

The attribution and the cherishing of bisexuality carries predictable confusions and inequalities between men and women. There are those who applaud bisexuality in men, while drawing back from the implications of bisexuality in women. For instance, in her essay, 'Hate, Greed and Aggression', the psychoanalyst Joan Riviere is anxious to console women with men's envy and emulation of them:

Men's desire for female functions comes openly to expression in painters and writers, who feel they give birth to their works like a woman in labour after long pregnancy. All artists, in whatever medium, in fact work largely through the feminine side of their personalities; this is because works of art are essentially formed and created inside the mind of the maker, and are hardly at all dependent on external circumstances.[23]

In that scenario it is the female in men which accounts for the artist in them, though it is the female in women which accounts for the artist which is not in them. Men even make off with wombs. The very organ which contains what women *may* produce becomes the instrument of men's creativity. 'They want it for themselves, of course,' as Angela Carter says,

But not, of course, a real one, with all the mess and inconvenience that goes with it. The womb is an imaginative locale and has an imaginative location far away from my belly, beyond my flesh, beyond my house, beyond this city, this society, this economic structure – it lies in an area of psychic metaphysiology suggesting such an anterior primacy of the womb that our poor dissecting tools of reason blunt on its magnitude before they can even start on the job.[24]

The hidden imbalance in the way metaphors of that kind are used is characteristic of the ambiguities with which women live.

I have not chosen Leavis's essay because it is a spectacular example of the muddled and patronising approach to their work which all women writers have expected and dreaded as their due. On the contrary. The essay is one which George Eliot could not but have found flattering and illuminating. There have, after all, been men who supposed that George Eliot must have enlisted the help of George Lewes in order to write *Adam Bede*. Leavis had reason to respect the energy of intelligent and creative women. The interest for me of his essay has two aspects. The first is that in its particular confusions it represents, in a comparatively mild form, the reason why women writers and women readers have needed to develop androgynous sensibilities. They have digested notions of exceptional women as fearful beings, who might be unfeminine 'monsters'. The masculinity of exceptional men is not, as a rule, impugned. The second has more to do with men's perceptions than with women's. When John Stuart Mill enunciated the impeccable sentiment, 'we are perpetually told that women are better than men, by those who are totally opposed to treating them as if they were as good',[25] he may not have been as far from Leavis's position as all that. He too felt that 'exceptional' women needed explaining, given the general state of their sex, and he too could only measure women's achievements in relation to men's. However, his association of women's liberation with general human progress at least signalled, as Leavis did not, that comparison between men and women was always and inevitably political. His book, *The Subjection of Women*, came out eighty years before Leavis's *The Great Tradition*.

Nearly forty years on, and it is hard to see changes in men's critical approaches as they affect women writers and readers as more than cosmetic. Wayne Booth has delivered a welcome *mea culpa*,[26] which implicates as well as himself the resurrected Russian critic Bakhtin, and by inference a line of traditional critics and innovative theorists; and Terry Eagleton ends his *Literary Theory*[27] with a vague but hearty affirmation of feminist theory as the hope for the future, since it is inevitably political. I shall be drawing on feminist discussion of particular authors and works in later chapters. At this stage I should like to mention the work of Elaine Showalter,[28] whose *A Literature of Their Own* and more recent essays have always combined a sense of the need for a feminist theory which is historical and cultural, with an honest facing up to the complexities of talking about anything as 'feminine'. With wit and wariness she has insisted on the dangers for feminist thinking of snatching whatever comes to hand from philosophies or psychologies which are not in the business of addressing women's issues at all, are not even in the business of considering the relation of literature to the real lives of most human beings. It was she who reminded us, for instance, that hermeneutics was actually 'hismeneutics' and warned that Lacanian theory might better be spelled 'Lackanian' in so far as it provides an explanation of the forming of female identity. Yet Showalter would not be surprised, I suspect, to find one of her admirers ignoring her counsel from time to time in order to listen to men who believe they speak for us all.

In an essay which helps us to read Charlotte Brontë through our own doubleness as women readers, Mary Jacobus finely sets out the agenda for a feminist criticism:

And what of the feminist critic? Isn't she in the same position as Charlotte Brontë, the writer, and her character, Lucy Snowe? – bound, if she's to gain both a living and a hearing, to install herself within the prevailing conventions of academic literary criticism. To this extent, hers must also be an ex-centric text, a displacement into criticism of the hunger, rebellion and rage which make Lucy an estranged image of self. Constituted within conditions essentially unchanged since those of Mary Wollstonecraft and Charlotte Brontë (i.e. patriarchy) and experiencing similar contradictions within herself and society, the feminist critic faces the same disjunction – removed, however, to the disjunction between literary response and critical discourse. The novel itself becomes the discourse of the Other, making its presence felt in the distortions and mutilations of critical selectivity (*Vashti*, *The Nun*, *Feminism and Romanticism*). What strategy remains, beyond unsettling the illusory objectivity of criticism? Surely also to unfold a novel whose very repressions become an eloquent testimony to imaginative freedom, whose ruptures provide access to a double text, and whose doubles animate, as well as haunt, the fiction they trouble. In the last resort, the buried letter of Romanticism and the phantom of feminism both owe their uncanny power to their subterranean and unacknowledged presence – to repression itself, the subject of Charlotte Brontë's most haunting novel (*Villette*), and fiction's special reserve.[29]

That agenda, with its expectations of dislocation and contradiction, certainly underlies my own. Just as women readers bring their own learned doubleness to the novels they read, so those novels can be seen to contain a new and secret life of division, repression and resistance.

The men in women's novels may reflect the shadowy and admonishing figures outside them, absorbed and internalised by women who, as they write, shuck off their own apparent invisibility. For women are not and have never been invisible, and reading their stories reminds us that notions of women's simply being stubbed out or rubbed out by men are inadequate, unhistorical, uncritical and reductive. They leave us with a ghostly and eternal Punch and Judy show, which begs questions about the sex and the purpose of the puppeteer. The problem is not invisibility, rather it is isolation. For women have been allowed to have in common only the fact that they are not men. We have been unarmed by what we are not and consequently faced by division, negativity and isolation when we consider who we are. No woman feels able to speak for all women, for as Viviane Forrester has put it:

We don't know what women's vision is. What do women's eyes see? How do they carve, invent, decipher the world? I don't know. I know my own vision, the vision of one woman, but the world seen through the eyes of others? I only know what men's eyes see.[30]

Slowly things are changing. We begin to recognise one another, to winnow out evidence of secret resistances and invasions. Sometimes those secret and coded signals are more exciting than the boldest declarations of mutiny, for they alert us to the kinds of accommodation women have made to their subordination and to the privacies and the powers they have snatched for themselves. We can begin to understand what they have made of the myths and stories which reduce them and which they retell with subtle differences. It has so often been in their own interests for women to accept, or seem to accept, the constraints put on them, as due to their natural inferiority, that they have not found it easy to deny the part they have played themselves in maintaining those determinations, which they have felt as oppressive and yet needed to welcome as inevitable and secure.

Sandra Gilbert and Susan Gubar have seen the preoccupations of women novelists in the nineteenth century with doubles, schizophrenia and madness as symptoms of what they call women's 'dis-ease'. *Diseases* too: hysteria, claustrophobia, agoraphobia, anorexia are allowed by them to be women's diseases in so far as they are responses to the restrictions and confinements of the lives out of which many women have written. It is all too easy to be persuaded as well as moved by Gilbert and Gubar's analysis of women's writing in terms of pathologies confronted or evaded but expressed as symptoms of anger and pain, injuriously controlled. I want to assume that doubleness and estrangement *are* characteristic of much of the writing I shall be looking at, though I shall want, in the end, to see those conditions less as ailments, symptoms of a pathology, than as a kind of experience which has enabled women to ally themselves with the majority of human beings, 'outsiders' too, who have struggled with the distorting and diminishing identities they have been required to live with.

A criticism which assumes the doubleness of women, their doubleness as readers and the contradictions embodied in women's writing could not be forged in isolation. Reading and writing are social practices, learned within a culture which produces individual and sexed identities. To deny that biological differences between the sexes explain the particular ways in which societies have marked and asserted those differences is not, of course, to deny that there are such differences. There are differences – there might even turn out to be differences of which human beings have so far been quite unaware – but they do not in themselves dictate who shall fight or cook, who shall wear skirts or preach from pulpits. That is social, cultural, historical.

Individuals become who they are historically, within the discourses of their own culture, or as George Eliot put it in *Middlemarch*, 'we all of us, grave or light, get our thoughts entangled in metaphors, and act fatally on the strength of them'.[31] Metaphors work by indirection, and women's entanglement in them is infinitely layered and snagged through their ambiguous relations to caste and class, to economic power and productivity, to men. There can be no understanding of the relations between men and women which ignores those other relations; the ones which carry the ways in which power is won and held within a particular society. The subordination of women and their consent or resistance to that subordination has to be seen alongside other forms of subordination, as continuous with them and illuminating of them.

Yet we still need to look at the perceptions women have had of the social arrangements organising their submission as specifically *women's perceptions*. Listening to women helps us to listen to other misheard or unheard groups and immigrants. It would be a mistake, though, to allow what women are saying to be subsumed once again within a voice or a chorus of voices which encourages a new version of the old deafness to women's speech.

For instance, in an essay which develops a critique of ethnocentrism in literary and cultural studies, Edward Said adds 'and women' to 'men' to indicate 'people', and yet fails to see that in his argument about cultural imperialism (and specifically the imperialism of Western culture over Eastern) he evades the issue of women's relation to *any* culture by suggesting casually that by tagging them on to men they become men. Yet the irony of that is that his account of the way in which dominant cultures maintain themselves is highly relevant to the argument I shall want to put, and I quote a short passage from his essay in the knowledge that I am doing what we all do when we make use of an argument offered by a man, who ignores its implications for women: asking for trouble:

in the transmission and persistence of a culture there is a continual process of reinforcement, by which the hegemonic culture will add to itself the prerogatives given it by its sense of national identity, its power as an implement, ally, or branch of the State, its rightness, its exterior forms and assertions of itself, and, most important, by its vindicated power as a victor over everything not itself.[32]

It is becoming possible to recover from nineteenth-century novels by women evidence of anger, frustration and argument with the ways in which their lives and their writing have been appropriated and judged by men and with the difficulty women have had in articulating their objections to such appropriation. That has been effected, as I shall want to show in later chapters, by a growing awareness by women writers of the political implications of their experience and their accounts of it. Projecting women's problems as apolitical, as personal and untheorised, has made women vulnerable to kinds of masculine political analysis, whether reactionary or revolutionary, which subsume women's concerns into more general ones, concealing their specificity and ignoring women's accounts of them. That awareness was always incipiently there, but in England, at least, it took writers like Jean Rhys, Christina Stead and Doris Lessing, who came to British culture from colonial variants of it, to show that sexual relations and their inequities were continuous with others forms of social relationship and depended on assumptions underlying imperialism and capitalism in both the societies they knew. It is significant that such understandings were first most clearly articulated by women who felt themselves to be outsiders in European societies and who were also trailed here by the anomalous entanglements of colonial worlds, where they had been born amongst white settlers. A less political outsider was Katherine Mansfield, who used her New Zealand childhood as an imaginative alternative to the limitations on her as an adult woman in Europe, without quite avoiding the blandishments of European superiority and snobberies.

Insights of the kind we get from Doris Lessing, for instance, were difficult, perhaps impossible, ones for women writers in the nineteenth century, not because they were insensitive to broader issues of injustice and inequality than the ones which affected them, but because the effect of those social evils on the position of

women was to divide them from each other and to encourage
them to seek refuge with men. This meant that women writers
were bound to submit themselves to men's views of them as
women and as writers to a greater or lesser degree. We would be
mistaken in looking to Jane Austen or Charlotte Brontë or
Elizabeth Gaskell or George Eliot for social or political analysis of
a kind to allow us to claim them as early, or inadvertent, feminists
or socialists, and even Harriet Martineau is not helpfully understood by anachronistic categorising of that sort. That does not
mean that we will not find in the work of these marvellous writers
evidence of resistance and criticism and of innovative thinking
and ways of feeling. We are bound to start, though, from the books
these women wrote and from what they can tell us about the
resources each writer had at her disposal for living and writing in a
society which implicitly and explicitly, and very uncomfortably,
defined her as abnormal.

So why does Jane Austen emerge from Virginia Woolf's *A Room of
One's Own* as exemplary?

Here was a woman about the year 1800 writing without hate, without
bitterness, without fear, without protest, without preaching. That was
how Shakespeare wrote, I thought, looking at *Antony and Cleopatra*; and
when people compare Shakespeare and Jane Austen, they may mean
that the minds of both had consumed all impediments; and for that
reason we do not know Jane Austen and we do not know Shakespeare,
and for that reason Jane Austen pervades every word that she wrote,
and so does Shakespeare.[33]

That is not an unfamiliar position; though it is an uneasy one to
arrive at in the middle of Virginia Woolf's witty, shrewd and often
angry polemic about the problems faced by women writers in her
own time and earlier. It can be, indeed has been, peremptorily
dismissed on several grounds: as rooted in a decadent theory of
art, in which works are seamlessly 'virtual'[34] rather than part of a
cultural practice, as redolent of classical aspirations and patrician
poise and, more recently, for its

tone of a woman almost in touch with her anger, who is determined not to appear angry, who is *willing* herself to be calm, detached, and even charming in a roomful of men where things have been said which are attacks on her very integrity.[35]

Jane Austen can certainly be baffling. Can any woman reading her feel absolutely sure that she is not hearing a cynical, witty, even frivolous voice adjuring a very young woman to settle for what is possible, to forget her own and other women's need for time, space, privacy, independence and scope for creativity? Do we really go on enjoying her because she has 'consumed all impediments'? Is there really no fear or rage or protest in these novels? And no preaching?

When Catherine Morland in *Northanger Abbey* anticipates that Henry Tilney will not have read the novels she has been reading so greedily, 'Because they are not clever enough for you; gentlemen read better books',[36] Jane Austen is teasing them both and alluding to the nature of her enterprise as a novelist. Catherine, we have been told, has a mind 'about as ignorant and uninformed as the female mind at seventeen usually is'.[37] It is a mind, nonetheless, which must interest Jane Austen, for it is the mind of a young woman embarking on her brief and only life's adventure. Henry's admission that he has read hundreds of novels, knows all the 'Julias and Louisas' in them and has relished having his hair stand on end, leads into his lecture to Catherine on the subject of her undiscriminating use of the word 'nice'. As he ebulliently teases her he reminds her, kindly – though the remark has its devastating implications – to 'Consider how many years I have had the start of you. I had entered on my studies at Oxford, while you were a good little girl working your sampler at home!'[38]

That scene is an early one in a novel Jane Austen is writing about an inexperienced, uneducated girl, whose reading of novels nearly leads her astray by offering a dangerously romantic model for judging the grown-up world she is entering. She is particularly vulnerable to novels because she was innocently working a sampler – or worse, in Catherine's case, tumbling thoughtlessly in the grass – when Henry, who is older than she, was reading 'better books'. At the end of this novel Catherine will marry Henry, and the reader may well feel encouraged to regard them both as having done pretty well for themselves. Catherine will have acquired position and security through marriage to a man of fortune and prospects, who will take care of her and perhaps become the father of a family as large as the one Catherine grew up in. Henry will have acquired a wife who is still naive, but who has shown herself capable of learning, especially, and gratifyingly, from him. She has also shown that she has some native common sense, if of a modest kind, in reacting to the loutish undergraduate, John Thorpe, as tiresome and stupid. With Henry's help, the danger of her spending her life as another Julia or Louisa has been averted. She is charming and unaffected, and there is a good chance that she will become a sensible, probably less busy wife and mother, like her own. Henry is lucky because he will be able to impress with his superior talents an innocent young wife, unspoiled by the world, by education or by literature. She may even make good his having lived for so long with no mother of his own.

Many a woman reader must have felt some anxiety when reading that passage and others like it in *Northanger Abbey*. What is Jane Austen actually saying about the inequality in the relationship between Catherine and Henry? Was she telling us that women's lives were like this, or might be, or should be? And how might an answer to that kind of question sit with the facts of her own life? Do we have to remind ourselves that this is a woman writing, let alone a woman who did not herself marry, perhaps by choice? Most men and women who love Jane Austen's novels have wanted to point out that Jane Austen was a realist and a humorous writer, who is being funny about youth, about the kinds of eighteenth-century novels which are parodied in *Northanger Abbey* (most of them by women), about herself as a writer of novels and about the young women she was to write about in her other novels.

The teasing and the ironies are unsettling, nevertheless, and it would be reductive to leave it at that, to regard such scenes as badinage, simply there to entertain. Jane Austen is laughing at women's novels (and at herself for writing one) and at young women's susceptibility to them. Yet even as she warns women of the dangers of believing such stories she is telling us that they are partly true and that men's stories and men's behaviour are no more trustworthy. The tension – and the anxiety it produces – of that scene stands for larger ambiguities in Jane Austen's work; ambiguities about stories and ambiguities about men's good faith and the trust women should put in it.

Jane Austen was not a feminist. She was not telling women that their problems were attributable primarily to their being women, though a modern reader might want to suggest that most of them were. She was, however, pointing out the lamentably restricted nature of women's lives, the pains and hazards of dependence, decorum, incompetence, ignorance and fear, women's vulnerability to men and to men's stories and to a world in which so indisputably women *were* inferior to men in their own eyes. Jane Austen is also reminding us that women have some consolations, that frustration, anger and ingratitude are unattractive emotions in women, and that coming to terms with what strong men want of women makes practical sense and is, besides, the only way by which women get even a toehold on power. Yet acceptance and submission, which a woman would be right to regard with suspicion in a man, can only be good qualities for a woman to cultivate on the assumption that women are not only different from men, but inferior to them.

Critics have often adjured us to read Jane Austen as her contemporaries did; and of course those contemporaries were quite unexercised by differences between the sexes! Anthea Zeman, for instance, makes a case for women writers, throughout history, feeling confident and secure enough in the position accorded them by men to want only to help their weaker sisters make the best of a bad job:

Where these most talented writers agreed in their attitude to the woman's novel was in a recognition that it was the perfect means of performing a function especially necessary to women: that of telling them accurately where they stood at a given moment . . . Here, in your time, if you are a woman, lie safety and satisfaction; there danger and disappointment. Disregard what you were previously taught; it probably no longer applies.[39]

Such a view, amiably complacent and complaisant, suggests that women have written novels out of quite different purposes from men: as instruction manuals, textbooks. It is not an uncommon view, of course. Rather than confront the difficult and the contradictory in women's novels many readers have preferred to read them in that way, or as escapist, bland entertainment, or even, in a few cases, as effortlessly continuous with the tradition of men's novels. To ask why Jane Austen did not recommend her own example to women is to ask a curiously unaskable question. In *Villette*, though, Charlotte Brontë does finally allow Lucy Snowe to settle for a working life on her own, and she certainly faced that as a reality for herself, from her youth onwards.[40] There are clever and imaginative young women in Jane Austen's novels, who read books if they do not write them, who might, as she did, have lived on very little, depending on the generosity of fathers or brothers, and made a life for themselves without a husband. Yet if that had happened to Elizabeth, say, in *Pride and Prejudice*, we would have regarded the novel as a tragic one, and so would Jane Austen. In order to make sense of that we have to remember that when Frank Churchill marries Jane Fairfax in *Emma* he rescues her from a life as a governess, a servant. That was a life lived by thousands of the young women who read the novel, by Emma's governess before she married and became Mrs Weston and by the Brontë sisters themselves. Marriage presented both the only chance for change, escape, adventure, and the end of the adventure.

There is more to all this than the common-sense realism of telling young women in the first quarter of the nineteenth century that they would have better lives if they married than if they did not. Inequality between the sexes could not have been maintained without women's consent to most of its manifestations and to those complex and shifting rationales which have used the obvious differences between the sexes to explain as 'natural' the ways by which men have controlled women, and women have let themselves be controlled. Yet that consent is barbed and complex and has always been. Reading women's novels helps us to understand the processes by which women have rationalised their own subordination to male values and male culture. Given the nature of those rationales, how are we to untangle women's psychology, their apparently negative account of themselves and their sex, within a history of what comes to look like duplicity and delusion?

Jane Austen was the most talented member of a talented family. Some might say that she was the most talented member of her whole society. Yet as a serious writer she was always determined on her amateur status. That has a parallel in her insistence in the novels that women need men, that as well as a husband a woman would do well to have a mentor. She shared with men and with most women a general contempt for values or lives which were exclusively 'feminine'. Yet, as I shall want to show, Jane Austen condemns men who assume their superiority over women to be unproblematic, natural. If we do judge the characters in *Emma* 'by Mr Knightley's standards' that is partly because he is almost the only man in the novels who is able to admit that he has patronised a woman and who cedes that and a good deal else to her. Of course, Jane Austen was also doing what most women have done and still do: focusing on the particular experiences, strengths and weaknesses of women and checking them against men's expectations of them. The necessity for that has been undeniable. Most societies are organised so that women's survival has depended on men, and that has meant that women must know and heed what men want from them in order to gain their protection. That will even include demonstrating, sometimes quite ritualistically, that women cannot do without such protection. Proving your vulnerability has meant different things for women in different cultures, though a canny understanding (conspiratorially shared with other women, whatever their class) and compliance with men's requirements of them may be said to have a long, and probably universal, history.

What we get from women's novels, however – and we get it strikingly from Jane Austen's – is an understanding of the tactics and of the private and lifelong negotiations women make with men in the giving of their consent. The morality women evolve, collectively and individually, is always partly oppositional and critical. Their novels may record defeats, compromise and apparently conciliatory moves. They also tell us how and why women put up with some ignominies and not others. Let us move forward from Jane Austen for a moment to a more recent writer and to an issue which preoccupied them both.

If, for instance, a community puts a premium on virginity (and most have), and on men marrying women who are younger, more innocent and less experienced sexually and socially than they are, we may want to know why and we may also want to know why women have given that intention their blessing, even as many of them register the fact that its disadvantages for them at times outweigh the advantages. Olive Schreiner, in her novel *From Man to Man*, makes the dilemma of women's ambivalent relation to authority and the sexual double standard central. That authority does more than limit the expression of women's sexual feelings. It ordains what women may do during their lives, when they are permitted to be sexually active and when they must grow old gracefully. It dictates their priorities and their loyalties and the spending of their time and energy. Yet, as Olive Schreiner shows, women who want and need to express their own sexuality or to study and write, and who live in a hypocritical, puritanical and patriarchal society, are defeated by more than the pervading cruelties of the society. They will have to contend too with the coercions of their own and other women's socialisation into the very values which have taught them how to question and resist them. Passionate or intelligent women, like Schreiner's two sisters, recognise that the tenets of their upbringing are dishonest and restrictive. Their tragedies follow from their own characters, which have been formed by and within a culture – touted inevitably as a communal agreement – which thrives on its power to assert itself against the flaws and misgivings of its members, through its influence on their own moral development and make-up. That cultural power has been exercised in a male interest in all the societies we know much about, and it has been backed by economic, legal and physical power. Women have only achieved power and any kind of individual freedom for themselves by working within the terrains marked out for them by men.

What women can tell us about a society comes from their ambiguous relation to the sources of power. We can learn from women's novels why, for instance, it has often been women who taught and upheld the very standards which have kept women subordinate to men. We learn about the kinds of resistance which are possible for the subordinated and about the kinds of modification of public moralities and values which the powerless contribute in order both to sustain the hegemony and to question it.

Women writers have been particularly sensitive to charges that they are ignorant of men's lives and natures and unlikely to understand, let alone live by, a male morality. While needing for a good deal of the time to concede the truth of such charges, women have also wanted to characterise such ignorance, or deviance, as prime examples of the circumstances of their lives and cultural conditioning. Jane Austen was not like George Eliot in tackling masculine *milieux*, nor was she like George Eliot in having personal experience of such *milieux*. She does not, though, appear to have expressed the difficulty in writing about men to which Charlotte Brontë admitted in a letter to her friend, James Taylor:

In delineating male character, I labour under disadvantages; intuition and theory will not adequately supply the place of observation and experience. When I write about women, I am sure of my ground – in the other case I am not so sure.[41]

It would be defeating my purposes to engage in a discussion of the relative capacities of various women writers to portray men in their novels. That would suggest that we all know a man when we see one. What I am interested in is women's sense of the difficulties they might have in writing about men, whether in their personal relations with women or as carriers of power in the society. All characters in novels are imagined out of what writers know of themselves, of other people and of characters in the novels or plays of other writers. At one point in his essay on George Eliot,[42] F. R. Leavis compares Henry James's Isabel Archer in *Portrait of a Lady* with Gwendolen Harleth. Leavis makes two points about this: a man could and did take as his starting point a character in a work of fiction by a woman; and the principal difference between the two characters lies in Gwendolen's being known from within, while Isabel is watched from without.

Why should it be supposed that women have difficulty in creating male characters if men are not thought to have an equivalent difficulty? Or rather, why is it legitimate for a man to watch his female character as a way of knowing her, but risky for a woman novelist to do the same thing? There are some answers to that. Most women have known little about those aspects of men's lives which were separate and different from women's, and were also the areas from which a good deal of men's authority and glamour for women derived. In Jane Austen's day it was possible for a woman of her class to know nothing at all at first hand about boys' schools or university education, or about the subjects they studied and most of the books they read. They might know little about travel or war or politics, little about solitude outside the home, virtually nothing about paid work and about the relationships which go with or depend on forms of working and professional life for men. Changes in industry and transport and agriculture, in urban and rural life, in political activity and in working relations had profound effects on the lives of women in all classes of society. The causes of those changes, let alone the chance to intervene or even to explain them, were not available to any woman, as of course they were not to most men. Mr Knightley in *Emma* derives his authority and those standards of his from a male world. He can appreciate Robert Martin's worth, when Emma frivolously and snobbishly dismisses him, because he knows Martin as a local farmer and within relationships across a far wider section of society, met through his involvement in local affairs, than Emma knows. Marriage to him will, amongst other things, allow her to share in some of that knowledge and, if more ambiguously, some of those relationships, though not all.

Where men *are* superior to women for Jane Austen, where their judgement, knowledge and understanding must be accepted by women, is in exactly those areas of life which were out of bounds for women. It takes Captain Wentworth in *Persuasion* years at sea, coping with danger and responsibility for other lives and other people's money, to become the equal in maturity and feeling of Anne, whose experience of life is narrowly constrained by family and convention. Jane Austen displays for us the anomalies in all this. Given the oppositions inherent in the way Anne and Captain Wentworth have spent the last seven years, how can Anne behave admirably? What kinds of concession and compromise can she allow herself in order to see herself as admirable and to be seen by Wentworth and by men and women readers as admirable?

It is not that men have *not* been at a disadvantage in writing about women, but that they have not needed to see themselves as at a disadvantage. Those aspects of women's lives which men do not share or know much about are not, and significantly, those for which men publicly value women, though their own lives have depended on them: planning, housework and the bringing up of children, all the rituals which women enter to make themselves desirable to men, relationships between mothers and daughters and between sisters, women's friendships with other women, their conversations. These have been allowed by men to be trivialities. Perfunctory tribute may be paid to such aspects of women's lives, but they are not the stuff of men's novels. Some of women's sense of the inequality between men's lives and their own lies there. Work, adventure, even war, have been seen by both sexes as ways of life which provide a challenge for men to develop their best qualities and their most useful skills: courage, stamina, leadership, responsibility, insight into human nature, under-standing of the natural and the social world (and not only their own), kinds of technical expertise, the ability to make money, win power and wield it. Those things are learned in the world, apart from women, outside the home. Jane Austen certainly thought women capable of possessing and developing admirable moral and intellectual qualities. The challenge for the women in her novels lies in the process of acquiring such qualities from the barren soil of an exiguous and unexciting life. More than that, the ways in which women could and should be virtuous were often in conflict with notions of manly virtue, notions to which women also subscribed.

In a powerful essay,[43] in which she argues that what she calls the 'bisexuality' of moral standards in Western societies issues in ambivalence and produces an 'explosively reactionary' effect, Frigga Haug points to an absolute difference between the traditional concerns of a woman's morality and a man's. Whereas a woman's morality has centred on love and the transactions of her own body in exchange for love, a man's morality has centred on law and on profitability. A woman may invoke the law, or even profitability, in support of her 'right' to love, and a man may invoke love (for his family or his country) as an argument for contravening the law. It is not only, therefore, that women and men have to listen to different moralities, but that each sex allows itself transgressions of morality in the name of different principles. This may help us to understand the kinds of contradiction facing Jane Austen's heroines, who must attend to love and be ruled by law and by money.

Some, at least, of the anxiety a woman may feel as she listens to Henry arrogantly lecturing the untutored Catherine stems from these kinds of contradiction. This is all more critical for Catherine than for Henry, as well as more difficult. If most women still sigh with relief at the end of *Northanger Abbey*, and at the end of a thousand novels, that at least the heroine has avoided the fate of Miss Bates in *Emma*, of Mary Bennet in *Pride and Prejudice*, of Jane Austen herself, it is a sigh, I want to suggest, with a kind of hiccup to it. Henry Tilney is neither attractive nor admirable as he teases and pontificates. Accepting that on the whole Catherine is lucky to get such a husband involves us in averting our gaze from all those insufferable husbands and fathers Jane Austen is good at who preach to and hector their wives and children, when they do not ignore them. Henry Tilney will not become a Casaubon or a Grandcourt, but he is very likely to become another John Knightley, Mr Knightley's clever brother in *Emma*, a lawyer and a family man, who lets no chance slip to put a woman right, to instruct. When poor Jane Fairfax, flustered because she has been caught furtively posting an illicit letter, prattles about the wonders of the post office, John Knightley, smiling, seizes the opportunity to inform her:

'The clerks grow expert from habit. – They must begin with some quickness of sight and hand, and exercise improves them. If you want any further explanation,' continued he, smiling, 'they are paid for it. That is the key to a great deal of capacity. The public pays and must be served well.'[44]

There are as few happy marriages in Jane Austen's novels as there are in real life. John Knightley's is very far from being the worst. Young women are brought up to see happiness as possible only within marriage, and yet 'Had Elizabeth's opinion been all drawn from her own family, she could not have formed a very pleasing picture of conjugal felicity or domestic comfort.'[45] We are going to want to ask whether we leave Elizabeth and Darcy at the end of *Pride and Prejudice* assured that they will be more fortunate, that the fulfilment of Elizabeth's personal moral quest, as it has been called, will be a marriage which, in Marilyn Butler's words, 'commits a couple to a responsible leading role in society'.[46] Is that what marriage means for Elizabeth, is that what Jane Austen looked to for her heroines?

The irony of that first sentence of *Pride and Prejudice*, 'It is a truth universally acknowledged, that a single man in possession of a good fortune must be in want of a wife' is that it is true – both Darcy and Bingley are 'in want of a wife' – and that it is what mothers of marriageable daughters, women like Mrs Bennet, know to be true. It is not, however, for gentry parents of the early nineteenth century, a seller's market, so that it is Mrs Bennet's manner of selling her daughters which is up for criticism. She will get no bargains that way, may even scupper the sale. The complication, of course, is that it is also Mrs Bennet's insensitivity to her daughters which demands our disapproval. Wives may always and really be wanted 'for the heavy work', but in any society with well-established social divisions and hierarchical and patriarchal traditions ways have been elaborately developed for eliciting the consent, or even coercing agreement, from those whose services are too essential to leave to chance. In serving men and the law women may ask for love. Marriage is a business deal, but it is women's part of the business, and their prerogative, to have it conducted humanely and with decorum. Men need wives because they need children and an establishment which provides a pastoral refuge from life's hurly burly. We may know why men wanted wives. Does Jane Austen tell us why women wanted husbands? In a letter to her niece Fanny, Jane Austen wrote about a young woman who was pregnant with her third child. 'Poor Animal, she will be worn out before she is thirty.'[47] Is that Catherine's future, Elizabeth's? Jane Austen wisely avoided answering questions like that,[48] and it is anyway in the nature of literary works that we as readers must not try to answer them for her.

I have wanted in this chapter to survey a difficult terrain through the kinds of questions which women have always asked, though they have done so circumspectly. That circumspection has been required and learned as part of men's ambiguous inclusion of them in a condition of dependence. And that dependence has been not only physical, social and economic but also impeding of assertions of anything resembling a specifically woman's viewpoint. Within such a dependence a woman's view of men can seem to recede as fast as it is pursued, for women writers, as women and as writers, have needed to cover their tracks. Yet taking this tangle as the starting point begins to reveal, I think, expressions of criticism and resistance in writers who have too often been seen either as kinds of men or as miraculously without the 'impediments' of anger or self-esteem.

   In the following chapters I shall consider the influence of

women's earliest knowledge of men on the view of men and of women's relations with men that women have offered in their novels. I begin with fathers: those precursors of husbands, replicas of God and repositories of authority, and I do so by revisiting Jane Austen, whose fathers were also gentlemen. I begin with her partly because she illustrates the dilemma underlying John Stuart Mill's remark: 'I deny that any one knows, or can know, the nature of the two sexes, as long as they have only been seen in their present relation to one another.'[49] That will remind us of the wayward invoking of nature to explain women, of history and of culture, of the understandings which have been available to particular writers and of the practices and forms into which they insert themselves. I begin with her too because her position as the daughter of a gentleman raises the issue of women's relation to class. It is usually accepted that Jane Austen was critical of many of the people and a good many of the arrangements of the society she knew; that, as D. W. Harding put it, the characteristic problem, which she shared with her heroines, was 'of being intensely critical of people to whom she also has strong emotional attachments'.[50] We cannot claim her as either a feminist or a reformer.[51] She found, nonetheless, ways of questioning the 'naturalness' of women's submission to men and ways of undermining the authority of men as fathers and as novelists.

2

Fathers and Gentlemen

Successful literary women are just as unlikely to prefer the cause of women to their own social consideration. They depend on men's opinion for their literary as well as for their feminine successes; and such is their bad opinion of men, that they believe there is not more than one in ten thousand who does not dislike and fear strength, sincerity, or high spirit in a woman. They are therefore anxious to earn pardon and toleration for whatever of these qualities their writings may exhibit on other subjects, by a studied display of submission on this: that they may give no occasion for vulgar men to say (what nothing will prevent vulgar men from saying), that learning makes women unfeminine, and that literary ladies are likely to be bad wives.

Harriet Taylor Mill[1]

Fathers in Jane Austen's novels are also gentlemen. They are men with some authority in the community. I have already suggested that when we are listening to women who are telling us about men we need to maintain a double focus, for fictional relationships between women and men will never simply resolve themselves into family ones or sexual ones or social ones. Whether Jane Austen's fathers are loved or feared or despised by her heroines they stand for more than themselves. They also stand for the tensions and difficulties young women experience in contemplating their present and future dependence and their prospects. Jane Austen has been called 'the gentry's greatest artist',[2] and there are anomalies in that which must be confronted if we are to understand what she is telling us in her novels about fathers, about marriage and about the kinds of men her heroines are likely to marry.

Not everyone would go so far as Peter Laslett does in insisting that until well into the nineteenth century England consisted of a single class, since all but the gentry were powerless and fragmented geographically. His emphasis is important, however, and so is the fact that he alludes to – though he does not explore all the implications of – the particular contradictions there were for those women who could not be said to belong to that one class, despite their having been born into it:

England was an association between the heads of such families (*of the gentry, that is*), but an association largely confined to those who were literate, who had wealth and status, those, in fact, who belonged, with their families as part of them, to what we have already called the ruling minority. Almost no woman ever belonged to England as an individual, except it be a queen regnant – scarcely a woman in the ordinary sense – or a noble widow and heiress or two, a scattering of widows of successful merchants and yeoman.[3]

We may pass over what 'a woman in the ordinary sense' might be, but hold to Laslett's account of women's relation to class. For if we accept without argument a view like Marilyn Butler's, that Jane Austen's brand of 'Toryism made it hard for her to countenance, even as much as Maria Edgeworth did, Enlightenment criticism of social constraints upon women',[4] we are left with questions concerning not only Jane Austen's views about women but also the particular contradictions there were for women who were born into, or married into, a powerful, ruling class. It is, I think, disingenuous to wonder whether Elizabeth Bennet falls in love with Darcy because of his house without considering the extraordinary contrast between the social and material advantages conferred on women by gentlemen and the lifelong dependence which accompanied those material advantages. That dependence, which was economic, political, social, physical and emotional is spelled out in painful detail in Jane Austen's novels, and it is the sub-text of her plots and of the finales to them.

Certainly we do not look to Jane Austen for political exhortation or for analysis of constraints on women, or indeed of other manifestations of constraint – the sorts, for instance, which made the vast majority of the population politically powerless and economically weak. What we do get in the novels, however, is a tension between the plots and their outcomes on the one hand and the family relationships within which the plots are enacted on the other. What are explicitly there in the novels are contradictions between those values and feelings hoped for and looked for in a marriage, a union between a man and a woman, and the values which operate within the society to determine what is actually possible in such a relationship. Jane Austen does not explain to us how and why a very small number of men could control the majority of men and all women, though she does demonstrate for us how that small number of men were enabled to do so in the name of the majority through the ways by which they could elicit a kind of consent from those who depended on them.

I want to suggest that if what have been called 'the failed paternalists'[5] of Jane Austen's novels are allowed to be no more than accidentals in the kind of social satire which could safely be made at the beginning of the nineteenth century by a self-confident writer unambiguously committed to the traditional and Christian values of the English gentry, we are in danger either of merging women with men and losing sight of them in a class from which they are importantly excluded, or of reading them as a man might and allowing a universalist reading to muffle the voice and the very particular perceptions of a woman.

With George Eliot, Jane Austen is probably the woman writer most successfully appropriated by men as their own. If Geoffrey Gorer's reading of her is not typical it is, nonetheless, a usefully characteristic one. In 'The Myth in Jane Austen'[6] he argued that in the first five of her novels, though not in *Persuasion*, Jane Austen's heroines hate their mothers, or mother substitutes, and love their fathers. They each proceed to reject a charming and worthless man for a fatherly husband, whom they love, though not passionately. In *Persuasion*, Gorer maintained, which was written after the death of her father, Jane Austen was released from the Oedipal fantasy and could tell the truth. Anne rejects her father and accepts the charming (and initially worthless-seeming) man, whom she does love passionately. Gorer's interpretation is intended to answer his own question: why is it that Jane Austen appeals to 'nearly everybody'? To show what he means he quotes four famous men and does not bother to wonder whether women (famous or otherwise) might share their views or have different ones. He also commits that familiar sleight of hand in assuming that a simple reversal of the Oedipus myth fits the 'facts' of women's subconscious life. At the very least, such an assumption ignores the probability that in most societies fathers are not to daughters what mothers may be to sons. It also ignores the probability that women read themselves as clearly into the role of Jocasta as the mother in that story as into the destiny of Oedipus the son. That itself is a hypothesis evaded even by those who have renamed the story *Jocasta's Crime*,[7] and it is one I shall return to in considering how women writers have dealt with the feelings of mothers towards their sons. Also at issue as a reading of Jane Austen is Gorer's assumption that her heroines do hate their mothers and love their fathers, and that they do go on to marry men who are in a fatherly relation to them. It is not difficult to read Gorer's interpretation as a theory of male consolation,[8] and he would not be the first or only man to have wished for that. It also leaves unexamined the crucial question of how women view authority and the figure of the father, for there is no question that for Jane Austen the two are never simply the same thing. Let us spend a little time with her heroines and their fathers.

A good many fathers in the novels, her heroines' and those of their chosen husbands, are dead or absent. Of those who are there the majority are ineffectual or worse as parents. The best mothers – Lady Elliot of *Persuasion* and Mrs Woodhouse of *Emma* – are dead. Mrs Morland is sensible, even sensibly negligent, and Mrs Dashwood of *Sense and Sensibility* is foolish, though undoubtedly well-meaning. A linchpin of the kind of conservatism which is usually invoked in connection with Jane Austen is the injunction to respect one's parents: to ensure continuity and practise obedience to those in authority. That is a possibility either denied or made very difficult for Jane Austen's heroines. Many of the young women who are not the heroines of the novels grow up impaired or impoverished because of unhelpful parents or because natural tendencies to headiness, vanity or ignorance have not been remarked or corrected by them. There are even some young women in the novels (Jane Fairfax is an example) who have flourished as a consequence of being orphans, or neglected, as Catherine Morland and Fanny Price and Anne Elliot have often been. It is worth remembering that a novelist like Maria Edgeworth, who is more critical generally of the social arrangements of her time than Jane Austen is, can, in a novel like *Helen*, make women and even men of the older generation repositories of experience, honesty and wisdom, from whom younger people are able to learn a great deal.

It is not, of course, that Jane Austen expected fathers to dote on their daughters. A doting parent is a bad one. Emma's sister Isabella is affectionately put down for her obsession with her children. Mary Musgrove in *Persuasion* and Lady Middleton and Fanny Dashwood in *Sense and Sensibility* are more severely taken to task for spoiling theirs. Young children are not seen to bring out the best in their parents, and only Isabella's are made at all attractive, which is due in part to the good influence on them of their father and their aunt. When, in *Sense and Sensibility*, the Middletons are introduced by the wonderful line, 'Sir John was a sportsman, Lady Middleton a mother',[9] there is not much doubt that Sir John comes better out of that than his wife. To be nothing but a mother is to be a bad mother. Children are not much helped by their parents' anxieties for their welfare. Mr Woodhouse worries about his daughters' health only as an extension of his own hypochondria, and Mrs Bennet's bustling strategies to marry off her daughters are counterproductive in that aim especially. Daughters can get into difficulties whether their mothers are as languid and indolent as Lady Bertram or as girlishly complicitous as Mrs Dashwood. Here then is a writer who is almost exclusively concerned with family life and women's possibilities within it, who could be said to catalogue its disadvantages as she simultaneously encourages its continuance.

There *are* good fathers, though they are not necessarily seen to be so in relation to their own children. Mr Gardiner, for instance, in *Pride and Prejudice*, is uncle to the Bennet girls. He is also represented as happily married. It is he who watches over Jane in London when she believes that she has been deserted by Bingley, he who encourages the relationship between Elizabeth and Darcy (though his motives for doing so are allowed to be as ambiguous as Elizabeth's change of tune), he of whom Elizabeth can feel proud when her family lets her down, and he who comes, with Darcy, most practically to the rescue of the absconding Lydia and the distraught Bennet parents.

Not the least of the faults committed by fathers in Jane Austen's novels is the mistake they made in choosing a wife, a familiar enough daughterly insight. That will resonate with the need for her heroines to do their own choosing, even as they concede that they must also be chosen and may in practice have only the choice of refusal. It must be, however, in the scheme of Jane Austen's moral world, that men who marry silly wives are at fault for doing so. As Mr Knightley puts it, 'Men of sense, whatever you may chuse to say, do not want silly wives.'[10] Men who have some choice – and Jane Austen's men do have choice – and let themselves be 'captivated', have only themselves to blame. Even Sir Thomas Bertram, who 'had to work against a most untoward gravity of deportment',[11] allows himself to be so captivated. Mr Bennet's marrying Mrs Bennet is held to be characteristic of his irresponsibility and nonchalance:

Her father, captivated by youth and beauty, and that appearance of good humour which youth and beauty generally give, had married a woman whose weak understanding and illiberal mind had very early in their marriage put an end to all real affection for her. Respect, esteem, and confidence had vanished for ever; and all his views of domestic happiness were overthrown. But Mr Bennet was not of a disposition to seek comfort for the disappointment which his own imprudence had brought on, in any of those pleasures which too often console the unfortunate for their folly or their vice. He was fond of the country and of books; and from these tastes had arisen his principal enjoyments. To his wife he was very little otherwise indebted, than as her ignorance and folly had contributed to his amusement. This is not the sort of happiness which a man would in general wish to owe to his wife; but where other powers of entertainment are wanting, the true philosopher will derive benefit from such as are given.[12]

Of course there is affection and warmth in that description, and we already know that Jane Austen sympathises with Mr Bennet's preferring Elizabeth to his other daughters, and with Elizabeth's responding to his preference. Michèle Roberts has written, 'If I had to be a daughter, I wanted to be my father's favourite daughter and there were three of us. I wanted my father to be my companion, to praise me for wit and intelligence as Mr Bennet praised Lizzy. Their fictional relationship compensated for what I felt I lacked in real life.'[13] We will return to favourite daughters and to daughters whose sense of men's treachery began with a father's delightful invitation to join him. Elizabeth does love her father, yet he is, even in her eyes, a bad father, and much closer to the charming and worthless young man of Gorer's schema than Darcy is. It is also the case that the difficulties and discrepancies of the Bennet marriage may be harder for the husband to bear than for the wife. His poor judgement, however, is at issue, and it is seen as a sign of his lack of seriousness about vital matters, with dire consequences for other people within his family and even within the community as a whole. All his children suffer in different degrees and in different ways from the carelessness which characterised his choosing of a wife.

Sir Thomas Bertram in *Mansfield Park* is an altogether more formidable figure, if possessed of considerably less charm and wit. He is awe-inspiring to his children and an important figure in the community, and yet he too fails his children and does so initially through letting himself be 'captivated'. Lady Bertram is 'guided in every thing important by Sir Thomas',[14] who allows her to hand over the control of her children to her greedy and indulgent sister,

Mrs Norris. Towards the end of the novel he admits to himself that his children have fared badly from 'the totally opposite treatment which Maria and Julia had been always experiencing at home, where the excessive indulgence and flattery of their aunt had been continually contrasted with his own severity.'[15] Sir Thomas is in fact one of the few parents in the novels who is capable of learning and changing. He learns too late for his daughters that his absences and his 'severity' have been side-stepped by them. It is Fanny, the niece he had coldly allowed to live with his children, who teaches him to feel paternal love and to recognise his faults as a parent. There is a thunderous self-importance in Sir Thomas, which we are allowed to find absurd, just as we can recognise as cruelly insensitive his refusal at first to let Fanny be treated as one of his children lest she nurse foolish hopes of marrying one of his sons. The qualities which terrify his children and impress the world are hollow and tyrannical ones at the beginning of the novel, and are only gradually transformed to the point where we can respect him as Fanny does, not least for his admission of failure as a father. He is in both manifestations, however, importantly a father, and it is significant that he should be so in *Mansfield Park*, in which Christian virtues, order, un-selfishness and respect are offered as spiritual and personal qualities as well as essential social ones. The regeneration of Sir Thomas from wooden figurehead of authority to something like the apotheosis of fatherhood makes an important statement, both about women's difficulties with their fathers and about their need to be heard by men if they are going to love and respect such men. It also reminds us that men may make better uncles than fathers.

D. W. Harding has suggested that there are two kinds of Austen heroine.[16] There are those who are good to start with, and Harding calls them Cinderellas, whose growing up involves patience, pain and self-denial. Those who are not Cinderellas must grope their way towards equivalent understandings through fogs of error and reticence. Of the first kind are Elinor, Fanny, Anne, perhaps also Jane Bennet and Jane Fairfax. They get little support from their elders and they marry men who are less morally and emotionally secure than they are. Her most loved, and perhaps lovable, heroines are lively girls with intelligence and good instincts, but with a good deal to learn: Elizabeth and Emma, Catherine and Marianne.

These young women get little help or example from their elders, of either sex, and are often put precociously into the position of acting as advisers to their contemporaries or even their parents. Elinor, at nineteen, is young 'to be the counsellor of her mother' and a mother to her two younger sisters. The trial for this kind of heroine is that she is the daughter of a parent she cannot respect. Elinor at least feels love and protectiveness for her mother. Anne Elliot can feel none of those things for her father:

Vanity was the beginning and the end of Sir Walter Elliot's character; vanity of person and of situation. He had been remarkably handsome in his youth; and, at fifty-four, was still a very fine man. Few women could think more of their personal appearance than he did; nor could the valet of any new made lord be more delighted with the place he held in society. He considered the blessing of beauty as inferior only to the blessing of a baronetcy; and the Sir Walter Elliot, who united these gifts, was the constant object of his warmest respect and devotion.[17]

Anne's predicament represents a central dilemma for Jane Austen's heroines between modesty and obedience on the one hand and realistic and critical intelligence on the other. A woman's double vision of her father entails a challenge to her intelligence and moral sense. It also announces the nature of the compromise women make as they leave one sort of dependence for another, a compromise that enjoins on them a calculation and balancing of profit and loss as they juggle with the possibilities of love and comfort, of passion and the rewards for duty. Emma, for instance, 'dearly loved her father, but he was no companion for her'.[18] The lesson learned from that admission will affect her choice of a husband and her expectations of marriage.

As stark an example of a disastrous father as Anne's in *Persuasion* is the case of Fanny's in *Mansfield Park*. That Lady Bertram's sister should have married 'in the common phrase, to disoblige her family, and by fixing on a Lieutenant of Marines, without education, fortune, or connections, did it very thoroughly,'[19] is not that sister's only lapse in Jane Austen's eyes. She proceeds to have more children than she can afford and to let her household and her family relations fall into chaos. By the time Fanny returns to visit her family in Portsmouth after eight or nine years, during which, rather unaccountably, she has not seen any of them but her favourite brother William, her father has deteriorated badly:

On her father, her confidence had not been sanguine, but he was more negligent of his family, his habits were worse, and his manners coarser, than she had been prepared for. He did not want abilities; but he had no curiosity, and no information beyond his profession; he read only the newspaper and the navy-list; he talked only of the dock-yard, the harbour, Spithead, and the Motherbank; he swore and he drank, he was dirty and gross. She had never been able to recal anything approaching to tenderness in his former treatment of herself. There had remained only a general impression of roughness and loudness; and now he scarcely ever noticed her, but to make her the object of a coarse joke.[20]

This encounter with her real father marks the turning point for Fanny's relations with Sir Thomas. She will return to Mansfield Park as to her home. There is an ugliness in this which is more than the ugliness Fanny finds in her family. Behind all the other inadequate and criticised fathers in the novels lies the spectre of the disintegrating Price father and his disintegrating family. Fanny cannot find it in her to love or forgive these parents, and there is no question but that Jane Austen approves of Fanny's recoiling from them in favour of all that Mansfield Park and the Bertrams stand for. It is, of course, poverty which Fanny is encouraged to recoil from as well as unhappiness and inadequacy, but her experience lends a desperate urgency to her rejection of Henry Crawford, to her need to consider feeling as well as comfort in contemplating her future. For if Jane Austen's heroines are by no means to be understood as being in love with their fathers they do learn from their own and from other people's what husbands are and might be.

Catherine Morland's fantasies about General Tilney derive, as we know, from her reading of novels. They are assisted by the genuine and, to Catherine, puzzling fear he inspires in his own children and, of course, by the ancient house in which he lives. The novel's final paragraph, in which 'Henry and Catherine were married, the bells rang and everybody smiled',[21] with its characteristically disconcerting shutter on the future, puts an interesting gloss on the usefulness of fathers in some of the novels:

It will not appear, after all the dreadful delays occasioned by the General's cruelty, that they were essentially hurt by it. To begin perfect happiness at the respective ages of twenty-six and eighteen is to do pretty well; and professing myself, moreover, convinced that the General's unjust interference, so far from being really injurious to their felicity, was perhaps rather conducive to it, by improving their knowledge of each other, and adding strength to their attachment, I leave it to be settled by whomsoever it may concern, whether the tendency of this work be altogether to recommend parental tyranny or reward filial disobedience.[22]

The tone is light-hearted, but the final ambiguity is important and has its relevance to others of the novels. Fathers can certainly not be relied on as models for their daughters of what husbands should be. Perhaps a daughter who found her father perfect as a husband and a father would find it difficult to leave him, let alone accommodate to another man. Fathers are not shown to be much good at protecting their daughters from marrying the wrong man. They are useful, though, in providing delays by their antics or absurd positions, in letting their daughters know that men are often erratic in their authority and arbitrary in their affections. General Tilney is no fanged and midnight murderer, but he is greedy and trivial and a man whose irrational moodiness and inconsiderate behaviour frighten his children and make it mandatory that they sometimes disobey him. The errors and weaknesses of fathers leave at least loop-holes for their children, chinks of light, which are necessary illumination.

Sir Thomas Bertram similarly makes gross errors of judgement which are not without their beneficial side-effects. He is wrong to encourage Fanny to marry Henry Crawford, whom she does not love and who, shortly after her rejection of him, elopes with Sir Thomas's married daughter, Maria. That very serious misjudgement does, however, allow Fanny to discover for herself, and to reveal to Sir Thomas and to Edmund, her determination to resist the ignominies of her dependent position in their family. Had she not done so she could never have been certain, and nor could they, that marrying Edmund was not simply continuous with her exploitation and submissiveness as their poor relation. Also, and crucially, it allows Edmund to hear Fanny as he could not when he was promoting Henry Crawford's claims as a husband, and doing so by urging her to listen to women's views of the advantages of such a marriage:

'That you could refuse such a man as Henry Crawford, seems more than they can understand. I said what I could for you; but in good truth, as they stated the case – you must prove yourself to be in your senses as soon as you can, by a different conduct; nothing else will satisfy them. But this is teasing you. I have done. Do not turn away from me.'

'I *should* have thought,' said Fanny, after a pause of recollection and exertion, 'that every woman must have felt the possibility of a man's not being approved, not being loved by some one of her sex, at least, let him be ever so generally agreeable. Let him have all the perfections in the world, I think it ought not to be set down as certain, that a man must be acccptable to every woman he may happen to like himself. But even supposing it is so, allowing Mr Crawford to have all the claims which his sisters think he has, how was I to be prepared to meet him with any feeling answerable to his own?'[23]

This conversation is important for showing Edmund that there are limits to Fanny's submissiveness, for allowing her to explain to him that if Mary Crawford cannot return his love another woman might; that she retains, if nothing else, the right to refuse a man and that the recognised desirability for a woman of finding a husband sets women against one another and allows both men and women to assume that women are governed by mercenary interests as men, apparently, are not. This is part of a much longer speech from Fanny, one uttered 'after a pause of recollection and exertion', a passionate, controlled and serious rebuke to the man she loves and will ultimately marry, who will need to know her better than he does now.

Mr Woodhouse in *Emma* is unable to understand why anyone should wish to leave home to get married. Mrs Weston and Isabella will be forever 'poor' to him for having done so. Anthea Zeman calls this trait in him 'one of the funniest jokes about sex ever made'.[24] It is funny. It also illustrates his inability to consider other people beyond his own convenience. He might have got his way with Emma and prevented her from leaving home (though it is hard to believe that) had not Mr Knightley brilliantly exploited the difficulty to display his perfect gallantry and his unequivocal superiority to his future father-in-law by offering to leave his own home and live in his wife's.

Jane Austen is concerned with the development and the destinies of women; and in all her novels, except *Persuasion*, she focuses on the brief period of their lives between childhood and maturity. They are still dependent on the example, the support and the protection of their parents; and they have had very few opportunities for learning about the world from anyone else. Mothers are important to them as models and guides. Fathers are important as protection, providers of status and money, as gentlemen, even leaders of the community, as representatives of the outside world, its ways and values, and potentially as models for the kind of men their daughters should be hoping to marry themselves. Marilyn Butler goes so far as to say that as Jane Austen's heroines chose their husbands so 'the village community's leader is being sought, the true hereditary gentleman'[25] (by some principle of matriarchal succession, presumably!). If Jane Austen could be said to prefer the young to the old and the weak to the strong she also preferred order to chaos and continuity to change.

Why then do Jane Austen's novels so insist upon the inadequacies of parents generally and upon the particular drawbacks of fathers? In some ways it is possible to see such ambivalence as characteristic of many women's attitudes to men and most particularly to their fathers. In a recent book[26] in which contemporary women writers (most of whom are feminists) write about their fathers, there is in many of the pieces one version of that ambivalence. From their position as adult daughters, fathers may be seen compassionately and affectionately as young people who have been thrust into uncomfortable roles of paternity and authority and who come to fill those roles for their children and even to embody their oppressive social realities in spite of themselves. If Jane Austen is able to feel some sympathy for her inadequate fathers she is also determined that her heroines should recognise that inadequacy and yet refrain from open defiance.

D. W. Harding wrote of what he called the 'regulated hatred'[27] in Jane Austen's work, and he drew attention to moments in the novels when bitterness suddenly threatens the work's, and the reader's, equilibrium for a moment. He suggests that too many readings have ignored such eruptions in favour of reassurances that Jane Austen liked and approved of the world she wrote about. Those kinds of disturbances are part of a more general uneasiness in the novels. For at the very moment when a young woman is leaving the parental home for her adult life with another man, she is also discovering the extent and nature of her own freedom and dependence. She is faced by the quality of male authority and by the unreliability of many of the men who wield it. She is also learning to find in the interstices of that authority the exact extent of her own possibilities for individual initiative.

Lawrence Stone charts the arguments which, during the seventeenth and eighteenth centuries, led to a questioning of the source and extent of paternal authority. He begins with Locke's disentangling of the authority of the king from the authority of the father in the family, which he summarises in this way:

It was argued that the power of the father over his children is merely a utilitarian by-product of his duty to nourish them until they can look after themselves. It is thus only a limited and temporary authority, which automatically ends when the child grows up. In any case, parental authority is irrelevant to the authority of a king, to which adults voluntarily submit on condition that he acts for their own good. The practical need to remodel the political theory of state power in the late seventeenth century thus brought with it a severe modification of theories about patriarchal power within the family and the rights of the individual.[28]

In developing the chapter which he calls 'The Growth of Affective Individualism', Stone describes what he regards as fundamental changes in the nature of marriage within the English ruling classes, which could be seen to derive from a century of discussion about the nature of political power. These changes, he maintains, were gradual and by no means universal, but in associating them with 'affective individualism' Stone suggests that they encouraged an expectation of companionship and affection in marriage rather than the benefits of a liaison which was either dynastic or something like a practical business partnership. That expectation, he claims, came to require a more permissive approach to the bringing up of children. One consequence of this was, in principle, greater freedom for children to choose their own marriage partners:

Once it was doubted that affection could and would naturally develop after marriage, decision-making power had to be transferred to the future spouses themselves, and more and more of them in the eighteenth century began to put the prospects of emotional satisfaction before the ambition for increased income or status. This in turn also had its effect in equalizing relationships between husband and wife.[29]

It is certainly true that in Jane Austen's novels marriages are not as a rule arranged by parents, and the hope is that marriage will provide young women and the men they marry with love and companionship. Yet there are grounds, I think, for treating with some scepticism Stone's assurances that everyone involved shared equally in this new individualism, and that it had anything like equalizing effects on relations between men and women. Rosalind Mitchison sharply articulates one of them:

Individualism may mean permissiveness. In the reaction to both formalism and puritanism it often did. But it could also mean the expression of the personality of the father at the expense of everyone else.[30]

Jane Austen's heroines are encouraged to develop and express their individuality – as she did – within what are presented as limiting and yet ambiguously limiting conditions. The forms of authority to which young women must listen in the novels are not in any simple way embodied in their fathers or in men. Authority as it affects them is more diffused than that, and more inescapable, for it is felt as the controlling direction of their lives, the accretions and learning which show them how to win men's approval. It is that approval which will ultimately make marriage a possibility. Where authority is straightforwardly embodied in a father or parent it is frequently so misused, and seen to be, and is in such flagrant conflict with the interests and needs of young women negotiating with men for the possibility of living anything but a cramped and wasted life, as to make a measure of daughterly disobedience acceptable.

The uneasiness we feel and find in the novels is sited precisely in that gap between the realities of fathers and families and the fairy-tale endings when one Cinderella gets her prince and 'the bells rang and everybody smiled'. It was Jane Austen above all who made of the woman's romantic novel a form which exposed as it soothed the pains of women's helplessness in taking control of their own lives. The tension which permeates the novels lies in the contrast between the realities of marriage and family life, boredom and ugliness, lack of privacy and lack of stimulation, and the merry wassail of those brief months of a woman's life during which everything seems possible and which will end in failure or a wedding. Jane Austen's apparently demure averting of her gaze from what follows stands for the difficult message she is giving to women. It is a message full of reminders and caveats and provisos, for her heroines have been warned that men get it wrong and are not to be trusted. Novels, however, and even life, for many women, do not offer favourable alternatives to marriage as the completion of a woman's adventure.

Will Jane Fairfax and Frank Churchill live happily ever after? What about Lucy Steele and Robert Ferrars, Lydia and Wickham, Harriet and Robert Martin? It is possible to feel that

Charlotte Lucas, who marries Mr Collins with her eyes open, will make a better go of it than many, enlarging her dairy and her garden and darning in public, as Jane Austen's mother is said so reprehensibly to have done.[31] Why do all these young women marry, after all? For money, for love, for sex, for security, for status, in order to have children, for companionship, or because that is the only way they can leave their own families and change their lives?

Anne Elliot's seven years of suffering are the consequence of her taking Lady Russell's advice to send Wentworth packing. It was bad advice; but Anne, Jane Austen's saddest and wisest heroine, needs to explain it to herself and to tell Wentworth why she took it:

'I have been thinking over the past, and trying impartially to judge of the right and wrong, I mean with regard to myself; and I must believe that I was right, much as I suffered from it, that I was perfectly right in being guided by the friend whom you will love better than you do now. To me, she was in the place of a parent. Do not mistake me, however. I am not saying that she did not err in her advice. It was, perhaps, one of those cases in which advice is good or bad only as the event decides; and for myself, I certainly never should, in any circumstance of tolerable similarity, give such advice. But I mean, that I was right in submitting to her, and that if I had done otherwise, I should have suffered more in continuing the engagement than I did even in giving it up, because I should have suffered in my conscience.'[32]

To wait for seven years is not the same thing as those 'dreadful delays' which attend the marriage of Catherine to Henry Tilney. What Anne cannot say to Wentworth is that those seven years allowed him to become a captain and a rich man, giving substance to what might otherwise have seemed, even to her, a perverse faith in his worth. Anne is suggesting in her letter what Jane Austen less solemnly insists upon at the end of *Northanger Abbey*. Marriage, the question of whom to marry, is the most critical decision of a woman's life. It is finally a decision which young and inexperienced women have to make for themselves and on their own. They may have the right of refusal, but they rarely get choice or a second chance. There is no great likelihood of getting useful advice. It may be, though, that the obstacles and delays, however casually or callously interposed by their elders, will offer young women a breathing space, an occasion for considering their own feelings and their implications for a lifetime. Even that pretty off-hand suggestion underlines the gravity of the situation, the horrifying likelihood of a woman's getting it wrong. *Persuasion* is shot through with pain as well as resignation. There is an outrageousness to Anne's predicament and to her need to be philosophically accommodating of it. That is not simply because she was offered bad advice and felt compelled to take it, but because that is symptomatic of the exiguousness of her chances, the obstacles there are to her taking the initiative. She must wait for Wentworth to make it possible for her to explain herself and clear up misunderstandings between them. She is in pain for what she may not say, may not do. She can admit neither to her total lack of confidence in her father, nor to her doubts about Lady Russell. Nor – and in this she is like most of the other young women in the novels – can she afford to make mistakes, test the ground, play the field, speculate aloud. Her feelings and her judgement must match, once and for all.

It is worth comparing Anne's ordeal with the latitude allowed to Edward Ferrars who, in *Sense and Sensibility*, is forgiven his engagement to a silly young woman he ceases to love. He can let himself be manipulated by his rich mother and he can tell lies. He is still acceptable to Elinor. She, to earn our admiration and deserve his, must be silently steadfast in loving him. Jane Austen is often applauded for her commitment to restraint, her stern insistence that if women complain they lose all (which may not be quite the same thing). Her robust backing of winners is always watched, however, against a backdrop of failure, of daughters and wives who have been lamentably misled and who lamentably deceive themselves.

There are chilling examples in the novels of the lives women lead if they do not marry or if they marry unwisely. There is not much to choose between the grimness of the future awaiting Mary

Bennet, who does not marry, and what happens to Maria Bertram, who marries without love, elopes with another man, and is divorced by the one and abandoned by the other almost simultaneously:

Mary was the only daughter who remained at home; and she was necessarily drawn from the pursuit of accomplishments by Mrs Bennet's being quite unable to sit alone. Mary was obliged to mix more with the world, but she could still moralize over every morning visit; and as she was no longer mortified by comparisons between her sisters' beauty and her own, it was suspected by her father that she submitted to the change without much reluctance.[33]

and

It ended in Mrs Norris's resolving to quit Mansfield, and devote herself to her unfortunate Maria, and in an establishment being formed for them in another country – remote and private, where, shut up together with little society, on one side no affection, on the other, no judgment, it may be reasonably supposed that their tempers became their mutual punishment.[34]

For Jane Fairfax, the most gifted woman in any of the novels, the alternative to marrying Frank Churchill would be working as a governess. One can imagine her taking to her bed when Frank fills the house with guests for his balls and barbecues and practising the piano during his lightning, unexplained visits to London, from which he will return bearing embarrassingly and suspiciously expensive gifts. Mrs Weston's career as Emma's governess is remembered as a happy time by her pupil, and a rosy glow is cast on it by the fact that it enabled her to marry above her station. Her teacherly skills will come in handy for her own daughter. Jane Austen did not, however, shirk the darker side to a woman's remaining unmarried, and though Emma's lecture to Harriet on the subject is partly there to show her at her most high-handed, the passage is also remarkable for its pain and intensity and for its attempts to curb such feelings:

If I thought I should ever be like Miss Bates! so silly – so satisfied – so smiling – so prosing – so undistinguishing and unfastidious – and so apt to tell every thing relative to every body about me, I would marry to-morrow. But between *us*, I am convinced there never can be any likeness, except in being unmarried . . . it is poverty only which makes celibacy contemptible to a generous public! A single woman, with a very narrow income, must be a ridiculous, disagreeable, old maid! the proper sport of boys and girls; but a single woman, of good fortune, is always respectable, and may be as sensible and pleasant as anybody else. And the distinction is not quite so much against the candour and common sense of the world as appears at first; for a very narrow income has a tendency to contract the mind, and sour the temper. Those who can barely live, and who live perforce in a very small, and generally very inferior, society, may well be illiberal and cross.[35]

It is easy to find examples from the novels of the misery of women forced to live alone or to live unmarried in their own families. There is the widow Mrs Smith in *Persuasion*, there is even Anne Elliot herself. Spinsterhood is a double spectre in Jane Austen's novels, of failure, souring loneliness and cramped proximity to aging relatives, and there is poverty, which is not always of a genteel kind. Jane Austen can never have expected to starve, though the £600 a year on which she, her mother and her sister are said to have lived is considerably less than she expected her heroines to aim for. Other forms of pain and frustration in her novels, which she must have known all too well, were the intellectual frustration of Jane Fairfax, too little space and privacy, the lifelong relationship with a mother she did not get on with, the deadly tedium of provincial life, of immobility, of uninteresting conversation. The 'hatred' for all this is indeed 'regulated'. Emma's speech to Harriet about Miss Bates has an operatic quality, moving between the frighteningly corrosive effects of such a life on a woman's personality and her own soaring confidence as she asserts that it could not be like that for her, and anyway she, like Jane Austen, will always have 'My nephews and nieces! – I shall often have a niece with me.' She will also have enough money.

Jane Austen must often have thought that her own life would have been easier if she had married. She seems also to have

contemplated women who were mothers and wives and shud-
dered with relief to have avoided that. Think of those words of
hers in a letter to her niece, Fanny: 'I shall hate you when your
delicious play of Mind is all settled down into conjugal and
maternal affections.'[36] That was not entirely a joke. Ambivalences
in her treatment of men stem from that paradox. Fathers can be
tyrannical or ineffectual, or even both. Their affection and concern for their daughters is often arbitrary and unreliable. An
intelligent young woman should not expect much support or good
sense from them. The best that can be said for Mr Bennet is that
his trusting Elizabeth has helped her to trust herself, and she has
inherited a sense of humour from him. The plots of Jane Austen's
novels involve young women in getting it wrong before they get it
right. In contemplating marriage to a gentleman they have little to
go on. Elizabeth Bennet is not alone in drawing pessimistic
conclusions about marriage from her parents' marriage. Fathers
are important in the novels as warnings. They may also provide
good reason for a young woman to exchange her dependence on
one gentleman for dependence on another.

As women sit – or even, amazingly and restlessly, stroll, as Miss
Bingley does – in drawing rooms, their hands empty of the
darning which their mothers, but not they, would have had to
employ them, men dart in and out. Women wait there, trapped
and trapping these bright and valuable creatures, who live and
thrive elsewhere. The men we are to admire do not belong in drawing rooms, are only inadvertently and casually there from time
to time. They leave to hunt, to ride, to travel, to see to the affairs
of the world outside; to make the money it is as tasteless for them
to refer to as it is imperative for women to know about. Stimulated
to a healthy glow by their activities – at sea, in offices, surveying
their property – they will occasionally join the ladies, look them
over, talk with them, guardedly woo them. They will give half an
ear to some indifferent piano playing and singing, half an eye to
the watercolours. Men who spend nearly as much time sitting
down as women do are not admired. Mr Woodhouse can barely be

prevailed on to leave his hearth, and Mr Collins is absurd at the dinner table or in the drawing room, abject, unmanly. Desirable men do not live in drawing rooms; they drop in between the excitements and the activities of their real lives. They may not have jobs or bosses, a daily routine or money troubles, but they do have work and cares and callings and professions. They are sailors like Captain Wentworth and Admiral Croft (and the two of Jane Austen's brothers who became admirals), they run huge estates or their smaller ones (like another Austen brother), and they earn love and respect and knowledge of the world as they do so. They go to university like Henry Tilney and Edmund Bertram. As women sit or stroll and wait they must show no impatience and must not appear to be considering the relative attractions of these lucky and glamorous intruders. Yet they *must* notice, they must keep their ears open for details of pasts and families, of property and entailments, of annual incomes and likely inheritances. They cannot help but register the beauty of Mr Elton, of Wickham and Willoughby. They must not be blinded by it.

It is possible to feel that Marianne in *Sense and Sensibility* is right to consider Colonel Brandon too old and dull for her, old enough at thirty-five 'to be my father'. A brutal realism, however, dictates that she marry him in the end. The novel is often read as a repudiation of sensibility in the name of sense. There is no question, though, that it is often no easier for Jane Austen than for her heroines to deny the attraction of beautiful and unmarriageable men. Fanny rejects Henry Crawford with more determination than Jane Austen does, and Elinor, against her better judgement, finds Willoughby irresistible. If he had made love to her rather than to Marianne, could she really have held out for Edward Ferrars?

She felt that his influence over her mind was heightened by circumstances which ought not in reason to have weight; by that person of uncommon attraction – that open, affectionate, and lively manner which it was no merit to possess, and by that still ardent love for Marianne, which it was not even innocent to indulge. But she felt that it was so, long, long before she could feel his influence less.[37]

And yet Elinor will settle for Edward, who

> was not recommended to their good opinion by any peculiar graces of person or address. He was not handsome, and his manners required intimacy to make them pleasing. He was too diffident to do justice to himself; but when his natural shyness was overcome, his behaviour gave every indication of an open, affectionate heart.[38]

And she will do so without the benefit of that 'intimacy' which might have given her a clearer view of his well-hidden charms. If a few young women in the novels marry fatherly husbands (and by no stretch of the imagination could Edward Ferrars be accounted one of those) they marry men who are better fathers than their own, ones at least who have the ability lacking in real fathers to detect the bounder, the meretricious and the plausible in other men. Mr Knightley knows that Mr Elton will want to marry a woman richer than Harriet, that Frank Churchill is not good enough for either Emma or Jane Fairfax. Colonel Brandon and Mr Darcy are in a position to have inside information as to the unsuitability of Willoughby and Wickham. Their motives for distrusting these men may not always be pure, but their experience of the world and of other men invites respect for their views. Women, without the benefit of knowing men outside the very terrain in which they may be, for women, at their most treacherous, must arrive, unaided, at similar judgements.

Jane Austen's heroines marry men who are older than they are. Some of them marry men as different as possible from their own fathers, others marry improved versions. Darcy's only failing in Elizabeth's eyes at the end of the novel is 'that he had yet to learn to be laughed at': a reminder that Mr Bennet's greatest charm is his ability to be amused and amusing. Captain Wentworth's adventurous, healthy nature is in obvious contrast with the vanity and the idleness of Anne's father. It is even possible to believe that he is in love. Certainly, Jane Austen's prospective husbands have something of the father in them, though that is not straightforward. Both Emma and Fanny have known the men they marry since childhood. Mr Knightley's relationship with Emma begins as a father and daughter onc, and the plot hinges on the stages by which they move from that history to becoming first brother and sister and then husband and wife. 'You have shown that you can dance, and you know we are not really so much brother and sister as to make it at all improper,' Emma says to him at last, and 'Brother and sister! no, indeed'[39] Mr Knightley startlingly replies: a moment as full of sexual feeling and its recognition as any in the novels. His behaviour to her and his thoughts about her have been a father's:

Emma has been meaning to read more ever since she was twelve years old. I have seen a great many lists of her drawing up at various times of books that she meant to read regularly through – and very good lists they were – very well chosen, and very neatly arranged – sometimes alphabetically, and sometimes by some other rule. The list she drew up when only fourteen – I remember thinking it did her judgment so much credit, that I preserved it some time; and I dare say she may have made out a very good list now. But I have done with expecting any course of steady reading from Emma. She will never submit to any thing requiring industry and patience, and a subjection of the fancy to the understanding.[40]

He has watched over her with concern and pride as she grew into a woman and has even allowed her to become herself. In retrospect he is prepared to tell her that he has loved her since she was thirteen in an exasperated, protective, anxious and fatherly way. That will need some modification now. He has lectured, corrected and occasionally encouraged her, all her life. He may have been a better father for her than her own. But as a husband he will need to concede that he is not her father, for that is not what Emma wants or needs. He must not let their marriage reverberate with those words he once spoke to her, during one of his fatherly harangues: 'I have still the advantage of you by sixteen years' experience, and by not being a pretty young woman and a spoiled child.'[41]

Many readers have felt that Emma's marriage holds out more promise than some of the other marriages in the novels. Part of that may be due to Mr Knightley's concessions to her, his admission that he is not her father and that loving her as a woman means more than lecturing and correcting.

My interference was quite as likely to do harm as good. It was very natural for you to say, what right has he to lecture me? – and I am afraid very natural for you to feel that it was done in a disagreeable manner. I do not believe I did you any good. The good was all to myself, by making you an object of the tenderest affection to me. I could not think about you so much without doating on you, faults and all; and by dint of fancying so many errors, have been in love with you ever since you were thirteen at least.[42]

There is also the fact that Emma is the only heroine who is marrying her social equal. As an heiress she has more than herself, her daughter-like, pupil self, to offer Mr Knightley. He must adapt to her. And as Emma puts it to Harriet, with not a little tactlessness: 'I have none of the usual inducements of women to marry.'[43] She is leaving her life as a daughter for a marriage in which she will have some power and some freedom, because she has already had some of both. For others of Jane Austen's heroines habits of deference and gratitude will be harder to shed. They will not write novels.

The difficulty in accepting Gorer's Oedipal account of Jane Austen's novels lies in the difference there must be between women's experience of authority and their expectations of submission to it (rather than a growing towards it) as intrinsic to their adventure. Jane Austen's heroines have learned that their fathers are fallible at the moment when they have to choose between short-circuiting their own adventure or accepting a lifetime's submission to another man, who will be likely, on the evidence, to share some of the failings of their fathers. Marilyn Butler asks us to see marriage for these young women as a 'consummation':

Jane Austen retained quite enough of the eighteenth century and quite enough respect for her own intelligence to give her heroines character and rationality. Yet the distinctive turns of her plots, unlike those of Maria Edgeworth, rebuke individualistic female initiatives, and imply that the consummation of a woman's life lies in marriage to a commanding man.[44]

The advantages to Catherine Morland of marrying Henry Tilney are at one level so obvious as to provide confirmation for Butler's point. But to see that marriage as 'the consummation of a woman's life' is to forget the alternatives, of which even Catherine would have been aware. The marriages of Jane Austen's heroines are not only better than all the clearly presented alternatives, they are, and spectacularly, better than the best, improbably fortunate. They are the exceptions. Most women born into the gentry would have been lucky to have Charlotte's life with Mr Collins. Maria Bertram's banishment as a disgraced wife, Mary Bennet's spinsterhood: these are serious and inescapable possibilities. The affirmation carried by 'the bells rang and everybody smiled' is the perfunctory and ritual one of fairy tales, in which everyone (or nearly everyone) lives happily ever after in a world where witches and ogres and wicked parents still stride the earth. The realities are there in Jane Austen: dependence on mean parents or brothers, loneliness, poverty, boredom, the servitude of governessing. It is the reality of women's experience and of their possibilities which impels young women in Jane Austen's novels into their adventures and towards an acceptance of men's plans for them. There is a parallel in Robert Martin's perceptions in *Emma* of the advantages of demonstrating, by imitation of his betters, that his social inferiority is just as 'natural' as their patronage. To read Jane Austen's novels as realistic *and* optimistic is wilfully to skate over the sense she gives of the constraints on women, the ignominies involved in any decision they make. As D. W. Harding put it: 'her books are, as she meant them to be, read and enjoyed by precisely the sort of people whom she disliked; she is a literary classic of the society which attitudes like hers, held widely enough, would undermine.'[45]

Jane Austen lived through a time of change; change which brought benefit to some sections of the population, despair and chaos to others, who were often adjured to bear it in the hope of a better future for their children or grandchildren. It is possible that some of the frustrations felt by women of her class, and by the women in her novels, were new ones. In her study of women workers beween 1750 and 1850, Ivy Pinchbeck[46] describes how the development of manufacturing industry altered women's work possibilities, their earning power and their family arrangements. She shows that though, characteristically, these changes affected most directly and devastatingly the poorest women, they entailed changes for richer women too, in their possibilities of work and in attitudes to how they should spend their time. These had some continuities with broader changes brought about by the beginning of the industrial revolution. Prosperity appeared to enjoin on the well-to-do imitation of aristocratic behaviour and of the ideal of beautiful idleness in women, promoted as a symbol of the breadwinner's capacity to sustain single-handed a style of life which had previously depended on the labours of a husband and his wife. Ivy Pinchbeck puts it like this:

Victorian ideas of 'refinement' prescribed a life of idleness for women, unless stern necessity ruled otherwise. Even then they were limited to the genteel but overcrowded trades of dressmakers and milliners, or to what Charlotte Brontë described as 'governessing slavery'.

By this time the effects of increased wealth and the exclusion of upper class women from industry and trade were easily discernible. 'A lady, to be such, must be a mere lady, and nothing else,' wrote Margaretta Greg in her Diary in 1853. 'She must not work for profit, or engage in any occupation that money can command, lest she invade the rights of the working classes, who live by their labour. Men in want of employment have pressed their way into nearly all the shopping and retail businesses that in my early years were managed in whole, or in part, by women. The conventional barrier that pronounces it ungenteel to be behind a counter, or serving the public in any mercantile capacity, is greatly extended. The same in household economy. Servants must be up to their offices, which is very well; but ladies, dismissed from the dairy, the confectionery, the store room, the still room, the poultry yard, the kitchen garden, and the orchard, have hardly yet found themselves a sphere equally useful and important in the pursuits of trade and art to which to apply their too abundant leisure.'[47]

Boredom is one of Jane Austen's most potent themes. It becomes something like a disease for Lady Bertram and Mr Woodhouse, and it has rather feverishly to be resisted by other characters. Yet it persists as a refrain. Chapter after chapter in *Emma* begins with details of the weather, the effects of these on plans to visit or receive visits, on delays, postponements, disappointments, on walks which might be taken or curtailed to ensure or avoid meetings, in which yesterday's meetings and conversations could be reviewed again and again. Time passes. People fill it as well as they can. Time is both urgent and wasted. The time span of the novels, of the heroine's adventure, is very short; yet within that time vast stretches are prodigally and impatiently given over to waiting. Suddenly there is a chapter in *Emma* which begins with the words: 'Human nature is so well disposed towards those who are in interesting situations, that a young person, who either marries or dies, is sure of being kindly spoken of.'[48] It is no wonder that marriage and death became the most common themes of nineteenth-century women's fiction. Marghanita Laski, in her biography of Jane Austen,[49] points to the differences between the domestic activities and responsibilities of a woman like Jane Austen's mother and the life of interested idleness expected of young women of the novelist's generation and of the women in her novels. It has always been difficult for women who are supported by men to complain of boredom. Yet Jane Austen often complained of boredom in her letters, and her heroines often do too. It is impossible not to feel that she would have been enraged by G. M. Trevelyan's contemptuous tone when he writes,

For the early Victorian 'lady' and her mother of the Regency period, too often had nothing in the world to do but to be paid for and approved by man, and to realize the type of female perfection which the breadwinner of the family expected to find in his wife and daughters. No doubt the ever-increasing numbers of leisured women usefully enlarged the reading public and the patronage of art and literature. Indeed, leisured women, like Jane Austen, Maria Edgeworth, and

Hannah More, had time and education enough to become authors and artists themselves. That was good.[50]

She would have been enraged because she would have agreed that it *was* like that for women. So long as that was what 'the bread-winner of the family expected' it could not be otherwise. It would be foolish to suggest that Jane Austen's treatment of boredom, as imaginatively polluting of her stories as Dickens's fog in *Bleak House*, meant that she (or her heroines) would have liked to serve in a shop or become an eye surgeon, as a certain Lady Read did in 1719.[51]

It is perfectly true that the best possible outcome for most young women born into the gentry at the end of the eighteenth century would have been marriage to a slightly older man with property, a position in the community, who was intelligent and benign. Jane Austen allows us to understand why that was so, why it did not always happen or turn out very well when it did, and what kinds of alternatives made it so improbably inviting. For Catherine, Elinor and Marianne, for Fanny and Elizabeth and Anne, negotiations leading to their marriages are at least as much to do with money as with love.

Ellen Moers begins her chapter on Jane Austen almost as the novelist might have done herself:

All of Jane Austen's opening paragraphs, and the best of her first sentences, have money in them; this may be the first obviously feminine thing about her novels, for money and its making were characteristically female rather than male subjects in English fiction.[52]

Women stand for love and think about money, while men like Willoughby and Wickham, who do the same thing, are disowned. Jane Austen knew, though it is possible to feel that she knew it with a sense of revulsion, that women *must* concern themselves with money. Without it their personalities could be stifled if not mutilated, their scope in the world undermined, their adventures short-circuited. A gentleman had money or made it, but did not discuss it. A lady had no money, thought and spoke continually of it and prepared to offer her body and her life in exchange for it.

That paradox stands for all the other paradoxes in the novels and underpins them. Fathers and indeed most men could not always be trusted, and women would do well to be wary of them. Women had at the same time to come to terms with their own dependence on men, for men's adventures were the real ones. If that involved some women in denying the reality of their own adventures we should not be surprised by that.

Those critics who have insisted upon Jane Austen's wit and sense, upon her stern opposition to the cults of individualism, sensibility and irrationality, and those who have felt it necessary to remind us that she was a Christian and a conservative, orthodox and unrebellious, have concentrated on 'the distinctive turns of her plots' at the expense of the quality of social and family life generating those plots, urging them forward and tripping them up. She made her novels sites of boredom, longing, constraint and frustration. Against that she set marriage, as an ambiguous escape, beset with dangers, but a possibility, and above all a possibility for ensuring your keep for the rest of your life. There might be a chance for a young woman to meet a man she could love, who was in a position to support her, to take over from the pains and limitations of girlhood, allowing her to become more than she is. It was not a chance most women had, but it stands as the organising principle of women's consent to their subjection to men, not a culmination so much as a hypothesis. At the end of *Pride and Prejudice* we get a glimpse of Darcy's younger sister, pondering the differences between a sister and a wife:

By Elizabeth's instructions she began to comprehend that a woman may take liberties with her husband, which a brother will not always allow in a sister more than ten years younger than himself.[53]

Might not that in itself provide one motive for a young woman to embark on her own short adventure?

In 1847, G. H. Lewes recommended *Pride and Prejudice* to Charlotte Brontë. In her reply to him she wrote:

And what did I find? An accurate, daguerreotyped portrait of a commonplace face; a carefully-fenced, highly-cultivated garden, with

neat borders and delicate flowers; but no glance of a bright, vivid
physiognomy, no open country, no fresh air, no blue hill, no bonny
beck. I should hardly like to live with her ladies and gentlemen, in their
elegant but confined houses.[54]

Charlotte Brontë is not the only reader to have recoiled from the
grimness of so much of the life Jane Austen writes about and to
have wondered about the after life of those of her heroines who
have achieved their 'consummation'.

3

Brothers

The day dreams in which you habitually indulge are likely to induce a distempered state of mind; and in proportion as all the ordinary uses of the world seem to you flat and unprofitable, you will be unfitted for them without becoming fitted for anything else. Literature cannot be the business of a woman's life, and it ought not to be. The more she is engaged in her proper duties, the less leisure will she have for it, even as an accomplishment and a recreation. To those duties you have not yet been called, and when you are you will be less eager for celebrity.

Robert Southey to Charlotte Brontë[1]

Patrick Brontë, parson and hypochondriac, outlived his wife and six children, yet fathers (and indeed husbands) make only occasional appearances in his daughters' novels. Agnes Grey starts out with a father, it is true, and so does Catherine Earnshaw, and there is Mr Yorke in *Shirley*. There is also Mr Home/de Bassompierre, the father of Pauline, that exquisite child in *Villette* who moves with such deadly tranquillity from daughterhood as Polly into a marriage of formaldehyde and perpetually preserved adolescence as Pauline. Agnes Grey has a mother too, and Caroline Helstone in *Shirley* finds hers: a mixed blessing, for if Mrs Pryor is rapturously recognised by her daughter she is also seen as potentially oppressive in her narrowness of experience and vision. Parents must be very nearly the only constraint which Brontë heroines are spared. As orphan children and orphan women their protagonists will be brothers: bad, spoiled ones and twins, warily watched as second selves and other halves.

Charlotte Brontë must always have been alert to the blandishments of the fatherly voice and its double-edged counsel, its
violence and its benevolence. She would not have been deaf to the
irony of Southey's later comment on his short correspondence
with her in her youth: 'Probably she will think well of me as long as
she lives.'[2] How predictably treacherous Thackeray's remarks
about her in a letter to a young woman friend would have seemed:

So you are all reading Villette to one another – a pretty amusement to
be sure – I wish I was a hearing of you and a smoking of a cigar the
while. The good of Villette in my opinion Miss is a very fine style; and a
remarkable happy way (which few female authors possess) of carrying a
metaphor logically through to its conclusion. And it amuses me to read
the author's naive confession of being in love with 2 men at the same
time; and her readiness to fall in love at any time. The poor little woman
of genius! The fiery little eager brave tremulous homely-faced creature!
I can read a great deal of her life as I fancy her in her book and see that
rather than have fame, rather than any other earthly good or mayhap
heavenly one, she wants some Tomkins or another to love her and be in
love with. But you see she is a little bit of a creature without a
pennyworth of good looks, thirty years old I should think, buried in the
country, and eating up her own heart there and no Tomkins will come.
You girls with pretty faces and red boots (and what *not*) will get dozens
of young fellows fluttering about you – whereas here is one genius, a
noble heart longing to mate itself and destined to wither away into old
maidenhood with no chance to fulfil the burning desire. Not that I
should say burning – les demoiselles ne brulent pas – Mais elles
s'ennuient voyez vous à être seules.[3]

Indeed, Charlotte could be said to have anticipated Thackeray's
letter when she made Shirley say to her friend Caroline:

'If men could see us as we really are, they would be a little amazed; but
the cleverest, the acutest men are often under an illusion about women:
they do not read them in a true light: they misapprehend them, both for
good and evil: their good woman is a queer thing, half doll, half angel;
their bad woman almost always a fiend. Then to hear them fall into
ecstasies with each other's creations, worshipping the heroine of such a
poem – novel – drama, thinking it fine – divine! Fine and divine it may
be, but often quite artificial – false as the rose in my best bonnet there.

If I spoke all I think on this point; if I gave my real opinion of some
first-rate female characters in first-rate works, where should I be? Dead
under a cairn of avenging stones in half-an-hour.'

To which Caroline replies,

'Shirley, you chatter so, I can't fasten you: be still. And after all,
authors' heroines are almost as good as authoress's heroes.'

And Shirley again:

'Not at all: women read men more truly than men read women. I'll
prove that in a magazine paper some day when I've time; only it will
never be inserted: it will be "declined with thanks," and left for me at
the publisher's.'[4]

If the spectre of fathers and of Patrick Brontë could be sidestep-
ped by Charlotte, Emily and Anne Brontë, the figure of their
brother Branwell could not. He is there in the cruel teasing of
Agnes Grey's young charges, in the delinquent Huntingdon and
in the vulnerable and addicted Lord Lowborough of *The Tenant of
Wildfell Hall*. He is there in Heathcliff, whom Catherine knows as
'more myself than I am'. He is there for Charlotte as her
childhood partner in fantasy and her equal, and as destroyer of his
own gifts and threat to hers, superior, wilful and suffering. Her
novels search for the 'semblable', the only man who might
ultimately be loved and trusted because he would 'know' her and
accept her. The men are tried out, tested. They cannot be trusted
until they have won an understanding of women's experience out
of failures and pains of their own. Such men must do more than
sympathise with women's difficulties. They must have known
fear, duality and exclusion themselves.

Marriage, in Charlotte Brontë's novels, is a kind of mirage, a
dream which recedes as it is approached. Its prospect and the
prospect of a husband, a man who could love and be loved, are
explored through the image of a brother, a phantom from childhood, who is resurrected in a variety of guises, and tried out.
Where Tom, in George Eliot's *The Mill on the Floss*, actually

stands between Maggie and her sexual fulfilment and marriage, the phantom brother in Charlotte Brontë's novels both promises that possibility and explains why it is likely to be withheld.

Mr Rochester is premature when he says to Jane, 'you fear in the presence of a man and a brother – or father, or master, or what you will – to smile too gaily, speak too freely, or move too quickly: but in time, I think you will be natural with me.'[5] Not yet, not while he is still able to believe that his loving her will be enough. He is still ignorant of the agonies of dependence and its necessary distrust, and he is unable to understand Jane's shrinking from the expansive future and the freedoms he is offering her when he asks, 'Are you anything akin to me, do you think, Jane?' and she replies, 'I have not been trampled on. I have not been petrified', and then, 'I am a free human being with an independent will.' Even Mr Rochester's words, 'my equal is here, and my likeness',[6] his proposal of marriage, are not enough. He will have to live with loss and solitude, blinded and crippled as a woman can feel herself to be, before Jane can trust herself with him. Not until then can Jane be sure that he will not treat her as he treated his first wife; for, she tells him, 'you are inexorable for that unfortunate lady: you speak of her with hate – with vindictive antipathy. It is cruel – she cannot help being mad'.[7]

How is Jane to know whether he would treat her as he treated his mistresses:

if I were so far to forget myself and all the teaching that had ever been instilled into me, as – under any pretext – with any justification – through any temptation – to become the successor of these poor girls, he would one day regard me with the same feeling which now in his mind desecrated their memory?[8]

It is not until Rochester can accept all of Jane Eyre, her potential madness, her sexuality and her vulnerability that he will become acceptable as a lover and a husband. The happy marriage which ends *Jane Eyre* is shot through with what could well be Charlotte's childhood memories of herself as the older sister of the charming and precocious Branwell:

He saw nature – he saw books through me; and never did I weary of gazing for his behalf, and of putting into words the effect of field, tree, town, river, cloud, sunbeam – of the landscape before us; of the weather round us – and impressing by sound on his ear what light could no longer stamp on his eye. Never did I weary of reading to him; never did I weary of conducting him where he wished to go: of doing for him what he wished to be done. And there was a pleasure in my services, most full, most exquisite, even though sad – because he claimed these services without painful shame or damping humiliation. He loved me so truly that he knew no reluctance in profiting by my attendance; he felt I loved him so fondly, that to yield that attendance was to indulge my sweetest wishes.[9]

The good marriage – and there are echoes of Emma and Mr Knightley in it – must start with a man's concessions, his acknowledgement of his own dependence and a brotherly admission of equality. That prospect is such an improbable one that in order to ensure it Charlotte Brontë resorted to tactics of brow-beating, physical assault and even manslaughter in her treatment of the men her heroines marry or contemplate marrying. In a later chapter I shall suggest that the appeal of 'romantic' fiction for women lies partly in its proposal that men give up as much for love of a woman as a woman is expected to give up; that 'romance' is a fantasy of female power, rather as pornography is a fantasy of male power. The image of the brother haunts such fictions as the embodiment of all that is forbidden and all that is known, intimate, recognisable from childhood, susceptible to taming and to the acknowledgement of equality between a man and a woman.

Adrienne Rich has written that 'The bond between Catherine and Heathcliff is the archetypal bond between the split fragments of the psyche, the masculine and feminine elements ripped apart and longing for reunion.'[10] There have always been difficulties in reading *Wuthering Heights* as a story of thwarted and thwarting sexual passion. If Heathcliff is Branwell as a boy and as a desperate young man, he is also Emily herself. He has some similarities, it should be said, to Emily's dog Keeper as well, which, as Mrs Gaskell put it, 'had come to the Parsonage in the fierce strength of his youth. Sullen and ferocious he had met with his master in the indomitable Emily. Like most dogs of his kind, he feared, respected, and deeply loved her who subdued him'.[11] The novel's violence is childhood violence, sibling rages of jealousy, covetousness, need. The passionate cry for union, completeness, howled and echoed by Catherine and Heathcliff, is a cry for a return to prepubescent innocence and confidence, when sister and brother were equal and children and threatened only by shifting and alternating allegiances within the family. That cry became for the adolescent and then the mature Emily a secret and mystical longing to be one with nature and the universe. Her poetry contains bright visions of that possibility and black despair when the power as well as the innocence of childhood seemed withdrawn and gone for ever. Winifred Gérin[12] suggests that after Emily's death Charlotte worked to disguise, even to destroy, all evidence of this side of Emily as pagan and freakish. Neither being a woman, nor men, were, in Virginia Woolf's word, 'impediments' for Emily, who may be thought to have come near to achieving Woolf's announced objective for the woman writer of the future: 'that curious sexual quality which comes only when sex is unconscious of itself'.[13] Whereas Charlotte recoiled from her brother Branwell during the last months of his dissolution before his death, Emily appears to have stood by him, to have procured drugs for him and to have hidden from her sisters aspects of his condition and her own sympathetic view of him. The adult love of Catherine and Heathcliff in *Wuthering Heights* alludes to and comes out of Emily's close identification with a brother who is both a part of herself, a reflection of herself and fierce even in his submission to her.

Anne and Charlotte can seem to treat women's relationships with men more straightforwardly. Their heroines admit to feeling love for men and admit that such love is physical and sexual. In some measure the difficulties and the contradictions of the relationships between women and men which they write about start from the difficulties and the contradictions there are in a sister's love for a brother. For if brothers stand behind the novels as models for relationships which might be familiar, close and equal partnerships within which the man will concede to the woman some power and even kinds of creative superiority, brothers also stand as warnings. Brothers can be dissolute bullies, spoiled and favoured siblings and, of course, images of men who are above all forbidden as lovers. The hateful, unhealthy John Reed is Jane Eyre's cousin and a kind of brother. So is St John Rivers, the perfect ivory statue and saint, who is also allowed to have a likeness to Jane, as Rochester believes he has. The marriage Rivers offers Jane is in every sense 'blanche': a cold, unintimate partnership between a master and his servant. It is not very hard for Jane to reject it:

Can I receive from him the bridal ring, endure all the forms of love (which I doubt not he would scrupulously observe) and know that the spirit was quite absent? Can I bear the consciousness that every endearment he bestows is a sacrifice made on principle? No: such a martyrdom would be monstrous. I will never undergo it. As his sister, I might accompany him – not as his wife.[14]

About eight years before Charlotte Brontë wrote that, in 1839, she wrote to her friend Ellen Nussey, whose brother, Mrs Gaskell suggests, she had just turned down:

I had a kindly leaning towards him, because he is an amiable and well-disposed man. Yet I had not, and could not have, that intense attachment which would make me willing to die for him; and if ever I marry, it must be in that light of adoration that I will regard my husband. Ten to one I shall never have the chance again; but *n'importe*. Moreover, I was aware that he knew so little of me he could hardly be conscious to whom he was writing. Why! It would startle him to see me in my natural home character; he would think I was a wild, romantic enthusiast indeed. I could not sit all day long making a grave face before my husband. I would laugh, and satirize, and say whatever came into my head first.[15]

He is Ellen's brother, but not Charlotte's, and he knew 'so little' of her.

Charlotte Brontë may have been ashamed of Emily's secret. She was also ashamed of her own, of her 'natural home character', which included romantic enthusiasms and an imaginative world, and would come to include the capacity to write novels. Anger, depression, wilfulness were aspects of herself she expected men to recoil from. She also expected them to abhor her initiative and her power as a writer. Only a brother might have come near to knowing who she was and accepting it, and Branwell knew her as the organiser of the family's games and fictions. Jane Eyre grows up knowing that bad, outspoken girls get locked into stifling red rooms and she will learn that mad women are locked in attics and become monstrous. Men may forgive plainness, but they do not forgive ugliness or unseemly energy. Thackeray was wrong. Neither Charlotte Brontë nor her heroines are looking for a Tomkins, nor even simply for a husband. In contemplating what life with a man might be like, they are firmly stating their conditions and acknowledging the likelihood that those conditions would not be met. In another letter to Ellen Nussey, which Charlotte wrote in 1843, she spells out the impossibility for her as a woman who could neither demand nor expect that her conditions be met:

Not that it is a crime to marry, or a crime to wish to be married; but it is an imbecility, which I reject with contempt, for women, who have neither fortune nor beauty, to make marriage the principal object of their wishes and hopes, and the aim of all their actions; not to be able to convince themselves that they are unattractive, and that they had better be quiet, and think of other things than wedlock.[16]

Charlotte Brontë knew, clearly, that such a protestation could not be made publicly, nor to a man like Thackeray, whose contempt she prefigures in her letter. Could a woman, her novels ask, who feels 'a knowledge of my own', reconcile that knowledge with a man's view of her, particularly if that man's view of her is that she is poor and 'unattractive'?

In her first novel, *The Professor*, she impersonates a man, as if to discover from within a man's body and clothes and career what he wants of a woman. She must have been discouraged that her hero should tell her, as it were, that in his marriage, 'it was her pleasure, her joy to make me still the master in all things'.[17] Charlotte gave up male impersonation after her first novel, as both Shirley and at one point Lucy Snowe do too, though she never wanted to relinquish her author's name, Currer Bell,[18] which was perhaps more androgynous than male anyway. If some form of impersonation was necessary as a disguise and for concealment, it was not in the novels themselves the way to deal with her inner divisions or with her curiosity about men's feelings for women.

In her review of *Villette* in *The Daily News*,[19] which put an end to a brief friendship with Charlotte Brontë, Harriet Martineau deplored 'the writer's tendency to describe the need of being loved'. There were, she insisted, 'substantial, heartfelt interests for women of all ages, and under ordinary circumstances, quite apart from love'. These charges went sharply home, touching Charlotte's vanity and the fears, which the three Brontës differently felt, about exposing their most secret selves and impulses in their writing. Charlotte must have felt no less hurt and reproved by Martineau's specific reference to *Villette*, in which 'the heroine, who tells her own story, leaves the reader at last under the uncomfortable impression of her having either entertained a double love, or allowed one to supercede another without notification of the transition.'[20]

Pairs of men figure, in fact, in all her novels. William Crimshaw in *The Professor* is defined as the opposite of his greedy and worldly brother, who excludes him from the family inheritance. In *Jane Eyre*, the warm, dark ugliness of Mr Rochester is illuminated by the ethereally pale and ascetic beauty of St John Rivers; and both are seen as 'akin', related to Jane Eyre herself, facets and adjuncts of her own contrary aspects. Robert and Louis Moore in *Shirley* are brothers, alike and unalike. Both are 'masters', Robert to his workers, Louis to his pupils. Both are proud and inaccessible, both brought low: Robert by his workers and the injuries they inflict on him and on his factory and machines, Louis by the humiliation he endures as a tutor (or male governess) who is in love with the rich young pupil, Shirley, who employs him. In *Jane Eyre* and in *Villette*, these pairs of men allow Charlotte Brontë to do more than explore different male types. They make it possible to focus on the contradictions in the heroines themselves, in terms of what these women want and expect of men and how they are caught by (and learn to evade) men's visions of them. *Shirley*, we know, was intended in some sense as a study of Emily, and the second half of the novel was written immediately after Emily's death. This may account for what is often thought perfunctory, indeed factitious, in *Shirley*'s resolving itself into a North of England *Così Fan Tutte*, in which the brothers serve merely as eligible husbands for two very different women, rather than as sites for an exploration of the differences themselves.

Villette is a novel of differences and divisions and contrasts. Lucy Snowe's life, her ordeal, takes her into two countries, two languages, two cultures, two religions. She is an immigrant, poised and powerless between two worlds, neither of which offers her a home. She wanders outside homes and families, sometimes exhilarated, sometimes terrified. The novel itself splits into moods and modes: uncanny happenings and nightmares and illness are the dark side of all the glitter and the resplendent flesh of the Catholic Church and the Belgian bourgeoisie. Reason and Feeling, like a pair of twirling, allegorical figures on the cathedral, take turns to admonish and exhort her. Feeling is physical: feverish temperatures, sudden change. On Lucy's journey to Villette,

The sky, too, was monotonously grey; the atmosphere was stagnant and humid; yet amidst all these deadening influences, my fancy budded fresh and my heart basked in sunshine. These feelings, however, were well kept in check by the secret but ceaseless consciousness of anxiety lying in wait on enjoyment, like a tiger crouched in a jungle. The breathing of that beast of prey was in my ear always; his fierce heart panted close against mine; he never stirred in his lair but I felt him; I knew he waited only for sun-down to bound ravenous from his ambush.[21]

Reason will tell her to control feeling, to distrust affection, treat glimmers of love and glimmers of ghosts with scepticism. Reason is often English rather than French and Protestant rather than Catholic.

Duality has for a long time been seen as a theme of Romantic literature,[22] which shapes plot and imagery and may stand for newly diagnosed pathologies as well as for newly perceived realities and conflicts in nineteenth-century life. Jeremy Hawthorn, in his study of multiple personality in literature,[23] suggests that where male duality has been expressed geographically, as, for instance, a pull between town and country, between work and play, between the street and the home, women have needed to internalise their contradictions, to make contrasts between inner and outer space, between secrecy, concealment and public display. In *Villette*, he writes, 'Charlotte Brontë explores the complex links between powerlessness, repression and self-division as they face the educated, poor, middle-class woman of her day.'[24] A central duality for Lucy Snowe is between the self that is seen, looked at or reduced to invisibility by men, and the self which watches. The two men in the novel, Graham Bretton and Paul Emanuel, are watchers and they are watched. And whereas in Charlotte Brontë's earlier novels, as in Jane Austen's, men are fixed by their names, their natures, their position, even their 'character', here these two men are as apt to deliquesce and transform themselves as Lucy is herself.

Kate Millett may have been right to regard *Villette* as 'a book too subversive to be popular',[25] but she is surely misunderstanding it when she claims that '*Villette* reads like one long meditation on a prison break.'[26] Certainly there are images of traps and prisons, of stifling attics and dormitories and classrooms which deny privacy. These, though, are very much features of her inner space as well as of her outer space. Lucy's prison is her own body. It is also her security and her refuge, from which she can view the world and its watchers, turning them into creations of her own mind, servants of her own wishes for herself. By the time Charlotte Brontë wrote *Villette* her two sisters and her brother were dead, and her cover as Currer Bell was blown. There is a new bravery in her last novel and new consequent terrors. If she is known now, exposed and watched, at least she will stare back. The tiger of her inner anxiety will be distanced and confronted.

Graham Bretton is an adolescent, 'the deeply-cherished son'[27] of Mrs Bretton, when Lucy first meets him. She is adopted by his mother, so that Graham becomes for Lucy the favoured, lucky sibling, handsome and dotingly loved by his mother, by his adopted sister and by the miniature Polly. He is charmed, spoiled and enviable. He is Dr John by the time Lucy is rescued by him on her arrival in Villette, a tall and handsome Englishman, who introduces her to the school run by Madame Beck, where she will teach and study. As a successful and eligible young English doctor abroad he is desired by the formidable *directrice* and is himself secretly and absurdly in love with the magnificently shallow Ginevra Fanshaw, for whom he is no more than a gullibly generous admirer she nicknames M. Isidore. His fluctuating manifestations, and names, are administered as a kind of punishment, just as his triumphant insensitivity to Lucy and to little Polly is reversed and mimicked by Ginevra's treatment of him. There is a langorousness to Graham's transformations, for they are performed on him by the invisible and meditatively watching Lucy, whom he does not recognise from his childhood. His 'masculine self-love',[28] the strength and stability conferred by his mother's conceding that 'my son is master, and must be obeyed',[29] foster a superb male hubris. It is this which Lucy undermines, through his blindness to her and to the real Ginevra. As his sister, his mother, his creator, Lucy Snowe loves him, for his beauty, his kindness and his maleness, but she does so privately and invisibly, allowing herself an inner flirtation, from which she can play tricks with him and on him and can also finally dismiss him. He can never know her, can never even see her. There is 'no notification of the transition'[30] to another love, for they overlap.

Paul Emanuel is utterly foreign, if always indeterminately and variably so, and he is small, ugly and a Catholic. As an inspired literature teacher at the school where Lucy studies and teaches, he seems to her to wear 'the mask of an intelligent tiger'.[31] His names are slippery. Lucy decorates the box she makes for his birthday, 'P.C.D.E. for Paul Carl (or Carlos) David Emanuel'.[32] The 'black and sallow tiger' becomes a saint, a knight, a Bonaparte, a monk, a subtle teacher, a ranting bully, a prig and whiner, a proud and kindly mentor. He too is often a brother, as Graham is; so that they are two loved alter egos, reflections and reflectors of the different aspects of herself. Dressed, for instance, in the surprising pink dress which Mrs Bretton gives her, Lucy is invisible to Graham still, but a scarlet woman to Paul Emanuel. 'Quiet Lucy Snowe', who is 'an inoffensive shadow'[34] to Graham, is a dangerous Protestant, *bas bleue* and free spirit, full for M. Paul of 'unfeminine knowledge',[35] fiery display and resistance.

As Lucy meditatively, and at first despairingly, contemplates these opposite reflections of herself, these viewers of her own oppositions, she also plays with her own creations, for she begins to see that these men are refracted through her vision as she feels herself to be through theirs. The difficulty in accepting Thackeray's or Martineau's views of *Villette*, or Kate Millett's Amazonian 'prison break' or even Jeremy Hawthorn's kindly diagnosis that 'it is the contradictory view of women taken by men that divides women into two'[36] is that though they are not wrong they all ignore the fact that these are men created by a woman and watched in the novel by a woman. They do not simply produce or reflect Lucy Snowe's ambivalence, they are themselves its products. It is she who learns to reduce their fixed, male solidity to the same insubstantiality which characterises the reflections of herself she constantly glimpses in mirrors throughout the novel. *Villette* is more than a record of one woman's 'dis-ease'. Charlotte Brontë developed through Lucy Snowe a theory of the female imagination as constructed out of resistance to men's control over women's bodies and women's vision. Graham, she realises, is the creation of her love and her creativity. Without her he is marble, a jest, a creature who cannot thrive outside her imaginings:

I recalled Dr. John; my warm affection for him; my faith in his excellence; my delight in his grace. What was become of that curious one-sided friendship which was half marble and half life; only on one hand truth, and on the other perhaps a jest? . . .

Good night, Dr. John; you are good, you are beautiful, but you are not mine.[37]

Disingenuously, Lucy announces early that 'Of an artistic temperament, I deny that I am.'[38] She prefers to see herself as a good student, doggedly conscientious with the *devoirs* M. Paul sets her to. If this is not the first woman's *Künstlerroman* it is a novel in which the possibilities for a woman to be artist as well as heroine, watcher as well as watched, are intricately and elaborately explored. As M. Paul's student she also struggles with opposing desires. She can simultaneously long to be clever enough to crush his 'mocking spirit' and ponder with a mocking spirit of her own his awful warnings about women who are clever, for

A 'woman of intellect,' it appeared, was a sort of *lusus naturae*, a luckless accident, a thing for which there was neither place nor use in creation, wanted neither as wife nor worker. Beauty anticipated her in the first office. He believed in his soul that lovely, placid, and passive feminine mediocrity was the only pillow on which manly thought and sense could find rest for its aching temples; and as to work, male mind alone could work to any good practical result – hein?[39]

During her recovery from a depressive illness Lucy is looked after by the Brettons, and Graham shows her Villette. He takes to leaving her at galleries for two or three hours, where she contemplates, alone, and with a good deal of asperity as well as pleasure, 'several very well-executed and complacent-looking fat women (*which*) struck me as by no means the goddesses they appeared to consider themselves'.[40] It is easy enough to picture Thackeray's knowing smile as he read this. One day she moves towards a painting which is cordoned off, the queen of the collection:

It represented a woman, considerably larger, I thought, than the life. I calculated that this lady, put into a scale of magnitude suitable for the reception of a commodity of bulk, would infallibly turn from fourteen to sixteen stone. She was, indeed, extremely well fed: very much butcher's meat – to say nothing of bread, vegetables, and liquids – must she have consumed to attain that breadth and height, that wealth of muscle, that affluence of flesh. She lay half-reclined on a couch: why, it would be difficult to say; broad daylight blazed round her: she appeared in hearty health, strong enough to do the work of two plain cooks; she could not plead a weak spine; she ought to have been standing, or at least sitting bolt upright. She had no business to lounge away the noon on a sofa. She ought likewise to have worn decent garments; a gown covering her properly, which was not the case: out of abundance of material – seven-and-twenty yards, I should say, of drapery – she managed to make inefficient raiment. Then, for the wretched untidiness surrounding her, there could be no excuse. Pots and pans – perhaps I ought to say vases and goblets – were rolled here and there on the foreground; a perfect rubbish of flowers was mixed amongst them, and an absurd and disorderly mass of curtain upholstery smothered the couch and cumbered the floor. On referring to the catalogue, I found that this notable production bore name 'Cleopatra'.[41]

Humour, amazement, disapproval, pain are all mixed here. This huge mountain of female flesh is a reproof to Lucy's insignificant figure. Cleopatra reminds Lucy of her robust pupils, fattened for marriage, who patronise her and are scornful of their studies and their teachers. Cleopatra is also and especially Gin-evra, the callous beauty loved by Graham, who can ask Lucy, 'But are you anybody?' 'Cleopatra' is a painful as well as a ridiculous spectacle for Lucy because she is a man's celebration of female sexuality, a woman's body relished and desired by men, a denial of the reality of her own small, withdrawn body and its containing of her, since it is neither beautiful nor fruitful. John Berger developed an interesting thesis in his *Ways of Seeing* about paintings of women and the ideology of ownership they carry and transmit:

Men look at women. Women watch themselves being looked at. This determines not only most relations between men and women but also the relation of women to themselves. The surveyor of woman in herself is male: the surveyed female. Thus she turns herself into an object – and most particularly an object of vision: a sight.[42]

Do women inevitably become for themselves the object of men's vision, a sight? And do they become 'men' by looking at women, and at themselves, as men might? There is a bleak determinism in Berger's account which is difficult for women to accept, and equally difficult to dispute. How can a woman value her body for being her perambulating, operational self, her place and space and solidity and history, if its surfaces have no currency with men, as sheath or container for their own desires? The dilemma for women confronted with images of themselves as 'sex objects' has always had two faces to it. It is reducing of women, expressive of their ambiguous value in the world. It is also the lure and the most devastating delusion for women, for it asks them to believe that if they were as beautiful as 'Cleopatra' they would be as powerful as she was, a queen. Lucy looking at 'Cleopatra' is caught and condemned for both her wishes and her failure, but she is also forewarned, so that she can detach herself. She can herself become a watcher of watchers, aware of herself as a woman who can make men the objects of *her* vision. As she sits 'wondering at' the painting and concluding that it is 'on the whole an enormous piece of claptrap' (and how surreptitiously Charlotte Brontë makes that phrase a reassuringly male remark) she is discovered by Paul Emanuel, outraged to find her there alone, left to her untoward devices, and looking at this of all pictures. Lucy, seeing him, can turn the tables on him, registering her sight of him with the eye of a Flemish master, the kind she admires, not Rubens:

M. Paul's hair was shorn close as raven down, or I think it would have bristled on his head. Beginning now to perceive his drift, I had a certain pleasure in keeping cool, and working him up.

  'Astounding insular audacity,' cried the professor. 'Singulières femmes que ces Anglaises!'

  'What is the matter, monsieur?'

  'Matter! How dare you, a young person, sit coolly down, with the self-possession of a garçon, and look at *that* picture?'

  'It is a very ugly picture, but I cannot at all see why I should not look at it.'[43]

And while M. Paul goes off, perhaps to join the crowd of gentlemen and ladies surrounding the 'Cleopatra', Lucy is packed off to scrutinise a set of four paintings, as demure and diminutive as she is, called 'La vie d'une femme':

The first represented a 'Jeune Fille,' coming out of a church-door, a missal in her hand, her dress very prim, her eyes cast down, her mouth pursed up – the image of a most villainous little precocious she-hypocrite. The second, a 'Mariée' with a long white veil, kneeling at a prie-dieu in her chamber, holding her hands plastered together, finger to finger, and showing the whites of her eyes in a most exasperating manner. The third, a 'Jeune Mère,' hanging disconsolate over a clayey and puffy baby with a face like an unwholesome full moon. The fourth, a 'Veuve,' being a black woman, holding by the hand a black little girl, and the twain studiously surveying an elegant French monument, set up in a corner of some Père la Chaise. All these four 'Anges' were grim and grey as burglars, and cold and vapid as ghosts. What women to live with! insincere, ill-humoured, bloodless, brainless nonentities! As bad in their way as the indolent gipsy-giantess, the Cleopatra, in hers.[44]

There is no doubt of Lucy's anger here, and if she is railing at women and at women's lives, she is also railing at men's representations of women, paintings of women by men, in which women have let themselves be traduced, have lent themselves to the reductive story men tell about good women. There is anger at women's acquiescence in such representations, but Lucy's response is also set alongside, and in equality with, the reactions of the men Charlotte Brontë has invented to the painting of Cleopatra. M. Paul shudders at Cleopatra's provocations: she may be 'une femme superbe', but he would have her 'ni pour femme, ni pour fille, ni pour soeur'. The fashionably vapid and 'pretty' Colonel de Hamal gazes admiringly and titteringly at the painting. Graham's unamused assurance that 'my mother is a better-looking woman' is wonderfully made the remark of an Englishman, and his adding to it ' "le voluptueux" is little to my liking. Compare that mulatto with Ginevra!' reminds us that he is as blind to the implications of 'Cleopatra' as he is to Ginevra. Lucy is reassured: not because these men's responses to the painting confirm her sense of it as 'claptrap', but because she can see, as they do not, the delusions and the ironies represented by such captive and captivating women. Her pain at not being one is neutralised by her understanding of the pains involved for women who settle for that.

This is an important scene, exuberant and poised. It marks Lucy's emergence from her summer fever, when loneliness made the charms and the festivities of other people, other women, so oppressive to her that she considered suicide. Its vigour signals the beginnings of recovery and discovery, of her own reality and creativity, of a faith in her own vision and her capacity to see herself, untethered by the limitations and perspectives of other people's views of her, and especially men's. The visit to the gallery is followed by the concert, to which she wears her ambiguous pink dress and catches disconcerting sight of herself in a mirror:

Thus for the first, and perhaps only time in my life, I enjoyed the 'giftie' of seeing myself as others see me.

This is a significant moment for her, because if

It brought a jar of discord, a pang of regret; it was not flattering, yet, after all, I ought to be thankful; it might have been worse.[45]

The central chapters of the novel have Lucy imagining herself in love with Graham. They are strangely hallucinatory, for her love is neither revealed nor received. She answers his banal though treasured letters in twos, ones to him dictated by Reality, ones for herself dictated by Feeling. She confides her sightings of the ghostly nun to him, secretly matching his scepticism with a scepticism of her own. Her happiness survives the clear and chilling reality of his indifference. She can love, dream, imagine, have visions, write letters. If it is not quite enough it is a good deal more than she has ever had before. She buries Graham's letters and her grief.

That 'notification of the transition' so sternly found missing by Harriet Martineau is in fact to be found in the chapter when Graham takes Lucy to the theatre to see a performance by the celebrated actress, Vashti, who is old now. Vashti is almost certainly based on the great Rachel, whom Charlotte Brontë was taken to see in London at about the time she was writing *Villette*. The experience is an extraordinary one for Lucy, at once liberating and monstrous:

It was a marvellous sight: a mighty revelation.
It was a spectacle low, horrible, immoral.[46]

Those two lines catch Lucy's and Charlotte Brontë's unresolved and perhaps unresolvable double focus on the woman artist. They hold the spectating Lucy's shock and excitement, her sensitivity to the kind of exposure of herself the aging actress was daring to make, the cruelty with which such courage in a woman might be received, her reaction to the performance as a wonderfully imaginative act and her sense of its dangerousness, the likelihood of its being dismissed or ridiculed as immodest, excessive, unseemly.

At one point in his *The Subjection of Women* John Stuart Mill speculates about women and art. He wonders why there have been no great women artists in exactly those areas where women have been encouraged to become accomplished. His hypothesis is fine as far as it goes. Women have not been allowed to become professionals, in the sense of having access to sanctioned support, training and competition with other professionals for money and patrons and audiences. He is able to explain the fact that acting and singing have been areas where women have excelled professionally by asserting that these arts do 'not require the same general powers of mind' as writing and painting and composing, and are, anyway, 'dependent on a natural gift'.[47] It is the old sleight of hand: historical, social determinants become natural ones by a process of elision. It is certainly interesting to speculate as to why it should have been that men have found women who made a living out of their bodies less threatening and less 'unnatural' than they have found women who made a living with their minds. We are returned to the 'natural' woman and the 'civilised' man.[48]

It may also be that women's failure to achieve 'greatness' in the other arts is better tackled by considering the use of the word 'great' when it is permissibly applied to women. A woman 'great' with child, even a 'great' lady, have greatness conferred on them by men. A 'great' woman novelist or thinker presents men with a spectacle of a woman achieving something entirely on her own, unwatched and unsupervised. Certainly many women writers have agreed publicly with Mill's point, and two of the 'greatest' of them, Charlotte Brontë and George Eliot,[49] chose as their 'great' artists an actress and a singer.

Vashti's performance is powerful and powerfully handled, extraordinary, exciting, moving and bizarrely intolerable too. It is made to stand in devastating contrast to 'Cleopatra' and to Rubens, who created her. 'Cleopatra' is a 'slug' by the side of the tigrish Vashti. The tiger of anxiety has been transformed into the tiger of creation. 'Where was the artist of the Cleopatra?' Lucy wonders, 'Let him come and sit down and study this different vision.' It is a woman's vision, and a vision of a woman, the most astonishing experience of Lucy's life for being a vision of female power unmediated by men and beyond their judgement and understanding. The moment makes it possible to relinquish Graham, to see him as the successful creation of her own imagination, the tamed brother. Graham can only judge Vashti 'as a woman, not an artist: it was a branding judgment.' It is a judgement which contains her judgement of him. He is no thinker, no artist. He is a good, sweet man, but 'unimpressible':

Dr John *could* think and think well, but he was rather a man of action than of thought; he *could* feel, and feel vividly in his way, but his heart had no chord for enthusiasm: to bright, soft, sweet influences his eyes and lips gave bright, soft, sweet welcome, beautiful to see as dyes of rose and silver, pearl and purple, embuing summer clouds; for what belonged to storm, what was wild and intense, dangerous, sudden, and flaming, he had no sympathy, and held with it no communion.[50]

Later, she will watch him fall in love with little Polly, now petrified into the heiress, Pauline, and she will end the silent love affair she has had with him in her head, 'Good night, Dr. John; you are good, you are beautiful, but you are not mine.'

Lucy is 'amused and enlightened' by her discovery of Vashti and her uncovering of Graham, and she is released. We wait, in vain of course, for her announcement that she is an artist herself, a writer, that her sense of her own strength makes it possible for her to require of a brother that he match her in insight and imagination. She does not make that announcement, but from now on she will know and say of herself, 'I am a teacher',[51] and she will turn to M. Paul, who is *her* teacher, as a student and an apprentice. The transition is not so startling because it is not just about love. It is a shift in Lucy's understanding of herself and her possibilities, a shift from a love affair lived in the head to one lived in the world, from seeing to doing, from dreaming to art and writing, from dependence to autonomy and from learning to teaching.

M. Paul may be her master, a tyrannical one and a tiger too. Yet he is not oppressive as Lucy's inner tiger has been: that diffuse anxiety about her capacity to be visible in the world if she is invisible to men. M. Paul provides Lucy with a new dimension to her struggle. Working for him, arguing with him, sharpening her wits against *this* tiger allows her to reveal what have seemed to her until now the possibly 'horrible, immoral' incongruities of her nature. M. Paul finally calls forth and appears to accept her passions and her intellect, her outspokenness and her modesty, her playfulness, humour and seriousness. He has changed himself, made concessions. She learns to stand up to his criticism and teasing, because she has allowed him to know her. He knows her so well, indeed, that he can flirtatiously propose that they are alike, even interchangeable:

'Ah!' he muttered, 'if it came to that – if Miss Lucy meddled with his bonnet-grec – she might just put it on herself, turn garçon for the occasion, and benevolently go to the Athénée in his stead.'[52]

She had resisted with fury his first suggestion that she act a boy's part in the school play. Now that is given a new meaning. His insistence on her playing a boy's role was less an obliteration of her as a woman than an invitation to consider aspects of their likeness as well as their differences, which M. Paul lists and ends by reversing. 'We are alike – there is affinity between us. Do you see it, mademoiselle, when you look in the glass?'[53] They will agree that differences and similarities define their friendship, as a bond between a brother and a sister. When she tells him her tale about the nun, the ghost, the mysterious rumours about him which she has heard,

> he smiled, betraying delight. Warm, jealous, and haughty, I knew not till now that my nature had such a mood; he gathered me near his heart. I was full of faults: he took them and me all home. For the moment of utmost mutiny, he reserved the one deep spell of peace.[54]

Paul Emanuel is a man who can accept Lucy's 'utmost mutiny', her rebellion. He makes it possible for her to start her own school, to practise her art, become economically independent. He gives her a room of her own, restoring her body to her as her own, the place where she lives and thinks and feels.

So why does Charlotte Brontë drown this man who has met her conditions and has returned her heroine to herself? Why does he not survive his mysterious crusade abroad and return to share her room and her life? Kate Millett is in no doubt that 'the keeper turned kind must be eluded anyway; Paul turned lover is drowned'.[55] Charlotte Brontë was clearly determined on this ending, and was only prepared to express it hazily for her father's sake, because, apparently, he begged her to give this novel a happy ending. Of course, it is possible to imagine that if he thought the endings to her other novels sad, the solitary and unmarried state of Lucy Snowe was, in fact, calculated to please him. The ending of *Villette* is certainly in marked contrast to the ending of *The Professor*, which has William sitting, pen in hand, while his wife makes the tea and a friend dandles their baby son. William is Charlotte Brontë's male impersonation, Charlotte Brontë and Lucy as a male version of themselves, and also a brother, for whom things might have turned out better. Perhaps by the time she wrote *Villette*, the ending of *The Professor*, or even a reversal of it (with Lucy writing while M. Paul makes the tea!), seemed as undesirable as it was unrealistic. The refusal to allow that 'the bells rang and everybody smiled' at the end of *Wuthering Heights* and of *Villette* is not the least of their authors' achievements, nor unconnected with their more significant ones. Mrs Gaskell believed that Charlotte wrote almost nothing from the day she married. If readers have regarded the ending of *Villette* as sad, that may say more about the traditional constraints on women's adventures in novels, about the anticipated target of a thousand women's trajectories, than about Lucy's adventure and Charlotte Brontë's notion of her reward for pursuing it:

My school flourishes, my house is ready: I have made him a little library, filled its shelves with the books he left in my care: I have cultivated out of love for him (I was naturally no florist) the plants he preferred, and some of them are yet in bloom. I thought I loved him when he went away; I love him now in another degree; he is more my own.[56]

The storm and the shipwreck which swallow Paul Emanuel are followed by sunlight and a curiously resigned peace. Paul Emanuel is Lucy's 'own' now, because she created him, one of the most precisely understood men in literature. She has no need to marry him.

Blurring author with heroine is often illegitimate, and yet it is hard not to think of Charlotte Brontë's professed dislike of Lucy Snowe, and her careful naming of her,[57] as an anxious dissociation of herself from what Lucy reveals about her nature in the novel. Mrs Gaskell told Charlotte frankly that she didn't like Lucy Snowe either, and that fits well with her own need to separate the woman from the artist in her biography of Charlotte[58] and to insist on Charlotte's womanly innocence and detachment from the darker revelations of her heroines. Mrs Gaskell once asked Charlotte how she managed to write about people and experiences she had never known herself, hoping perhaps for Charlotte to reveal that opium was responsible for the writer's 'coarser' imaginings as it is for Lucy's hallucinatory breakdown. Charlotte denied having ever used opium, but she was ready to describe the working of her imagination in a way which probably satisfied Mrs Gaskell, and which may explain Charlotte's own fears about what her novels might inadvertently reveal about herself:

She had thought intently on it for many and many a night before falling to sleep, – wondering what it was like, or how it would be, – till at length, sometimes after the progress of her story had been arrested at this one point for weeks, she wakened up in the morning with all clear before her, as if she had in reality gone through the experience, and then could describe it, word for word as it had happened.[59]

Charlotte Brontë's secret, the one she feared to expose, to have recognised as her own, was the one Lucy Snowe discovers and reveals. It is the secret of her creativity, of its source in her own body and mind, of her independence and her nature, which is as mutinous and murderous as Vashti is, bounding and fierce as a tiger. That nature could not be revealed to men, who might ridicule it as incongruously set within a body and a demeanour which she expected them to find 'unattractive'. Modesty was a protection. That was why she wrote to G. H. Lewes:

I wish you did not think me a woman. I wish all reviewers believed 'Currer Bell' to be a man; they would be more just to him. You will, I know, keep measuring me by some standard of what you deem becoming to my sex; where I am not what you consider graceful, you will condemn me.[60]

It is the gracelessness of *Villette* which has been especially deplored, by Matthew Arnold 'because the writer's mind contains nothing but hunger, rebellion and rage',[61] by Leslie Stephen, Virginia Woolf's father, for its 'unhappy discord, which leaves us with a sense of something morbid and unsatisfactory'.[62] There are men in *Villette* apart from Graham Bretton, Paul Emanuel, the tricky count, who is sometimes colonel, and M. de Bassompierre who is sometimes Mr Home. They are the men in Charlotte Brontë's own life and the men she was asking, with a suitable timidity and fear, to join and be judged by. Her novel is a quest, a woman writer's quest for a brother, a 'semblable', and through him for herself. Its ending predicts its own rejection by many of the male readers who found it too full of 'unfeminine knowledge'. It also records a mutinous denial as well as a lifetime's agreement with those remarks of Southey's in the letter he wrote to her before she had ever written a novel:

The daydreams in which you habitually indulge are likely to induce a distempered state of mind; and in proportion as all the ordinary uses of the world seem to you flat and unprofitable, you will be unfitted for them without becoming fitted for anything else.[63]

Those echoes of Hamlet would have reminded her that as an Ophelia she had even less to look forward to. If *Villette* is a novel which grows out of a woman's sense of her own divisions and fragmentations as pathological, it also and emphatically proposes a resistance and expresses a capacity for survival.

The brother has been for many women novelists the first remembered object of a woman's love for men and envy of them. Harriet Martineau herself remembered her relationship with James, the brother who was younger than her by three years, as the most passionate and painful of her life:

All who have ever known me are aware that the strongest passion I have ever entertained was in regard to my youngest brother, who has certainly filled the largest space in the life of my affections of any person whatever. Now, the fact, – the painful fact, – in the history of human affections is that, of all natural relations, the least satisfactory is the fraternal. Brothers are to sisters what sisters can never be to brothers as objects of engrossing and devoted affection. The law of their frames is answerable for this: and that other law – of equity – which sisters are bound to obey, requires that they should not render their account of their disappointments where there can be no fair reply. Under the same law, sisters are bound to remember that they cannot be certain of their own fitness to render an account of their own disappointments, or to form an estimate of the share of blame which may be due to themselves on the score of unreasonable expectations. These general considerations decide me to pass over one of the main relations and influences of my life in a few brief and unsatisfactory lines, though I might tell a very particular tale.[64]

The brother is all that the sister might have been but for her sex. His are the life and the possibilities she might have had. He may also be the one man she has unconditionally loved, the one by whom she is known.

Charlotte Brontë imagined lovers and husbands as brothers, twins, alternative versions of herself, who would know her, accept her and who were themselves knowable and intimately related. She also doubted the brother's good faith towards her, suspected his maleness and apartness, and tested and punished these brothers for the pains of being a woman in a world where men controlled women's vision as well as their lives. In later chapters I shall suggest that as women writers learned to see their own predicament within broader analyses of social relations, it became necessary to transcend this concentration on the inequalities between women and their brothers. For that concentration left intact the social relations, the class conflicts, the sources and nature of power within the society which they inhabited so uncomfortably.[65]

4

Sons

The grand function of woman, it must always be recollected, is, and ever must be, *Maternity*: and this we regard not only as her distinctive characteristic, and most endearing charm, but as a high and holy office.

G. H. Lewes[1]

Half the sorrows of women would be averted if they could repress the speech they know to be useless.

George Eliot[2]

Of all the descriptions of themselves with which women have had to grapple, those which define them as mothers, and especially as the mothers of sons, have been the most contradictory and the most silencing. All sons have had mothers, and a good many sons have written about theirs. They have written out of love and loss and frustration, and women have sometimes written about their mothers in similar ways. What is much harder to find are women who have written as mothers, or of sons from a mother's point of view. Many of Jane Austen's mothers are either culpably indulgent of their sons, or cruelly domineering, as, for instance, Mrs Ferrars is towards hers in *Sense and Sensibility*. In *Villette* Charlotte Brontë makes the relationship between Mrs Bretton and her son Graham ostensibly healthy and undamaging. Mrs Bretton cherishes and fosters her son's talents, with the wish and the expectation that he will outstrip her. When he is grown up they are able to tease one another about the difficulties for them both in contemplating that she will ultimately be replaced for him by a younger woman. She prepares him expertly for marriage and for fatherhood by encouraging him to practise being 'master' in his mother's household. Yet Lucy's final disappointment with Graham, her impatience with his 'masculine self-love', must implicate his mother's complaisance.

George Eliot filled her novels with sons and their mothers. Two of her most stalwart sons, Adam Bede and Felix Holt, are loved by mothers who look somewhat foolishly to their sons for the love and support their husbands did not give them. Pride in their sons is overlaid by a need to collect reflected glory from their sons' achievements. Both mothers are represented as simple, ignorant women, irritants and gnats, who impede for a time their sons' trajectories into the adult, masculine world and independence. Even the likelihood that both Adam and Felix have learned from their mothers' dependence on them a gentle and chivalrous wish to protect and love women as weaker than themselves could only be grudgingly conceded and has certainly contributed sentimentality for some critics to the already flawed natures of these dubiously craggy heroes. I want to consider how George Eliot moved towards an understanding of mothers as the site of conflict for women as well as for men, and to speculate more generally as to the resources and messages available to women from myth and from literature if they are to represent truthfully their relations with their sons on terms of their own. I need to start with what I have called the contradictions and the silences of 'motherhood'.

Words like 'motherhood' and 'maternity' are not really about women who are mothers. They are abstractions developed historically within discourses rarely entered by women who are mothers. They could be said to mark out processes, values and relationships, and in doing so to assign roles and powers to women in specific relationships with men. These roles and powers carry beneficent as well as malign potential, as it is accorded by men to women. Within those discourses, mothers have, for instance, been portrayed as goddesses and queens and witches, even as virgins. They have been adored and feared, protected and cursed, reverenced and envied. And whether they are worshipped or diminished by these stories about them, mothers as mothers have been silenced; or rather the words they may utter have been put into their mouths. Accorded, apparently, a divine creative power, whose sources are seen as natural and universal (and shared with half of the entire animal kingdom), women have found it nearly impossible to speak out of that role as themselves, as particular women. They have dreaded hearing their own voices announcing that their bodies and 'instincts' have a reality and functions which may, for them, be in conflict with, or at any rate different from, the superficially tempting account of what mothers, especially good ones, *are* within a particular culture. Even the beauty and the fecundity for which they are valued may sit oddly with the qualities they are prepared to accord themselves.[3]

The ambiguity of women's collusion with male domination is at its most intense in the promise and the experience of motherhood. For the very discourses which offer a prospect of female power, facilitated and supported by male love, are above all the discourses controlled by men as sons; and men will often insist on that power, while reminding us that it is also a snare and a delusion, for mothers and for their sons. Those famous words of Aeschylus, 'The mother of him who is called her child is not the creator, but merely the nurse of the young life which is sown in her', are spoken, after all, in justification of a son's murdering his mother. Clytemnestra kills her husband, Agamemnon, in revenge for his killing their daughter. That requires and gets no such justification.

Several recent feminist treatments of the subject[4] have returned us to Greek, and to other, mythologies in order to trace what is seen as a gradual undermining of mother worship in the name of patriarchal arrangements and the values and laws which underlie and maintain highly organised modern societies. Robert Graves, in his tellings and interpretations of the Greek myths, suggests that the change itself, from matriarchies to patriarchies, is a central theme in many of the stories. In his discussion of early versions of the Oedipus story, for instance, he goes so far as to say that 'it may once have run something like this':

Oedipus of Corinth conquered Thebes and became king by marrying Iocaste, a priestess of Hera. Afterwards he announced that the kingdom should henceforth be bequeathed from father to son in the male line, which is a Corinthian custom, instead of remaining the gift of Hera the Throttler. Oedipus confessed that he felt himself disgraced as having let chariot horses drag to death Laius, who was accounted his father, and as having married Iocaste, who had enroyalled him by a ceremony of rebirth. But when he tried to change these customs, Iocaste committed suicide in protest, and Thebes was visited by a plague. Upon the advice of an oracle, the Thebans then withheld from Oedipus the sacred shoulder-blade, and banished him. He died in a fruitless attempt to regain his throne by warfare.[5]

Freud developed his interpretative theory of the Oedipus complex from his reading of the *Oedipus Rex* of Sophocles.[6] His 'Family Romance' is elaborated out of his stated principle that 'The first choice of object in mankind is regularly an incestuous one, directed to the mother and sister of men.'[7] It is a theory expressly offered as universally explanatory; indeed, Freud quotes his own 'suspicion' (expressed in *Totem and Taboo*) 'that perhaps the sense of guilt of mankind as a whole, which is the ultimate source of religion and morality, was acquired in the beginnings of history through the Oedipus complex.' Its universality is reaffirmed from a different perspective by the structuralist anthropologist, Lévi-Strauss,[8] who offers this particular story as demonstration of a fundamental and universal human structuring of experience in terms of forbidden relationships and their antitheses: a mode of thought common to all myths and found in all cultures. Just how abstracted an abstraction the Oedipus complex was for Freud can be illustrated by the ease with which he performs a simple reversal of the incestuous drive when he comes, with some belatedness, to account for the development of sexuality in girls.[9] For the assumption must be that the relation between a boy and his mother is allowed to be virtually equivalent to the relation between a girl and her father, regardless of historical realities. There can be few, if any, societies, after all, that Freud knew about, where such relations were, in fact, materially equivalent.

My purpose, it should be said at this point, is not to offer alternative theories of the social and psychological construction of female identity, nor to quarrel with Freud's theory, which I have anyway characterised very sketchily here. What I am after is some understanding of the narratives about women as mothers which have made it so difficult for women to think and write about that role from within it.

It is bewildering to return from Freud to Sophocles. The power of *Oedipus Rex* lies somewhere within the contrast between human beings living their lives as well as they can and the destiny, of which they are ignorant (as we are all ignorant of the future), which has been prophesied for them and which then hurtles them towards its fulfilment. In the play, Oedipus has grown up as the son of Polybus and Meropé, so that his first reaction to hearing the prophecy that he will one day kill his father and marry his mother had been to flee from the parents he knows and loves in order to avoid his (unavoidable) fate. Freud turns the ignorance of Oedipus as to his relations with the man he has murdered and with the woman he has married into 'repression' of guilt. If the complex were a matter of children's real feelings for the parents they grow up with, and of their possibly real need to attack and undermine parental authority in adolescence, Oedipus would be repressing his murderous and incestuous feelings towards Polybus and Meropé and transferring them to the unknown Laius and Jocasta. It is essential, of course, to Freud's theory that the Oedipal transgression be unconscious and transformed, so that the 'events' of the Sophocles play become secondary to the form in which they are revealed. By translating the fate in the play to guilt, Freud finds himself uneasily subverting the actual terms of the conflict in the play, so that it becomes for him 'immoral' because 'it sets aside the individual's responsibility to social law, and displays divine forces ordaining the crime and rendering powerless the moral instincts of the human being which would guard him against the crime.' Freud's revision of the play allows him to question its 'virtues' and morality and to pass over those realities of family life as they are present in the play in all their tragic vulnerability to the patterns of divine destiny. Just as the Oedipus of Sophocles has grown up with a particular mother and father and not idealised ones, so his marriage with Jocasta and his life with his children is concretely presented:

> But the girls, poor little mites,
> Have never known a meal without their father;
> Everything was shared between us.[10]

There is nothing illegitimate, of course, about Freud's 're-vision' of Sophocles. Indeed, it is exactly what I am up to myself.[11] The difficulty lies in ignoring the purposes which underpin such an enterprise and in extracting as a general truth about all human beings those meanings in the story, and its tellings and retellings, which are embedded in a particular history and culture. That difficulty is compounded as well as illustrated if we ponder the meanings of the Oedipus complex for women. If we focus on Jocasta, for instance, we may want to ask how her marriage to her son is to be read. A simple reversal of the story, and the process would involve changing the sex of each of the characters in the story. A girl kills her mother and marries her father. Such a version surely falters on the problem of endowing the female protagonist's adventure with the larger social meanings of the Oedipal transgression while maintaining the traditional patriarchal power structures, within families and whole societies, which would give it its meaning.

The Electra myth[12] is sometimes invoked, though not by Freud, to account for the woman's Oedipal drama. Electra's hatred for her mother and her support of her brother, Orestes, when he murders their mother, are explained in terms of her incestuous love for her father, Agamemnon. Yet there are crucial differences from the Oedipus story. Electra does not murder her mother. She supports her brother when he commits the murder. Nor does she marry Agamemnon, who is anyway dead. Electra's destiny, it could be said, is to support men against women – and particularly against her mother – rather than to fulfil a destiny of her own. That would sit quite well, it is true, with an incapacity in her, resulting from penis-envy and an incestuous love for her brother, to act on her own behalf.

Women play, of course, an absolutely critical role in both myths as mothers. Clytemnestra is condemned for murdering her husband in revenge for his sacrificing their daughter, Iphigenia, and for her adultery.[13] Jocasta is more comprehensively condemned, and especially by Freud. He describes her role in the play from the moment when the evidence is building up to convict Oedipus of the murder of Laius:

> In the dialogue the deluded mother-wife, Jocasta, resists the continuation of the enquiry; she points out that many people in their dreams have mated with their mothers, but that dreams are of no account. To us dreams are of much account, especially typical dreams which occur in many people; we have no doubt that the dream Jocasta speaks of is intimately related to the shocking and terrible story of the myth.[14]

Jocasta, who in Sophocles is queen and 'equal partner in rule and possession' with Oedipus, has become for Freud the 'mother-wife', who is 'deluded' rather than ignorant, cynically wise to the frequency with which men have incestuous dreams, yet unwilling to pursue an enquiry which may deliver the truth she also expects and dreads. She is convicted of knowingness in this version as well as of moral and intellectual cowardice. What Freud does not contemplate is that she knows that she is implicated in that dream, that it holds her moral responsibility too. Her dismissing it as of no account is a last-ditch attempt to avert disaster and avoid a truth, which 'we' as Freud puts it, are bent on revealing. Yet Oedipus is also anxious at several points in the play to back down from a 'continuation of the enquiry'. Since that enquiry is likened by Freud to the process of psychoanalysis, it is possible that Freud is petulantly remembering those other words of Jocasta's, which in one translation of *Oedipus Rex* read, 'a fig for divination!'

Sophocles at least registered Jocasta as a character in the play in her own right, joined with Oedipus and equally punished. The attendant who describes her death points to the eclipsing of Jocasta's fate by that of Oedipus as to a noticeable anomaly:

Her death was hidden from us.
Before we could see out her tragedy,
The King broke in with piercing cries, and all
Had eyes only for him.[15]

When finally they stumble into the room where Jocasta has hanged herself they find

a knotted pendulum, a noose,
A strangled woman swinging before our eyes.[16]

If this sight is followed by one more moving to its reporter as Oedipus snatches Jocasta's brooches to blind himself, it would still be fair to say that Sophocles makes Jocasta a visibly conscious and suffering participant in the drama in a way that Freud does not.

In an essay which is doubly illuminating, Caren Greenberg makes the myth of Oedipus itself analogous to the critical uses which have been made of it by men to examine their own sexual development. She argues that:

Oedipal reading suffers from many limitations. The very elements which make the Oedipus myth so useful in the discussion of male sexuality tend to deny the importance of the woman, since she acquires meaning only as the symbol of the father's power. Woman is the text in the Oedipus myth, and if we pursue the analogy, the fate of the text (and therefore of language) in the Oedipal reading process parallels the fate of women in the patriarchy: both are without intrinsic value and gain importance only to the extent that they signify something other than themselves.[17]

The suggestion here is that there has been a tradition in which men read myths as Oedipus 'reads' Jocasta, as a body signifying something other than, and outside, itself. I shall want to take from that the hypothesis that, as androgynous readers of myths, women have, until very recently indeed, allowed the body of Jocasta (their own body), alive or dead, to mean something only for those who pass through it as fathers or husbands or sons. This has effectively dictated what mothers could say about their relations with their sons. Most women writers have echoed the accounts that sons have given of mothers, and where they have wanted to represent the consciousness of a mother they have been driven towards a female image as damaged and as damaging as Clytemnestra or Jocasta.

When I was that young mother who was feeding her baby son and reading Proust on the first page of this book, I thought I knew a thing or two about Jocasta and Jewish mothers in novels and even about my own mother, who was Jewish but had no sons. I had read some Freud, and when I doubted my maternal capacities I would turn to Dr Spock, who told me sternly to pay for a baby-sitter and go to the cinema when I became overwrought. I remember that I never saw a film quite through to the end in those days as, choked with panic that my small son might have shrivelled to dried orange peel in my absence and sustained as well the onset of some life-long trauma, I ran home, to find him sleeping. He did not, in fact, do a lot of sleeping in those days, and when he did I sometimes woke him to check that he was still alive. I often marvelled at the love I felt for this person, which was beyond any feeling I had known or imagined. And like all protective and possessive loves it was threaded with fear and with premonitions of danger.

While I was still in hospital with him I instructed my husband, unavailingly, I think, to sweep under the bed. I did not want my new son to discover that his mother was a slut. It was not only Proust that I read when I fed him. I read the newspaper too, and it would gently brush his face and get in his eyes as he sucked. I even smoked occasionally, and if I had company I talked and laughed across him. I was quite often reproved as well as guilty: told that I spoiled him, let him get away with murder, or that my reading and smoking and talking while he fed was upsetting to him. *He* needed peace. Long before he could talk back I would apologise to him for my deficiencies, expecting his forgiveness as I had never expected any other man's forgiveness. I loved a man (a rather small one, it is true) who loved me back unconditionally. What greater power could a woman have? Yet when I remember that time I also remember feeling pain. A new confidence was always threatened by anxiety. I can still revisit those double feelings, though my sons and my daughter are now grown up. There was the terror of damaging these creatures who had burst out of me into separateness and daylight. There was shame; for my breathless love for them was always tainted for me by the selfish wishes I persisted in having for myself. I wanted to read, to work, to earn money. I wanted to walk down roads on my own, to love adults as well as children, be loved back. I wanted my body restored to me as it had been before its amazing swellings and productions had transformed it from my body to my children's mother's.

I did not talk much about these things, for I feared disapproval. Men, I believed, were squeamish, even as they applauded my maternal achievements. It would in those days have seemed disingenuous or crowing to have displayed my confusions to women without children. I was sure that I was luckier than they were. Most of the women I knew were, I think now, as I was, too guiltily aware of their own ambivalence to admit to any conflict beyond what could be met by common sense and practical solutions. We were a practical generation: young mothers in the fifties and the early sixties. We had jobs as well as babies, and we cooked and cleaned and converted and gardened and worried about schools and skills for our children. I remember baths, taken irregularly and after the children were in bed. They felt like ha-has, invisible trenches separating days of endless activity, movement and exhaustion from evenings. Surveying my long, white woman's body (not, of course, the one I would have chosen for myself), a foot resting on the tap, I would dream of another world; one where I would be taken to be something other than a mother and a wife and a worker with an eye on her watch for the end of school and collecting time. Multiplicity was enjoined on women, and many of us accepted it (though not without effort and tears), just as many of us accepted living with guilt and the one certainty: we deserved rejection for our duplicity and would be rejected. We would be found out; for we were not the genuine article.

And of course I read books, most of them, I suppose, by men: *Anna Karenina* regularly every four years, and *Madame Bovary* and *Tess of the d'Urbervilles*, in which I found pictures of women which were disturbing but reconciling too. For they confirmed in me a sense that women could only expect to see themselves at all by attending to what had been glimpsed of them by men, what was filtered through men's views of women and plans for them. It did not even seem surprising to me that many of them, like Proust, simply made women disappear. If these were the wives and mothers and lovers and daughters men wanted I would simply try harder and keep quiet. I used sometimes to think that men just wanted us to be more like them. That was attractive, but hard, because men seemed to know who they were and we didn't. There was a part of me which would have agreed with Lionel Trilling in his assessment of women characters in novels and the view they reflect, and promote, of women in the real world:

Women in fiction only rarely have the peculiar reality of the moral life that self-love bestows. Most commonly they exist in a moon-like way, shining by the reflected moral life of men . . . They seldom exist as men exist – as genuine moral destinies. It is only on the rare occasions when a female character like Emma confronts us that the difference makes us aware of the usual practice. Nor can we say that novels are deficient in realism when they present women as they do: it is the presumption of our society that women's moral life is not as men's. No change in the modern theory of the sexes, no advances in the status that women have made, can contradict this. The self-love that we do countenance in women is of a limited and passive kind, and we are troubled if their self-love is as assertive as man's is permitted, and expected to be. Not men alone, but women as well, insist on this limitation . . . But there is Emma, given over to self-love.[18]

As I write this I am anxious and even ashamed. Anxious still that men, my sons, my husband, my father, will disapprove; ashamed of my cowardice and of my toleration of injustices, which had they not involved me as they did would have earned my utmost indignation. It was one of my sons who explained to me my earliest pussy-footing response to what was then called (mostly by men, I remember) 'Women's Lib'. He rightly saw this as being my first encounter with a politics which was for myself. Perhaps he couldn't know that I also feared the Amazonian confidence of those days, was worried that the peculiar dilemmas of mother-hood would be ignored or by-passed by the rush of younger women towards a childless freedom, which would short-circuit my own search for a solution. I was sceptical too: of a programme of discarding and divestment. Instead of the pure and untram-melled woman which, it was hoped, would be revealed by this pro-cess, might I not discover nothing there at all, or, more probably, a shrunken replica of the split and muddled person I had started out as?

In considering how women have presented men in their novels I want to suggest that their representations of sons have most often been evasive because there is no story which tells them why and how they love their sons. They have had to make do with stories which tell them only why their sons' love for them is potentially dangerous, why sons must go beyond them, beyond mother-love and towards fathers, the great wide world and its doings and its laws. Mothers have been warned that their power over their sons is dangerous and that it must be transmuted or relinquished. They have not been told why Jocasta loved Oedipus as well as Laius, and perhaps more than Laius. Is the love of a mother for her son the consequence of *her* incestuous love for *her* father, *her* brother? Does it come from penis-envy?

I shall not be long. There may be few examples of women who have dared to imagine Jocasta's life, but there *are* one or two, and before we turn to them we should return to history. For in recent years there have been women who have shown more courage than I in facing the ambiguities for women who have sons. Nancy Chodorow's *The Reproduction of Mothering. Psychoanalysis and the Sociology of Gender* is by now a classic study of the subject, and I shall quote one of her concluding passages:

The sexual division of labor and women's responsibility for child care are linked to and generate male dominance. Psychologists have demonstrated unequivocally that the very fact of being mothered by a woman generates in men conflicts over masculinity, a psychology of male dominance, and a need to be superior to women. Anthropologists argue that women's child-care responsibilities required that the earliest men hunt, giving them, and not women, access to the prestige and power that come from control over extra-domestic distribution networks. They show that women's continued relegation to the domestic, 'natural' sphere, as an extension of their mothering functions, has ensured that they remain less social, less cultural, and also less powerful than men.[19]

Her book explains how women make mothers of their daughters and men of their sons, and how they do so in response even now to edicts which are often inaudible, though they are devastatingly inescapable. Chodorow contributes rational analysis to a terrain inevitably marked by anger and fear. She rightly insists that any feminist theory which confronts history, economics, culture and ideology in its understanding of women's relations with men must start from 'mothering' and other unpaid work done by women to support the family and allowed to be peripheral to most social and economic theories. Differently, and also usefully, writers like Tillie Olsen,[20] Judith Arcana,[21] Jane Lazarre,[22] and Adrienne Rich,[23] have moved from their confessions as the mothers of sons to explorations of myth and literature, history and anthropology and psychoanalysis, which might help them to understand what Adrienne Rich has called 'the obscure bodily self-hatred peculiar to women who view themselves through the eyes of men'.[24]

I want to look at three novels which deal with sons and with their mothers, in ways which demonstrate women's fascination with, and fear of, Jocasta. They are Rebecca West's *The Judge* and George Eliot's *Felix Holt* and *Daniel Deronda*. I shall start, confusingly, with Rebecca West, because her novel was written with a knowledge of Freud's theory as George Eliot's were not. The readings themselves will, I hope, make the significance of that clear. Rebecca West's novel was published in 1922, when she was thirty. She must have meant it to be shattering – and occasionally, it must be admitted, it is shatteringly bad – for it becomes, quite simply, Jocasta's story. It was received with varieties of outraged excitement: disapproved of for its dependence on 'psychoanalysis and its slimy exponents'[25] and for having an unmarried mother as its heroine; and accounted 'blindingly brilliant' by one critic, who wrote, 'I do not think any female genius has eviscerated the unspeakable male so mercilessly and so savagely.'[26] Its scope and grandeur are meant to be Sophoclean (and one might wish that to have had more irony to it), and this works to remind us how much more wonderingly and tenderly Sophocles managed such themes in his intense, spare dramas. It is not, of course, that the agonies of a mother in love with her son have not been written about. Racine's *Phèdre* is just one example of a work in which the mother's emotions are blamed for the destruction of a son and, through him, of the natural and the social moral orders.

More recently, Samuel Hynes has described *The Judge* as 'a long, melodramatic story of sex, guilt, and power, interesting for the autobiographical beginning in Edinburgh, and for remarks about the nature of man–woman relations, but imaginatively lifeless.'[27] That is not entirely unfair, if inappropriately laconic, though one might want to replace 'lifeless' with 'uncontrolled'. What does, nonetheless, make this a fascinating novel from my point of view is that it is a courageous and flawed attempt to face up to the implications of the Oedipus complex, and the traditions which have fed it, for a woman. Here is a woman who is confronting the Eve, the Jocasta, the Clytemnestra, the Phèdre in herself. If, as Adrienne Rich puts it, 'A woman is for a man both more and less than a person: she is something terribly necessary and necessarily terrible',[28] is it possible for a woman to explore the experience and the psychology of a woman's love for her son, and to demand a hearing for her even as she acknowledges her dangerousness for men?

In the first half of the novel, Marion Yaverland, the tortured and unmarried mother of Richard, is off-stage. The central character is a magically understood seventeen-year-old typist, poor, flamingly and eccentrically beautiful and a committed suffragette, who lives with her sad bird of a mother in a dank quarter of Edinburgh. Ellen's wit and intelligence, her appetite for knowledge and experience, are made palpable, and so is her life with her touchingly defeated mother, who had for a moment been beautiful too and known things, as she reminds her daughter:

'You took me up so sharply when I thought Joseph Chamberlain was a Liberal. And he *was* a Liberal once, dear, when your father and I were first married and he still talked to me. I'm *sure* Joseph Chamberlain was a Liberal then.'[29]

Into the small legal office where Ellen types, oblivious of the lustful fantasies woven round her by her employers, the Mactavish James, father and son, strives the Titan, Richard Yaverland. He is built on a heroic scale:

His black hair lay in streaks and rings on his rain-wet forehead and gave him an abandoned and magical air, like the ghost of a drowned man risen for revelry; his dark gold skin told a traveller's tale of far-off pleasurable weather; and the bare hand that lay on his knee was patterned like a snake's belly with brown marks, doubtless the stains of his occupation; and his face was marked with an expression that it vexed her she could not put a name to, for if at her age she could not read human nature like a book she never would. It was not hunger, for it was serene, and it was not greed, for it was austere, and yet it certainly signified that he habitually made upon life some urgent demand that was not wholly intellectual and that had not been wholly satisfied. As she wondered a slight retraction of his chin and a drooping of his heavy eyelids warned her, by their likeness to the controlled but embarrassed movements of a highly-bred animal approached by a stranger, that he knew she was watching him, and she took her gaze away.[30]

Richard is in his thirties, a scientist who works in the dynamite business, and a traveller, full of tales. He falls in love with Ellen, wooing her triumphantly and with such profusion of roses as to exhaust her poor mother's meagre supply of vases. Indeed, this excess and the strain it imposes seem to Ellen 'to have deprived of urgency all her other longings'.[31] The first half of the novel ends with the death of this mother from diphtheria in a pauper's bed of Edinburgh Infirmary's public ward. So far the novel has maintained a tension between the reality of Ellen's life and the grandeur of her dreams, with Richard as their overbearing fulfilment. When he tells her shyly that he is illegitimate and we are allowed to know that 'though his mother had suffered great pain from sleeplessness for thirty years, she had never bought peace with a drug. Nothing would make her content to tamper with reality'[32] and that he had always wanted to 'share the sorrow of the woman who was enduring pain because she had given him life', we still read him, as Ellen does, as a powerful man, a lover, who must necessarily be more than a son by now.

The second half of the novel begins when the orphaned Ellen is sent by Richard to his mother in Essex, where he will join them in a few days. Marion is an intense, squat, brusque, middle-aged Englishwoman, whom Ellen tries, and fails, to like. We do not learn Marion's story through her telling of it, but through her remembering it during her long nights of sleeplessness, as she wrestles with her jealousy of her son's remarkable fiancée and her knowledge that Richard's only hope of redemption lies in this liberating love. Marion's story is melodramatic and self-consciously literary and mythic. After a furtively idyllic love affair with the local, married squire, she had conceived a son. Her lover was posted abroad and was consequently unavailable to protect her from either the hostility of her family or the violent attacks on her made by the villagers. She had been an orphan, and it was her grandmother who accepted Peacey's offer to marry Marion. Peacey was the squire's butler, loathsome and servile, and he had writhingly reassured his young bride that they need never live together. Eventually Marion gave birth, painfully, to Richard. He was everything she had anticipated, and for a brief period she had been entirely happy. Her bitterness – which echoes Clytemnestra's words: 'the child whom he had begotten, at little cost of course compared to mine who bore her'[33] – was temporarily assuaged. Then Peasey had reappeared and raped her. This time she had given birth, with horrible ease, to a palely unlovable and legitimate son, come, it has seemed to her, to interrupt her perfect maternal marriage to the magnificent Richard.

Her atavistic pride in bearing a son, and this son, her glorying in his love for her, her confusing of this love with the more ambiguous and withheld love of his father, her excited power over the boy, are presented from his babyhood, through his childhood and youth and into his adult life and culminate in the moment when she recognises in herself 'an insane regret that being his mother she could not also be his wife.' The novel's portentous refrain, 'Every mother is a judge who sentences the children for the sins of the father' has been taken, a little mysteriously, I think, to be 'a life sentence, not a death sentence'.[34] In fact, it stands for, and heralds, with a good deal of thunderous drum-rolling, a conclusion as corpse-littered as any Greek or Jacobean tragedy. Marion drowns herself to save Richard from his love for her and to prevent her sons killing each other. This she fails to do. Richard stabs his pathetic sibling, who is by now an incompetent 'child of Jesus' incompetently preaching for the Salvation Army, and Ellen is dragged by the wild-eyed Richard to banishment (or death) on a small island off the Essex coast. It is excessive and grotesquely operatic, but not unintentionally so, as Ellen's wistful remembering of her own mother – 'that was how a mother ought to be, little, sweet, and moderate' – reminds us.

Rebecca West attempted the impossible and proved that it was impossible. For Jocasta *is* impossible for women. It is not bearable to embody the rages and passions of a woman who takes the mother's legendary role literally. How, the novel seems to ask, can a woman first match and satisfy a man's sexual need of her with a total giving of herself, when it is required of him that he subordinate love to law, sexual passion to paternalism? How can she control her own love and transform it to supportive steadfastness once she has discovered that her body and its sexuality are her only power? How can she simply serve male power while denying herself her one opportunity of wielding power herself, over a boy child? The only obstacle to a mother expressing her incestuous love for her son, it is suggested, is her knowledge that she will lose him, indeed lose all, if she exposes her 'inexorable womb'[35] and her horrifying fantasies to men. A socially inculcated inhibition serves as a prohibition; and Jocasta's tale is prohibited. When Marion tells Richard the story of the villagers stoning her when she was in her seventh month of pregnancy with him she knows she has done the one unforgivable thing. ' "Have I lost him?" she wondered. "Harry did not like me so much after horrible things had happened to me." '[36] Men cannot tolerate knowing that they damage women, drive them into impossible dilemmas. They will stone or reject the woman who tells them that this is so.

Jocasta's curse in the novel is passed from mother to daughter and through sons to daughters-in-law. Ellen has learned it from her submissive mother too. Women must not use the humiliation of their submission to men, the agony of childbirth, the ambiguity of mother love, to elicit men's pity. Richard Yaverland hates the thought of his dead and barely known father. He is jealous that his mother loved this other man. He is damaged by this hatred because it implicates him in harming his mother, forces him to love and pity her out of guilty complicity with the father who damaged her. He is incapacitated, literally made impotent, by loving and pitying and resenting his mother, and Ellen will receive the consequences of this, through what will have to be a kind of rape, devoid of love; and she in her turn will pass those consequences on to her children.

For all its sometimes windy posturings and bellowings *The Judge* is an extraordinary novel, often unbearable to read, which does provide a woman's version of the dilemma posed but not faced by Freud in his Oedipus complex. Marion's tragedy is conducted as if in some gusty amphitheatre lovingly replicated in the home counties. Ellen's is more subtly and touchingly understood against its exactly seen Athens of the North. For her wonderfully frail energy and vision, her common sense and her political idealism, her intelligence and humour are roughly, arbitrarily, destroyed by her titanic hero and his inescapable charms. Her adventure has been eclipsed, merged into his. It is as if Rebecca West were begging Ellen, as a gloriously imagined incarnation of her younger self, to resist the blandishments of all striding giants, and then admitting exhausted defeat on her behalf. How can a woman resist the offer of a hero's love and its promise to her of motherhood, when that looks like her only access to and prospect of power for herself? Rebecca West is not condoning women's exercise of that power. Indeed, she sees that as damaging to sons and crushingly limiting for mothers too, because there is no escape for women who exert it, and its effect on men is to incapacitate them as lovers of women. In her biography of St Augustine,[37] written some years later than *The Judge*, Rebecca West suggests that his mother's oppressively incestuous love for him explains what was stunted and death-dealing in Augustine as well as what was enlightened in him and inspiring to the Church. His mother's 'shuddering alarm' at his growing up, 'her desire that her son should not become a man',[38] are allowed to stand for the particular tensions which have produced modern, civilised men: a denial of the physical in the mother and of female power, and a seeking after those refinements of thought and feeling which have been allowed to be the special province of the male celibate.

It would be possible to see as defensive the tendency in some women writers to represent mothers as figures of pathos or comedy. Certainly, mothers are amongst George Eliot's best comic creations. Mrs Poyser in *Adam Bede* is garrulous and opinionated, yet she is also able to be wise and effective. Mrs Tulliver in *The Mill on the Floss* is superbly embedded in the practical and the literal, so that it does not seem far-fetched that her litigious husband should have carefully chosen her as his wife 'because she wasn't o'er 'cute'. I have already suggested that the mothers of Adam Bede and Felix Holt, men of heroic moral potential in the novels, are less dangerous to their sons for their love than for their dependence and limitedness of vision. These mothers are made part of their sons' difficult life choices and are symbolic of the moral hazards inherent in their sons' having ambitions and aspirations for themselves. Felix Holt has learned through his mother that 'women ... hinder men's lives from having any nobleness in them'.[39] He will not change his mind about that until he is confronted by Esther's capacity for renunciation. Both these mothers are poor, and their dependence on their husbands and their sons has been that of women who are physically, socially and economically weak. It was not until George Eliot began to tackle higher social *mileux* in her novels, worlds in which women could be said to have broader experience, greater scope for choice and discrimination, and considerably more power over their own lives and other people's, that she created mothers through their own consciousness of who they are. In such worlds mothers might be people who bore responsibility for their own actions rather than women compressed by cramped destinies, scarcely more than their role; or comic, as the Dodson sisters are in *The Mill on the Floss*, for the wonderfully idiosyncratic seriousness with which they each take that role. The mothers George Eliot invests with tragic potential are Mrs Transome in *Felix Holt* and the Princess Halm-Eberstein in *Daniel Deronda*.

Leavis, in accounting that part of *Felix Holt* which centres on Mrs Transome 'astonishingly finer and maturer than anything George Eliot had done before', is also persuaded that it is so because 'She has not here ... a heroine with whom she can be tempted to identify herself.' She is presented, Leavis insists, with 'complete objectivity'.[40] Mrs Transome's attachment to her second son, Harold, the child of her adulterous love affair with the family lawyer, Jermyn, has been described by most critics as Oedipal and by Rosemary Ashton, more precisely, because Mrs Transome is 'forced to watch him set about, Oedipus-like, the discovery of a fact it would have been better for him not to know'.[41] What makes this Oedipal story quite different from most is that, as in Rebecca West's novel, the triangular relationship and the full knowledge of its history and consequences are communicated to us through the experience of the woman in the triangle.

It is always risky to suppose an author's identification with her character. George Eliot was not a mother and certainly did not resemble Mrs Transome. Yet I find it impossible not to invoke some suggestion of identification, if only because of the sheer force of imaginative sympathy with which Mrs Transome is understood. Mrs Transome's nature and her adventure are made a part of the novel's exploration of the possibilities women have for rising above the trivial preoccupations expected of them. She is made clinching to Esther's final decision to renounce her right to the Transome estates and to her realisation that position and money hold particular dangers for women who are tempted by them. Mrs Transome carries one version of the constraints on women's impulses to achieve heroic, tragic status; Esther carries another. I shall want also to suggest – by tracing an extension of the treatment of Mrs Transome to the much more explicit messages delivered in the figure of Daniel Deronda's mother – that George Eliot came to locate in the role of the mother particular as well as more general conflicts for women. We may take from her novels the sense, I think, that there are always hazards and pains for women who live their lives expectantly through their children. We may also assume a particular conflict for a woman artist: between creating children and, in George Eliot's case, creating the human population of her novels.

Mrs Transome is a handsome woman in her middle fifties, married to an older man who has become senile and childish and has allowed the family estates to disintegrate. The oldest son, and heir, sickly and unlovable, has died of desultory excesses. The mother waits, with the most intense anticipation, for her favourite son to return from abroad after fifteen years and to restore the family's fortunes and her own:

She sat still, quivering and listening; her lips became pale, her hands were cold and trembling. Was her son really coming? She was far beyond fifty; and since her early gladness in this best-loved boy, the harvest of her life had been scanty. Could it be that now – when her hair was grey, when sight had become one of the day's fatigues, when her young accomplishments seemed almost ludicrous, like the tone of her first harpsichord and the words of the songs long browned with age – she was going to reap an assured joy? – to feel that the doubtful deeds of her life were justified by the result, since a kind Providence had

sanctioned them? – to be no longer tacitly pitied by her neighbours for
her lack of money, her imbecile husband, her graceless eldest-born,
and the loneliness of her life; but to have at her side a rich, clever,
possibly a tender, son? Yes; but there were the fifteen years of
separation, and all that had happened in that long time to throw her into
the background in her son's memory and affection. And yet – did not
men sometimes become more filial in their feeling when experience
had mellowed them, and they had themselves become fathers? Still, if
Mrs Transome had expected only her son, she would have trembled
less; she expected a little grandson also: and there were reasons why
she had not been enraptured when her son had written to her only
when he was on the eve of returning that he already had an heir born to
him.

But the facts must be accepted as they stood, and, after all, the chief
thing was to have her son back again. Such pride, such affection, such
hopes as she cherished in this fifty-sixth year of her life, must find their
gratification in him – or nowhere. Once more she glanced at the
portrait. The young brown eyes seemed to dwell on her pleasantly; but,
turning from it with a sort of impatience, and saying aloud, 'Of course
he will be altered!' she rose almost with difficulty, and walked more
slowly than before across the hall to the entrance-door.[42]

There are several significant ways in which Mrs Transome
resembles Marion Yaverland, the mother of Rebecca West's
novel. She loves her illegitimate son and has never loved the son
born of her marriage. For both mothers, this failure to love one
child becomes as much the focus for their guilt as loving the other
son. Mrs Transome too looks to this favourite son for the love
once given her by his father and then withdrawn. The character of
his begetting and the demands she has made on her son are
blamed for his cold sensuality and his inability to love another
woman generously and completely. Harold returns with a son of
his own, whose mother, it is hinted, had been bought by him and
disposed of, as a slave. Mrs Transome is also like Marion
Yaverland in entreating the young woman her son comes nearest
to loving to exert herself, so that he may be liberated from the
curse transmitted to him by his mother. A curious bonding is
proposed in both novels between the mother and the young

woman the son might marry; it is a complicity between the older and the younger Jocasta. In loving a man, a woman takes on, and offers to compensate for, his unfinished love for his mother. Both sons in the novels have confined their relationships with other women to sex, the only aspect of the relationship with their mothers which was not realised. Both writers see sons as incapacitated by their mothers' love for them. As lovers of women they are emotionally divided, unable to love one woman sexually and with the kind of need they have had for their mothers. Incompletely loved herself, the younger woman will turn to her own son.

Where George Eliot's treatment of Mrs Transome differs most importantly from Rebecca West's of Marion Yaverland is in the quality of the mother's hopes for 'gratification' from her son. Mrs Transome's hopes have undeniably sexual overtones to them, but they are also characterised as continuous with everything that is generally gratifying to her essentially trivial nature. The expression of what she longs for from Harold accords with her reliance on hollow superiorities and the narrowness of her emotional resources. Harold will somehow fulfil *her* destiny. While Rebecca West condemns a mother for holding her son's affections through eliciting his pity for her, working on his guilty complicity with his father, Mrs Transome's hands are tied, as it were, by her own nature. Her desire for her son is infected above all by her need to be triumphantly envied in a world where by now she might all too easily be seen as an object of pity. She 'had not the feminine tendency to seek influence through pathos; she had been used to rule in virtue of acknowledged superiority.'[43] The character of her incestuous feeling is marked by her nature, and it is in her nature to assume her 'acknowledged superiority', and to fail to admit to age, to the degeneration of dignity, to a crumbling social order, seen here as unhealthy and rightly vulnerable to disintegration and decay. 'Acknowledged superiority' rests on birth and class and money, without which it cannot survive. The tragedy of *this* mother is grander in its scope than her own contained and explosive feelings. It is the tragedy of people who are blind, as King Lear is blind, to the bases and the motives of the allegiance and love shown to them: people who misunderstand the limitations and the arbitrariness of their own power. The poignancy of Mrs Transome's position is that she does not enjoy the ardent, if disabling, reciprocity of feeling between mother and son, which is at the heart of Rebecca West's novel. Her arrogance makes it impossible for her to ask for his love. Mrs Transome's Oedipal drama has been reduced to a parasitic dependence on the son she has damaged, but whom she has had to watch 'growing into a strong youth, who liked many things better than his mother's caresses'.[44]

His mother's overwhelming impression, when Harold returns, is that he is a stranger; nearly as much a stranger, it might be said, as Oedipus is when he returns unrecognised to the mother who put him out on the hillside in babyhood. He has become for Mrs Transome the image of his father, and Jermyn is by now a hated and fearful figure for her. She recognises instantly that any hold she might have over this son will not be through love. Her only hope lies in her public role as 'a mother who was to be consulted on all things, and who could supply his lack of the local experience necessary to an English landholder.'[45] That hope is just as quickly dissolved. Harold's announcement that he intends to stand as a Radical candidate for the county is, therefore, doubly shocking to his mother. It demonstrates his independence and apparent perversity and makes it clear to her that 'his busy thoughts were imperiously determined by habits which had no reference to any woman's feeling.'[46]

Soon after his arrival, Mrs Transome sits at breakfast with her son and the family lawyer, the father of her son, though Harold does not know that yet.

There were piteous sensibilities in this faded woman, who thirty-four years ago, in the splendour of her bloom, had been imperious to one of these men, and had rapturously pressed the other as an infant to her bosom, and now knew that she was of little consequence to either of them.[47]

The grandeur which Rebecca West felt it necessary to infuse into her novel in order to make tolerable, and give credibility to, her impossible theme had, astonishingly, nearly sixty years earlier, been understood as an overweening 'imperiousness'. Mrs Transome, the 'clever sinner',[48] expert at subterfuge, can permit herself an evasion of conscience and penitence, feel guilt only as fear, because of her 'imperiousness'. Her sufferings issue from anger and pride, from the 'imperiousness' which characterises all her social relations and which was even intrinsic to her adulterous transgression. Her nemesis is not only the consequence of her transgression and her incestuous love; it lurked for her always in the quality of her contempt, transmitted to her son and returning to her as retribution.

George Eliot grounds this woman's tragedy in an understood and particular world, not an idealised or abstracted one.

Here she moved to and fro amongst the rose-coloured satin of chairs and curtains – the great story of this world reduced for her to the little tale of her own existence – dull obscurity everywhere, except where the keen light fell on the narrow track of her own lot, wide only for a woman's anguish.[49]

Neither the mother nor the son are convicted as sinners against laws grandly older or higher than those of the society and the relationships they actually inhabit. The mother is not entirely beyond redemption, and the son is neither completely nor irrevocably damaged. Their sins are potentially the sins of all human beings who have a responsibility to imagine and respond to the reality of other people's lives. The mother's frozen torment is the penalty for failure of imagination, and her redemption is made possible at the end of the novel when she lets herself be loved by Esther, who is her rival, the woman loved by her son. George Eliot did not need to be a mother to understand the pains of a mother in love with her son. Her sympathy for Mrs Transome can be understood as the sympathy of a novelist who must release her own male creations into a world which excluded her.

It is a fact perhaps kept a little too much in the background, that mothers have a self larger than their maternity, and that when their sons have become taller than themselves, and are gone from them to college or into the world, there are wide spaces of their time which are not filled with praying for their boys, reading old letters, and envying yet blessing those who are attending to their shirt-buttons. Mrs Transome was certainly not one of those bland, adoring, and gently tearful women. After sharing the common dream that when a beautiful man-child was born to her, her cup of happiness would be full, she had travelled through long years apart from that child to find herself at last in the presence of a son of whom she was afraid, who was utterly unmanageable by her, and to whose sentiments in any given case she possessed no key. Yet Harold was a kind son: he kissed his mother's brow, offered her his arm, let her choose what she liked for the house and garden, asked her whether she would have bays or greys for her new carriage, and was bent on seeing her make as good a figure in the neighbourhood as any other woman of her rank. She trembled under this kindness: it was not enough to satisfy her; still, if it should ever cease and give place to something else – she was too uncertain about Harold's feelings to imagine clearly what that something would be. The finest threads, such as no eye sees, if bound cunningly about the sensitive flesh, so that the movement to break them would bring torture, may make a worse bondage than any fetters. Mrs Transome felt the fatal threads about her, and the bitterness of this helpless bondage mingled itself with the new elegancies of the dining and drawing rooms, and all the household changes which Harold had ordered to be brought about with magical quickness. Nothing was as she had once expected it would be. If Harold had shown the least care to have her stay in the room with him – if he had really cared for her opinion – if he had been what she had dreamed he would be in the eyes of those people who had made her world – if all the past could be dissolved, and leave no solid trace of itself – mighty *ifs* that were all impossible – she would have tasted some joy.[50]

As a portrait of a mother Mrs Transome is neither sentimental- ised nor wholly scorned. Yet she is punished for her love and for her expectations of her son, and for the sexuality which produced him and is transmitted to him. That sexuality is allowed to seem an unwarranted assertion of her own needs, for which she will pay. If the portrait prefigures Freud's Jocasta it is also the portrait of a woman who is sympathetically understood and realised.

In *Daniel Deronda*, George Eliot created a mother who was an artist and a powerful advocate. Daniel Deronda is thirteen when it occurs to him that he may be illegitimate, that Sir Hugo Mallinger, whom he has called uncle and thought of as his guardian, may be his father. It becomes 'the habit of his mind to connect dread with unknown parentage',[51] and out of his secret anxieties as to his mother and her fate to develop the 'deepest interest in the fates of women'.[52] His own adventure, towards self-discovery, is also Oedipal, as he scrutinises the faces and the lives of women in search of the mother who will tell him who he is. George Eliot admires Daniel Deronda for his beauty, his kindness and for being the sort of tolerant, speculative and adventurous intellectual she was herself. It may be, indeed, that what has been felt by some readers as 'unimagined' in him comes from the author's too serenely identifying herself with him:

It happened that the very vividness of his impressions had often made him the more enigmatic to his friends, and had contributed to an apparent indefiniteness in his sentiments. His early-wakened sensibility and reflectiveness had developed into a many-sided sympathy, which threatened to hinder any persistent course of action: as soon as he took up any antagonism, though only in thought, he seemed to himself like the Sabine warriors in the memorable story – with nothing to meet his spear but flesh of his flesh, and objects that he loved. His imagination had so wrought itself to the habit of seeing things as they probably appeared to others, that a strong partisanship, unless it were against an immediate oppression, had become an insincerity for him. His plenteous, flexible sympathy had ended by falling into one current with that reflective analysis which tends to neutralise sympathy. Few men were able to keep themselves clearer of vices than he; yet he hated vices mildly, being used to think of them less in the abstract than as a part of mixed human natures having an individual history, which it was the bent of his mind to trace with understanding and pity. With the same innate balance he was fervidly democratic in his feeling for the multitude, and yet, through his affections and imagination, intensely conservative; voracious of speculations on government and religion, yet loath to part with long-sanctioned forms which, for him, were quick with memories and sentiments that no argument could lay dead.[53]

If that account of Deronda at twenty-five, and I have quoted only a third of it, reads like the obituary George Eliot might have wanted for herself, it is no accident. He is both her son and herself in the role of the son. He is also, and importantly, as I shall argue in the next chapter, her hero. He has the makings of a novelist and a thinker, and he has also, as his guardian points out, an enviable array of choices as to how he will spend his life. The questions he asks himself about Gwendolen in the first lines of the novel, as he watches this unknown girl gambling, as it seems, her life away, suggest the intensity of his scrutiny:

Was she beautiful or not beautiful? and what was the secret of form or expression which gave the dynamic quality to her glance? Was the good or the evil genius dominant in those beams? Probably the evil; else why was the effect that of unrest rather than of undisturbed charm? Why was the wish to look again felt as coercion and not as a longing in which the whole being consents?[54]

Always his sympathies for women will be seen as themselves 'feminine'. When he is 'priestlike' he is so for women, possessed of a special sensitivity to their natures and an almost morbid pity for and horror of their vulnerability to men. His love for Gwendolen grows with his realisation that her marriage to Grandcourt is cruelly disabling to her and that she could not have had the strength to stand out against it. His love for Mirah starts from pity too, pity that she has been driven to attempt suicide, pity at her father's treatment of her and pity for her long-lost mother. Mrs Glasher, Grandcourt's discarded mistress and mother of his four children, is another focus for Deronda's compassion, as a woman in the position his unknown mother may also have been driven into. His sensitivity to women's suffering could be seen as preparation for the guilt he expects to feel about his own mother. The cool letter he is finally to receive from her, summoning him to a meeting in Genoa, is not what he had expected:

The tender yearning after a being whose life might have been the worse for not having his care and love, the image of a mother who had not had all her dues whether of reverence or compassion, had long been secretly present with him in his observation of all the women he had come near. But it seemed now that this picturing of his mother might fit the facts no better than his former conceptions about Sir Hugo.[55]

The mother he meets is old and dying, but she neither asks for pity nor expects it. The story she has to tell the son she left on the hillside in babyhood, or at least left to be brought up by her admirer, Sir Hugo Mallinger, is the story of a great artist, a great singer and actress, who relinquished her child to pursue her career. Deronda is not confronted by *his* guilty secret but by his mother's.

In this, the last of her novels, George Eliot posed questions about art and about artists, men and women artists, in ways she had not done before. Small talents and accomplishments are put in their place by the great musician, Klesmer. Mirah has a delicate and domesticable talent as a singer, while Hans Meyrick, Deronda's friend from Cambridge, has a versatile and probably commercially exploitable talent as a painter, which is likely to be, it is suggested, unserious and even meretricious. In the Princess Halm-Eberstein – for Deronda's mother has remarried and into the European aristocracy by the time he meets her – George Eliot has created a great woman artist, one with enough self-love to satisfy Lionel Trilling, and one who provides a new reading of Jocasta, a woman who has been a daughter, a wife, a mother, and who is also an artist. She replies angrily to Deronda's questions.

'You are not a woman. You may try – but you can never imagine what it is to have a man's force of genius in you, and yet to suffer the slavery of being a girl. To have a pattern cut out – "this is the Jewish woman; this is what you must be; this is what you are wanted for; a woman's heart must be of such a size and no larger, else it must be pressed small, like Chinese feet; her happiness is to be made as cakes are, by a fixed receipt." That was what my father wanted. He wished I had been a son; he cared for me as a makeshift link. His heart was set on his Judaism. He hated that Jewish women should be thought of by the Christian world as a sort of ware to make public singers and actresses of. As if we were not the more enviable for that! That is a chance of escaping from bondage.'[56]

That anger is reminiscent of the nine-year-old Maggie's in *The Mill on the Floss*, when, on bold impulse, she chops off her hair. An act of rebellion rebounds, becomes self-destructive. The Princess reveals that her talent and her confidence in her decision deserted her at one point, so that she married again and even bore her second husband five children.

Deronda is most hurt by his mother's secrecy, by her long silence. That too is answered by his mother: 'When a woman's will is as strong as the man's who wants to govern her, half her strength must be concealment.'[57] She has feared that her son would see her creativity, her energy as monstrous too, as her father did. She is right. Deronda is as appalled by the unnaturalness of this mother as he is by her denial of Jewishness, which is the character of the identity he gathers from her revelations. Above all, he believes that she has lost in the battle with her father. For him, her destiny has been, as her father meant it to be, to provide the 'makeshift link', to produce a son, himself, who will inherit his grandfather's legacy and carry Judaism into the future:

Your will was strong, but my grandfather's trust which you accepted and did not fulfil – what you call his yoke – is the expression of something stronger, with deeper, farther-spreading roots, knit into the foundations of sacredness for all men. You renounced me – you still banish me – as a son . . . But that stronger Something has determined that I shall be all the more the grandson whom also you willed to annihilate.[58]

The second meeting between mother and son ends, and there will not be another one. For a moment George Eliot allows us a glimpse of that self in a mother which is larger than her maternity but must yield to that maternity in the end. That self has needed to be silent and concealed from her son, for it is monstrous in its egotism. We are returned to Daniel and to the effect of this meeting on him:

He felt an older man. All his boyish yearnings and anxieties about his mother had vanished. He had gone through a tragic experience which must for ever solemnise his life, and deepen the significance of the acts by which he bound himself to others.[59]

The son is at last freed from the mother and from the disablingly feminine sympathies gathered from his search for her throughout his childhood and his youth. His mother's revelations – about herself, about his Jewishness and his destiny – expel him from her influence, become a second birth. George Eliot has held on to the hero who is most herself, but has, just in time, launched him on his male destiny: an act which repudiates the mother as it exonerates her.

The Jocasta of Sophocles, 'A strangled woman swinging before our eyes', has struggled in these novels by women to speak to us out of the myth's contradictions, its prohibitions and obligatory silences. She has begged for a destiny of her own and been granted one only as a corpse. Rather than face the image of the mother who exerts power over men and damages them, women have more often turned to blander, more comforting accounts; ones which applaud mothers and damagingly confine them. For as Angela Carter puts it, 'this theory of maternal superiority is one of the most damaging of all consolatory fictions and women themselves cannot leave it alone'.[60] The good mother is the good woman and a temptation, the begetter of heroes and messiahs, who sits capaciously lapped at the heart of the problem, wanting no more than her due. Women writers have found her an impossible dilemma and have too often ducked behind men's accounts of her. It has been easier to challenge the heroes and the messiahs, and the next chapter will consider some women's heroes and the difficulties men have often had with them.[61]

5

Heroes

The hero of my story I will now describe.

    Leslie Woodcock was about 6 feet in his stockings and fine and well built. He had very dark brown hair neatly parted at one side, a curly moustache of the same shade and deep brown eyes always half shut. He had a large straight nose and mouth to correspond, and white well shaped hands and feet, that set off this good looking young man.

Daisy Ashford[1]

A hero who did no more than get married would not be a hero and would not be worth marrying. Men in novels become something as well as husbands, while women become something by becoming wives. Not only does this reflect the historical realities and the opposite notions of achievement for a man and a woman, but it makes women's novels significantly different from men's, even where the scope and the subject matter are alike. Heroines are not heroes, for ultimately they are judged by their creators, whether they are men or women, and by their readers and critics, according to how and whom they love, for that will be crucial to who they are and to what becomes of them. Marriage in novels, as in life, presents a different prospect for a woman than for a man. What is often called the bourgeois novel has always been concerned with marriage; and Jenni Calder,[2] in her book about marriage in Victorian fiction, shows how illuminating of writers like Thackeray, Tolstoy and Meredith a consideration of their treatment of marriage and family life can be of their own and of their societies' wider values and attitudes. The kind of energy and sensitivity a hero brings to his choice of a woman to love, to his marriage and to his family life will contribute to our understanding of him as a character with a moral destiny in the world. But whereas a woman faces in the question of whom she will marry the principal test of her life, which in practical terms will determine how that life is spent, a hero will be judged by other criteria. Heroines are not heroes, and nor as a rule are their husbands. If a woman loves a hero that is more likely to make her a wife or a mistress than a heroine. This, I think, has presented male readers with difficulties, for if they approve of a heroine they would like her to marry a man's hero. They are disconcerted to find that women do not propose such men as the husbands for their heroines. Indeed, many women's novels centre on the dangers for a young woman of loving or marrying her hero.

Here, for instance, in Alexandra Kollontai's novel, *A Great Love*, is the hero of the Russian Revolution and a young woman who aspires to be one of its heroines:

'Oh, come on now! It won't be such a tragedy if you're a little late! They'll manage very nicely without you, you know.' Moving closer to her he'd started to nibble her ear and then, with mounting passion, to kiss her neck. But she hadn't responded. His words had stung her and she thought of all the other occasions when he'd referred so disparagingly to her work for the Party – *their* Party; she wondered if he'd ever understand that it was only out of a sense of total commitment to her political work that she derived the strength to endure their separation for good.[3]

The nibbling and insensitive lover is Senya. The ear and neck are Natasha's. When this story was published in 1923 Kollontai had already held office in Lenin's government and was beginning a long period of political isolation, which lasted until her death in 1952, for her views on feminism and for her bold stand against Lenin's New Economic Policy. She wrote and spoke out on both issues, and was in a way both a hero and a heroine. The story, however, is set in the period before the Revolution, when Lenin and some of his followers were living in exile in France. Senya is the leading intellectual of the exiled Bolshevik Party. Natasha works, less exaltedly, for the same cause. The couple are presumed to be portraits of Lenin himself and of Inessa Armand, who was Kollontai's friend and was politically active on behalf of women. Lenin is thought by many, and Kollontai appears to have made no bones about believing it, to have had an adulterous affair with Armand between 1911 and 1913. Kollontai is usually exhortatory rather than subtly exploratory in her fiction. She is here too; but this story, for all its moralising and partiality, is often funny as well as serious, and though 'mounting passion' is not its only solecism, the irony of the title seeps into the story itself.

Senya, round-shouldered and rarely seen without his floppy peaked cap, is married in the novel to Anyuta (less a Krupskaya than an ailing and querulous wife and mother). Natasha has been welcomed into the family as Senya's young, pretty and well-born supporter. The story begins when the affair has seemed to be over for several months. Senya has ponderously reminded Natasha of his marital obligations, and they have agreed (or rather she has agreed to agree with him) to end it all. Although she has written – but not posted – passionate letters to him, she is just beginning to recall the affronts of the affair more readily than its delights. Now she receives imperious orders to join him in the South of France. Exasperated, but unable to refuse, she goes about the difficult task of borrowing money for the trip and for her stay with Senya. She cannot admit to her colleagues her reason for needing money and she is embarrassed to leave the group she works with, since her commitment to them has grown partly out of a need to make herself indispensable to them and to counter their criticism that 'Lady Natasha's nothing but a dilettante!'

Despite 'those wonderfully intelligent eyes of his' and his brilliance and originality as a political thinker – qualities we are required to take on trust – Senya, Natasha's hero and lover, is an absurd figure as well as an insensitive one. Their reunion after a long separation begins uncomfortably and deteriorates during the weeks they spend together. He makes her walk behind him to the hotel in case they meet anyone they know. Once in the shabby bedroom he has booked for her, he fells her to the bed before she has removed her hat and then sets about her like some leery dog, playful without being endearing. He has booked another room for himself, since he plans to fill his days working at the home of a professor living in the town. He will need nights uninterrupted by what he likes to believe are Natasha's insatiable demands. Kollontai does not bless her heroines with lovers of much charm or talent as a rule. Senya is an intellectual, whose authority and rousing speeches first seduced Natasha. It is not much of a surprise when before long he is even denying her the fruits of his intelligence (such as it is). His days with the professor stretch into evening and night time, and he woundingly exults in the 'real intellectual stimulation' the professor is able to provide. Cut off from her work and her friends, Natasha is confined to the hotel with nothing to do. She has always known that Senya could be obtuse, naïve, silly. She begins to realise that there may not be enough to compensate for that. She rehearses having things out, delivering sober explanations of her resentment. When she wakes him one night to do this she is dismissed with the words: 'Surely that's enough kisses for one night.'

Blundering affection, sexual crassness and failures of understanding in men collide in all Kollontai's stories with women's protection of men from such truths about them. Senya has the vulnerability of someone who, for most of his life, is acclaimed and powerful. Sexually he is inept, inexperienced and without confidence, and Natasha is touched by and attracted to exactly the part of him which exhibits his dependence on her, even his deference. He is allowed to realise, fleetingly and secretly, that both his wife's and Natasha's unhappiness might be the consequence of his 'inability to relate sexually to women', though he is not able to admit this to either of them. Natasha's resentment grows from the discrepancy between his public arrogance and his private uncertainties, and also from her own participation in this muddle. She has loved him for being a great man who also grovellingly needed her.

The best passage in the story describes the three days when

Senya fails altogether to return to the hotel. Natasha's anxiety and anger suspend her from her own life, and expose shockingly her possessiveness, intolerance and dependence. Eventually a brief note alerts her to his having been ill. His concern for her had been quite outweighed by his wish to keep their affair from the professor. A gasp of outrage turns instantly to maternal tenderness for a man so childish and self-centred in his treatment of her. Her own vanity, the knowledge that a discussion of her feelings will be blocked by charges of hysteria, of behaving just like his wife, make it impossible for her to continue with the affair. The 'great love' is over. Natasha goes home, settling into the train and to her papers with relief.

A Great Love works best when the author is exploring Natasha's confusions rather than inveighing against male failings. The love affair is undermined by her expectations and needs, by her vanity in wishing to behave better than Senya's wife, by her loving his fame and power, by her needing to be taken seriously as an intellectual, by her longing for romantic decorums and post-coital tenderness. Has she simply fallen in love with the wrong man for the wrong reasons? Kollontai had a long affair with the considerably younger Dybenko, who was famously romantic and a military hero. Apparently Lenin said of that liaison, 'I will not vouch for the reliability or endurance of women whose love affairs are intertwined with politics.' How marvellously ironically that resonates with the quite different reasons Natasha offers for thinking the same thing. Stalin was more explicit and sneering. Trotsky remembered that 'Stalin, with whom I had never before had a personal conversation, now came up with unusual jauntiness, and jabbing with his shoulder at the partition, said, leering: "that's him in there with Kollontai! He's in there with Kollontai!" His gestures and laughter seemed unendurably vulgar and out of place.'[4] Natasha gets off more lightly than some women who love or marry their heroes. Her 'great love' with her hero has not destroyed her, though it has wasted several weeks of a busy life. The story raises interesting questions: about hero worship and love, about the possibilities for a woman who is successful in a man's world combining such achievements with romance and love and marriage; about the discrepancy, finally, between men's heroes and women's heroes.

In *Middlemarch*, Dorothea Brooke's decision to marry Casaubon when she is nineteen is very nearly a catastrophe. It is so disastrous that initially George Eliot can treat it only with almost satirical off-handedness. She mercifully spares us the Casaubon wedding-night and honeymoon in Rome, which have been prefigured in a conversation they have before their marriage:

The season was mild enough to encourage the project of extending the wedding journey as far as Rome, and Mr Casaubon was anxious for this because he wished to inspect some manuscripts in the Vatican.

'I still regret that your sister is not to accompany us,' he said one morning, some time after it had been ascertained that Celia objected to go, and that Dorothea did not wish for her companionship. 'You will have many lonely hours, Dorothea, for I shall be constrained to make the utmost use of my time during our stay in Rome, and I should feel more at liberty if you had a companion.'

The words 'I should feel more at liberty' grated on Dorothea. For the first time in speaking to Mr Casaubon she coloured from annoyance.

'You must have misunderstood me very much,' she said, 'if you think I should not enter into the value of your time – if you think that I should not willingly give up whatever interfered with your using it to the best purpose.'

'That is very amiable in you, my dear Dorothea,' said Mr Casaubon, not in the least noticing that she was hurt; 'but if you had a lady as your companion, I could put you both under the care of a cicerone, and we could thus achieve two purposes in the same space of time.'

'I beg you will not refer to this again,' said Dorothea, rather haughtily. But immediately she feared that she was wrong, and turning toward him she laid her hand on his, adding in a different tone, 'Pray do not be anxious about me. I shall have so much to think of when I am alone.'[5]

Time, it should be said, is a symptomatic and essential difficulty for any woman who wishes to mate with her hero, a man with important things to do in the world. There will be a good deal of hanging about. Dorothea plans to learn enough Greek to be able to read aloud to her husband, whose eyes are, amongst other things, failing. In marrying her hero, Dorothea 'was not in the least teaching Mr Casaubon to ask if he were good enough for her, but merely asking herself anxiously how she could be good enough for Mr Casaubon.'[6] The comment is lightly made, but it is also a serious indictment of both of them and of the prospects for their marriage. Mrs Cadwallader consoles Sir James Chettam for losing Dorothea to Casaubon with the words, 'you are well rid of Miss Brooke, a girl who would have been requiring you to see the stars by daylight'.[7] That reminds us of George Eliot's ability to sympathise with Casaubon, as a man who does not claim heroism for himself but has it thrust, incongruously, upon him by a young woman who is as blind to his real nature as she is still ignorant of her own.

None of her friends and relations find the prospect of Dorothea marrying Casaubon an attractive one; but because he is a man of the church, a man of property, who has led a blameless life and is forty-five, they are bereft of expression of their unease. Only Celia, Dorothea's younger sister, speaks out and is able, momentarily, to disturb Dorothea. 'Can't you hear how he scrapes his spoon? And he always blinks before he speaks. I don't know whether Locke blinked, but I'm sure I am sorry for those who sat opposite him, if he did.'[8] Dorothea quickly dismisses this as frivolous irreverence. In her dreams of acquiring sanctity as kneeling handmaiden to her husband, and learning something or other from him as an added bonus, she has not only become blind to his appearance and to his habits and behaviour, but blind too to his having no sexual interest in her of any sort, to his being an arid and unimaginative scholar and a humourless man. She has ignored her own sexual nature and allowed it to be so utterly and unspecifically subsumed into her hero worship that it has not seemed worth dwelling on. When Ladislaw, Casaubon's nephew, collapses with helpless laughter after his first meeting with his uncle's bride, we recognise with a shock the kind of vitality and awareness that Dorothea is dooming herself to do without.

George Eliot's novels are about women's sexual feeling and

about how a woman can intelligently manage such feeling in relation to love, to morality and integrity, and to her own creativity. It has not always been easy for men to accept this in her or in other women novelists. Some of George Eliot's most devoted admirers have, it seems to me, misread her as a result. They have expected this phenomenally intelligent writer to recommend that her heroines marry men's heroes rather than their own, and they have ignored the possiblity that it was her intelligence, which was a woman's intelligence, not a male accretion, which demanded that a woman understand her own sexual nature and needs when she offered to spend her life with a man. Hanging about, alertness to the needs of a remarkable man, are not good enough for George Eliot's heroines. Antonia Byatt explains this well:

Of all the great English nineteenth-century novelists George Eliot best understood and presented the imperative need to come to terms with, to recognize, sexual energy and sexual desire. Critics who judge that Stephen Guest, handsome and provincial, or Will Ladislaw, boyish, emotional, wayward, are 'unworthy' of those complex moral women, Maggie Tulliver and Dorothea Casaubon, ignore the fact that both Stephen and Will have what the other men in their novels (Philip, Casaubon, even Lydgate) notably lack: they have a direct, instinctive, powerful sexual presence, and in matters of sex they are driven to know what they desire and to develop love from desire. Both Stephen and Will behave *well* to the women they come to love, though both are in positions where their love is substantially prohibited by custom, social propriety, good taste. They are sexually honest, and they communicate their sexual feelings clearly to the women they love, and they develop morally through contact with them.[9]

In according respect and admiration to George Eliot and to a few other women writers, men have applied their own standards, and not only to their art, their subject matter, their sensibilities and their moral attitudes. They have applied male standards to the men imagined by women as men their heroines might love, and they have often found them wanting. Even the terrifying Grand-court, who marries Gwendolen Harleth, seemed to Leslie Stephen 'rather the cruel woman than the male autocrat'[10] (a view unlikely to be shared, I should have thought, by women readers). Whether the men in women's novels have been intended as realistic portraits, romantic fantasies or a mixture of both, they have not always been recognised for what they are: men seen, desired and understood by women.

The notion of men's heroes is, of course, more complicated than I have allowed it to seem. There is a world of difference between the divine hero and the romantic hero, just as there is a difference between a society's heroes and the heroes of literature. Nor have those women writers who have wanted to redefine a hero in terms of his relations with a woman been deaf to the bugles of heroism which can be bemusing for them as well as defeating.

When Charlotte Brontë was thirteen she wrote about a play called the 'Islanders', which she, Branwell, Emily and Anne had planned two years earlier:

We then chose who should be chief men in our islands. Branwell chose John Bull, Astley Cooper, and Leigh Hunt; Emily, Walter Scott, Mr Lockhart, Johnny Lockhart; Anne, Michael Sadler, Lord Bentinck, Sir Henry Halford. I chose the Duke of Wellington and two sons, Christopher North and Co., and Mr Abernethy. Here our conversation was interrupted by the, to us, dismal sound of the clock striking seven, and we were summoned off to bed. The next day we added many others to our list of men, till we got almost all the chief men of the kingdom.[11]

Mrs Gaskell, who quotes this fragment from the Brontë childhood manuscripts, comments on the fact that the list includes for the most part staunch Tory politicians of the day. She does not comment on the fact that though the island is to include a school for a thousand children it will not, apparently, include women, heroic or otherwise. There is nothing very surprising about that. For instance, in an illuminating ethnographic study of her own girls' boarding school, Judith Okely shows how even in the 1950s (and almost certainly still) middle- and upper-class girls, taught almost entirely by women, were educated to be 'failed men'. They were taught to admire heroes they were not to emulate but to marry:

Famous men, not women, were to be our heroic models. The school was divided into four cosmological 'houses', not represented by buildings but as groups of girls competing for cups in sport, conduct, drama and deportment – but not academic performance. The houses were named Shackleton, Scott, Livingstone and Rhodes, after male explorers and chauvinists of the colonial kind whom we, as Penelope to Ulysses, could never imitate. We could only marry and beget these kind of men and the Bishop's heroes (*who were, incidentally, Mr Baldwin, Field Marshall Earl Haig and Francis Drake*). Aspirations were stimulated which were simultaneously shown to be impossible for women to attain. Our impotence was confirmed. Even our classrooms were named after male, not female, writers: Shakespeare, Cowper, Kingsley (not Brontë, nor Eliot, certainly not Wollstonecraft).[12]

It is common nowadays to find posters on classroom walls which illustrate the career of a woman pilot or a Black woman brain surgeon. Another poster shows the Brontë sisters, demure and depressed, against a sketched-in background of Yorkshire moors and Haworth parsonage. The shift is undoubtedly well intentioned, but it is nonetheless foolish and insulting. The history, the traditions, the very idea of heroism – of superior human beings, with superior powers or luck, triumphing over social and environmental odds, and over each other – have been inhabited by men. That Black woman brain surgeon is being congratulated for doing as well as a white male brain surgeon, not for what may well be an impressive contribution to brain surgery. The exceptions to this prove the rule. The few women who have become queens or prime ministers or, even, great writers, are admired for doing as well as some men, very few men, in fact. The irony of those posters, and of their simple-minded propaganda, is that it confers retrospectively an honorary place for the Brontë sisters on an island from which they deliberately excluded them-selves and all women.

What have women made of the paradox which encourages them to admire as heroes men whom at best they could only 'marry and beget'? Young women's adventures in many of the novels I have been discussing are often brief make-or-break affairs. There are few novels by men or by women in which women are followed into middle age or old age as people who are still developing and acting on the world. The substance of that short adventure is the search for a man to marry, a man who is at least admirable. At the same time, it has not always been easy for women to gain access to the information which might determine whether a man was admirable or not. In their search they are looking neither for a hero nor for heroism, but for a life which might allow them to develop and to use their gifts. That this short adventure requires, nonetheless, a sort of heroism I have already, I hope, made clear; for young women undertake it alone, with little knowledge or experience, and the consequences of getting it wrong can stain the whole of their lives.

The bad marriages women knew or read about in the novels of Jane Austen, for instance, may for some have operated as simple deterrents against predators or fools; and the rigid discriminations of the class system alerted some young women to the kinds of men who were certainly to be regarded as out of bounds. It is interesting to hear Jane Austen offering advice to a young woman on these matters in her own life. Fanny Knight was in the middle of her brief adventure when she received two long letters from her aunt, Jane Austen, on the question of whom her niece should marry. The older woman's agitation and uncertainty display both her affection for the younger woman and her sense of how critical a time this is for her:

. . . tho' I did not think you then so *much* in love as you thought yourself, I did consider you as being attached in a degree – quite sufficiently for happiness, as I had no doubt it would increase with opportunity. And from the time of our being in London together, I thought you really very much in love – But you certainly are not at all – there is no concealing it. What strange creatures we are! It seems as if your being secure of him (as you say yourself) had made you Indifferent. – There was a little disgust I suspect, at the Races – & I do not wonder at it. His expressions there would not do for one who had rather more Acuteness, Penetration & Taste, than Love, which was your case. And yet, after all, I *am* surprised that the change in your feelings should be so great. He is, just what he ever was, only more evidently & uniformly

devoted to *you* . . . Poor dear Mr. J.P.! – Oh! dear Fanny, your mistake
has been one that thousands of women fall into. He was the *first* young
Man who attached himself to you. That was the charm, & most
powerful it is. Among the multitudes however that make the same
mistake with yourself, there can be few indeed who have so little reason
to regret it; *his* Character and *his* attachment leave you nothing to be
ashamed of. Upon the whole, what is to be done? You certainly *have*
encouraged him to such a point as to make him feel almost secure of
you – you have no inclination for any other person – His situation in
life, family, friends, & above all his character – his uncommonly
amiable mind, strict principles, just notions, good habits – *all* that *you*
know so well how to value, *All* that really is of the first importance –
everything of this nature pleads his cause most strongly. You have no
doubt of his having superior Abilities – he has proved it at the
University – he is I dare say such a scholar as your agreable, idle
Brothers would ill bear a comparison with. Oh! my dear Fanny, the
more I write about him, the warmer my feelings become, the more
strongly I feel the sterling worth of such a young Man & the
desirableness of your growing in love with him again. I recommend this
most thoroughly. There *are* such beings in the World perhaps, one in a
Thousand, as the Creature You and I should think perfection, Where
Grace & Spirit are united to Worth, where the Manners are equal to
the Heart & Understanding, but such a person may not come in your
way, or if he does, he may not be the eldest son of a Man of Fortune,
the Brother of your particular friend, & belonging to your own County.
Think of all this Fanny. Mr. J.P. has advantages which do not often
meet in one person. His only fault indeed seems Modesty. If he were
less modest, he would be more agreable, speak louder & look
Impudenter; and is not it a fine Character of which Modesty is the only
defect? I have no doubt that he will get more lively & more like
yourselves as he is more with you; he will catch your ways if he belongs
to you. And as to there being any objection from his *Goodness*, from the
danger of his becoming even Evangelical, I cannot admit *that*. I am by
no means convinced that we ought not all to be Evangelicals, & am at
least persuaded that they who are so from Reason and Feeling, must be
happiest & safest. Do not be frightened from the connection by your
Brothers having most wit. Wisdom is better than Wit, & in the long run
will certainly have the laugh on her side; & don't be frightened by the
idea of his acting more strictly up to the precepts of the New Testament

than others. And now, my dear Fanny, having written so much on one side of the question, I shall turn round & entreat you not to commit yourself farther, & not to think of accepting him unless you really do like him. Anything is to be preferred or endured rather than marrying without Affection; and if his deficiencies of manner &c &c strike you more than all his good qualities, if you continue to think strongly of them, give him up at once. Things are now in such a state, that you must resolve upon one or the other, either to allow him to go on as he has done, or whenever you are together behave with a coldness which may convince him that he has been deceiving himself. I have no doubt of his suffering a good deal for a time, a great deal, when he feels that he must give you up; – but it is no creed of mine, as you must be well aware, that such sort of Disappointments kill anybody . . .[13]

Clearly, Jane Austen considers Fanny's suitor acceptable. He will be rich, and the two families are already connected. He has done well at university and is a good Christian. He is sensible, kindly and fond of the girl he is thinking of marrying. What might be called the sub-text of Jane Austen's letter, however, is that Fanny thinks him dull, shy, humourless and unattractive. He is not remarkable, and she is not in love with him, though she had initially been excited by his attentions to her. The problem is not just that he is not perfect, is not a hero. He is not Fanny's hero. What should she do? A second letter from her aunt, sent only a fortnight later, withdraws some of her earlier enthusiasm for Fanny's suitor. Clearly Fanny is not in love. 'It is very true,' Jane Austen writes, 'that you never may attach another Man, his equal altogether, but if that other Man has the power of attaching you *more*, he will be in your eyes the most perfect.'[14]

Jane Austen advised her niece and her heroines from a vantage point of pessimism about marriage and love and women's dependence on men. The dilemma is carefully spelled out in her letters to Fanny, and it was the theme of her novels and the theme, more or less intelligently confronted, of most women's novels; even of recent ones, where sex is made explicitly central to the dilemma, and authors are prepared to scrutinise the marriage itself. There are aspects of that dilemma and of the choices it compels which an unmarried woman writing to an unmarried girl in 1814 found it difficult to allude to. The passionate love of Marianne for Willoughby in *Sense and Sensibility* may not, it is suggested, be of the kind to survive a marriage, let alone a marriage which is financially insecure. Yet the prospect of this lively young woman sharing the bed and bearing the children of Colonel Brandon is not an easy one to accept, and is likely to be felt as deserved punishment for earlier rashness or as penitentially making the best of a bad job. It would be unfair to suggest that Jane Austen altogether evades the question of what happens if a young woman finds her admirable husband impossible as a lover and a companion, though that eventuality might be thought fudged in favour of his probably having had moral deficiences in the first place, which it is a woman's duty to detect. Jane Austen's unwillingness, however, to look hard at the marriages she has arranged for her heroines does indicate, as the uncertainties in her letters do, that she could not persuade herself that love did necessarily survive marriage or ensue from a marriage based on good sense or even on admiration. What is clear from her letters and from her novels is that she was advising young women to marry a man for the life he could offer her, that liking him or even loving him might be made possible by that. She does not seem to have been optimistic about even that happening very often, and she appears to have been unwilling to risk it for herself.

Charlotte Brontë was warier and more ambitious. Her heroines look for a man they love physically, whom they are able to trust and who might understand them sufficiently and love them enough to bear even with a woman's 'utmost mutiny'. Her heroines are older and more experienced than Jane Austen's when they fall in love and marry, and they are orphans. Some have travelled, worked for a living. They are surer of what they want and what they do not want. In her last novel, *Villette*, she firmly settled for Lucy's living alone for the rest of her life. Courage, heroism,[15] for the young woman in most nineteenth-century novels, will not mean an exceptional life, a hero's life, garlanded with achievements. It will mean coming to terms with what is possible, loving the man who will have her or else accepting that love is not for her, dealing with emotional and intellectual frustration, attending to her 'duty' (which will not be the same thing as a man's duty), developing courage and controlling pain in the face of the sad and the dull and the trivial. She will find these grand achievements (and, of course, they could be grand) less difficult if she loves and is loved by a man. Gwendolen Harleth's 'ideal was to be daring in speech and reckless in braving dangers, both moral and physical',[16] and it is thwarted because she has misunderstood her own nature and her possibilities as a woman. Courage and duty can seem to mean different things for men and for women.

So heroism is not heroism; and yet it seems important to remember that most men's lives are a good deal more like those of the women in novels than like the men's. Most men's achievements are not the achievements of heroes, any more than women's are. We need to understand, therefore, why the realism of many women's novels has often been read as 'sordid' or as 'romance' and why men have found the men in women's novels unacceptable for that reason.

George Henry Lewes, who lived with George Eliot for twenty-four years, wrote a long, intelligent review of Charlotte Brontë's *Shirley* in the *Edinburgh Review* in 1850. I shall quote the whole of the passage in which he deals with the Moore brothers for its intrinsic interest and because it was written by the man who, years later, and as her lover, leapt to George Eliot's defence when her heroes were criticised, with these wise words:

We only see what interests us, and we have only insight in proportion to our sympathy. Now both these fundamental principles are forgotten by critics who ask, 'Who can be expected to feel interest in the Jews?' – 'Who can believe in such a prig as Deronda?' – 'Mordecai is a Shadow,' etc . . .[17]

In his review of *Shirley* Lewes takes the opportunity to elaborate a theory about 'female literature'. This is the part of the review which deals with Charlotte Brontë's heroes:

The two heroes of the book, however, – for there are two – are not agreeable characters; nor are they felicitously drawn. They have both something sordid in their minds, and repulsive in their demeanour. Louis Moore is talked about as if he were something greater than our ordinary humanity; but, when he shows himself, turns out to be a very small person indeed. Robert, more energetic, and more decisively standing out from the canvas, is disgraced by a sordid love of money, and a shameless setting aside of an affection for Caroline in favour of the rich heiress. *He* will be universally condemned: for all our better instincts rebel against him. The authoress will appeal in vain here to *the truth* of such sordidness – the truth of thus discarding a real passion in favour of an ambitious project. True it is: *true of many men*; but *not true of noble natures* – not true of an ideal of manhood. In a subordinate character such a lapse from the elevation of moral rectitude, might have been pardoned; but in a hero – in the man for whom our sympathies and admiration are almost exclusively claimed – to imagine it possible, is a decided blunder in art – as well as an inconsistency in nature. A hero may be faulty, erring, imperfect; but he must not be sordid, mean, wanting in the statelier virtues of our kind. Rochester was far more to be respected than this Robert Moore! Nor is Louis Moore much better. On any generous view of life there is almost as much sordidness in his exaggerated notions of Shirley's wealth, and of the *distance* it creates between his soul and hers, as there is in Robert's direct and positive greed of the money. That Louis, as a tutor, should be sensitive to any personal slight, should deeply feel that he was no 'match' for the heiress, we can readily understand; but if he thought so meanly of *her* as to suppose that her wealth was any barrier to her affection, then he was unworthy of her.[18]

The only difference between the disapproval expressed here by Lewes and the sort which was directed by some at George Eliot's heroes is that the 'failure' is not so simply attributed to Charlotte Brontë's being a woman. Lewes finds a great deal to praise in her writing and in her treatment of two others of the male characters in the novel: Mr Helstone and Mr Yorke. Lewes also argues with Shirley's view that male novelists are bad at portraying women. He lists six women novelists (including Maria Edgeworth, Jane Austen and Miss Mitford) who, he maintains, 'are second only to the first-rate men of their day; and would probably have ranked

even higher, had they not been too solicitous about male excellence, – had they not often written from the man's point of view,
instead of from the woman's.' In a well-argued section of the essay
he denies the writer's invoking of 'reality' or 'fact' to justify what is
unrealised, unimagined and unbelievable in a character. There
are important questions raised by this passage, whether or not we
want to agree with its assessment of the Moore brothers and its
general dislike of *Shirley* as a whole.

There is a difficulty in requiring heroes or heroines to fall in
love only with 'noble natures'. I have suggested that for women
that difficulty is exacerbated. Whose 'ideal of manhood' might the
Moore brothers be expected to represent? Of course, Lewes uses
these terms aesthetically as well as morally. Yet in assuming that
women will be at one with men in both their aesthetic and their
moral judgements of male characters in novels he evades the
dilemma. For in generally concurring with men who are their
contemporaries as to who might be thought a hero, whether in
politics or literature, women have also been divided. If they have
been 'too solicitous of male excellence' and have failed to give the
woman's point of view, it is because they have been denied the
right to invoke their own 'truth' or their own reality in defence of
their vision of men. So that they are hopelessly and helplessly
exposed to a male critic, even one as sensitive and sympathetic as
Lewes.

The 'truth' in Charlotte Brontë's life as in her novels was that
young women knew very few men, let alone potentially marriageable ones, and they had little experience of men's lives or, indeed,
of their natures, noble or otherwise. There is also the possibility
that since Charlotte Brontë created these men, imagined them for
her heroines, she believed that they were as good as or better than
most men, certainly the best the two young women in the novel
were likely to encounter, and that they were like men were in the
world for her: unreliable, unadmirable, erratic, opaque, keenly
interested in money and infinitely necessary to a woman. It is clear
too that in these portraits of two men who must work hard to make
a living in their different spheres, elements of 'sordidness' were an

inescapable fact of their lives, as they were of most people's and all women's. Charlotte Brontë was open about her intention in creating William Crimsworth, her professor:

I said to myself that my hero should work his way through life as I had seen real living men work theirs – that he should never get a shilling he had not earned – that no sudden turns should lift him in a moment to wealth and high station; that whatever small competency he might gain, should be won by the sweat of his brow; that, before he could find so much as an arbour to sit down in, he should master at least half the ascent of "the Hill of Difficulty"; that he should not even marry a beautiful girl or a lady of rank. As Adam's son he should share Adam's doom, and drain throughout life a mixed and moderate cup of enjoyment.[19]

Louis Moore is obliged to be the servant of people who are unable to appreciate him except as that. Perhaps his sensitivity to Shirley's superior wealth and status is a more characteristically 'female' sensitivity. Robert Moore is engaged in manufacturing industry of a kind which inevitably meant exploiting other people's lives and labour, and this is specifically, if ultimately ambiguously, criticised by Brontë.

There are several things which are conspicuously unconsidered in Lewes's account of *Shirley* – good as it is in other ways – and in the judgements of many other critics of women writers' heroes. There is the sheer difficulty of giving any male character a setting and a context for his life, when women knew so little about men's lives outside the family. There is the nature of women's actual relations with real men in their own lives. There is the ambiguous identification they make with men, and there is the doubt as to the desirability for a woman of a marriage to a man who is in *every* way her superior. Finally, and crucially, there is the question of sexual love and its relation to the kind of romance in which women may take refuge and for which they may also be condemned. At the very least it is likely, for instance, that strong and creative women who long for love and a sexual relationship with a man are not going to envy, let alone emulate, the fate of Penelope. Passive acquiescence, as the wife of a hero or indeed of any man who is successful and impressive in a man's world, promises something even worse than boredom. Dorothea's marriage to Ladislaw, after the terrible emotional impasse of her marriage to Casaubon, has to be understood as a recognition of the deludedness of believing, if you are a woman, that your fulfilment could possibly be found *through* an attachment to a man whose career is more important to him than you are. He will need a younger and sturdier helpmate before long, anyway.

When Lewes was defending George Eliot's treatment of Daniel Deronda he was referring particularly to Henry James's dramatised review, *Daniel Deronda: A Conversation*, in which one of its three *dramatis personae* replies to another's, 'He must have been delightfully handsome', with the words:

Never, my dear, with that nose! I am sure he had a nose, and I hold that the author has shown great pusillanimity in her treatment of it. She has quite shirked it. The picture you speak of is very pretty, but a picture is not a person. And why is he always grasping his coat-collar, as if he wished to hang himself up? The author had an uncomfortable feeling that she must make him do something real, something visible and sensible, and she hit upon that clumsy figure. I don't see what you mean by saying you have been *near* those people; that is just what one is not.[20]

This passage is at least as remarkable for its anti-semitism as for its dismissing of Deronda as a hero whom women could plausibly love. It is certainly not to be taken as James's only thoughts on the novel. I quote it because it chimes with the views of many male critics that Daniel Deronda was not *a real man* and could not therefore be attractive to women. Robert Louis Stevenson thought Daniel Deronda a 'melancholy puppy and humbug ... the Prince of Prigs',[21] and Leslie Stephen uses Deronda to illustrate his belief that it was as a creator of men that George Eliot's 'femininity' invariably betrayed her:

I must repeat that George Eliot was intensely feminine, though more philosophical than most women. She shows it to the best purpose in the subtlety and the charm of her portraits of women, unrivalled in some ways by any writer of either sex; and shows it also, as I think, in a true perception of the more feminine aspects of her male characters. Still, she sometimes illustrates the weakness of the feminine view. Daniel Deronda is not merely a feminine but, one is inclined to say, a schoolgirl's hero. He is so sensitive and scrupulously delicate that he will not soil his hands by joining in the rough play of ordinary political and social reformers.[22]

I argued in the previous chapter that Daniel Deronda is, above all, a son; that for most of the novel he is searching for his mother, who will be able, he expects, to explain him to himself and to release him from a search which has deflected him from some grander purpose in life. That portrait and that destiny contain a mother's focus on her son and a woman writer's male hero. His appeal for a good many readers, men as well as women, lies in his 'deepest interest in the fates of women', for without his need of women he would remain outside their knowledge and unimaginable. For Gwendolen, who fears men and sex in anticipation of her own vulnerability to them, Deronda is the one man who does not threaten her as a woman. He is a hero who has time to hear her and to hear other women. We are returned to the irreducible difference between a man's hero, who would put achievement before love, and a woman's hero, who would be a rare and extraordinary man, prepared to love her and to hear her first.

The irony is that George Eliot herself seems to have found happiness with just such a man, for Lewes devoted himself to her and to her career at least as much as to his own. Much harder for some of us to accept than Deronda's being 'a schoolgirl's hero' (to return to Leslie Stephen, who would presumably have preferred him to be a schoolboy's) is the ending, when, after his last meeting with his mother, he is sent off by George Eliot to get on with his real man's life, to marriage, his nobly unspecific projects in the East, his destiny as a man in the world. George Eliot, as we are unlikely to forget, knew her duty, and mothers know it too. It is to see that sons stop worrying about women and get on with serious matters. Deronda's destiny *will* involve marriage, though it will not be the kind of partnership George Eliot enjoyed with Lewes. Deronda tells his mother that Mihra, whom he loves, is not ambitious. She (unlike his mother) will be prepared to give up her career as a singer when she marries him. His mother is contemptuous, but also relieved. She has done her son no lasting damage.

For some critics this is too late. There has been too much shilly-shallying. Deronda has spent too much time listening to women and fidgeting with his coat collar. This beautiful, epicene creature should have been ejected from his mother's womb and into the world of men years earlier, for as Leslie Stephen put it, 'In the Cambridge atmosphere of Deronda's day there was, I think, a certain element of rough commonsense which might have knocked some of her hero's nonsense out of him.'[23] Clearly George Eliot did not know that, may even still not have known it when she walked at the end of her life with F. W. H. Myers in Trinity Fellows' Garden and is alleged to have taken 'as her text the three words which have been used so often as the inspiring trumpet-calls of men, – the words *God, Immortality, Duty*, – (and) pronounced, with terrible earnestness, how inconceivable was the *first*, how unbelievable the *second*, and yet how peremptory and absolute the *third*.'[24] The last laugh may be said to be on Myers himself, not only for subsuming George Eliot's 'duty' in the trumpet-calls of men, but because he has often himself been proposed as the model for Casaubon.

Leslie Stephen ends his anathematising of Deronda with the words, 'But, in any case, one is sensible that George Eliot, if she is thinking of real life at all, has come to see through a romantic haze which deprives the portrait of reality.'[25] Romance as an evasion of reality is often invoked in discussions of novels written by women (indeed whole sections of libraries are devoted to 'romances' which, if they are not always by women, are invariably about them and intended for them). I shall want to argue that whether 'romance' is intended pejoratively or not, it has been allowed to obscure the meanings it may have had for women writers and still has for women readers. Certainly, as Stephen uses it here, 'romantic haze' is allowed to adhere in a special way to the feminine in George Eliot, even to the elderly and feminine in her, while reality is the reality of Cambridge and its common sense, from which George Eliot protected her hero, as any mother might, and particularly if that mother could never have studied there herself.

Leslie Stephen is no less scathing about Stephen Guest, the young man with whom Maggie Tulliver falls so passionately and disastrously in love in *The Mill on the Floss*, which was written sixteen years earlier than *Daniel Deronda*:

George Eliot did not herself understand what a mere hairdresser's block she was describing in Mr. Stephen Guest. He is another instance of her incapacity for portraying the opposite sex. No man could have introduced such a character without perceiving what an impression must be made upon his readers. We cannot help regretting Maggie's fate; she is touching and attractive to the last; but I, at least, cannot help wishing that the third volume could have been suppressed. I am inclined to sympathise with the readers of *Clarissa Harlowe* when they entreated Richardson to save Lovelace's soul. Do, I mentally exclaim, save this charming Maggie from damning herself by this irrelevant and discordant degradation.[26]

In quoting this passage, F. R. Leavis was sufficiently incensed by the snobbery in it to overcome his own prejudices for a moment, though not for long:

That the presentment of Stephen Guest is unmistakably feminine no one will be disposed to deny, but not only is the assumption of a general incapacity refuted by a whole gallery of triumphs, Stephen himself is sufficiently 'there' [Leavis is referring to Stephen Guest here] to give the drama a convincing force. Animus against him for his success with Maggie and exasperation with George Eliot for allowing it shouldn't lead us to dispute that plain fact – they don't really amount to a judgment of his unreality.[27]

Having stepped back for a moment in order to take a swipe at Leslie Stephen, Leavis moves in for the kill. Guest, he insists, is all too convincingly suited to Maggie's weakness, the 'soulful side' of her, the 'yearnings' and their renunciatory history, derived from Maggie's teenage reading of *Thomas à Kempis*. It isn't just Stephen Guest that is the trouble, it is George Eliot's culpable identification with Maggie, her seeing her from within, her uncritical acceptance of Maggie's loving Stephen, her refusal to come clean and say that Maggie's finding Stephen irresistible is a mark of her immaturity. For in the end – and Leavis has not wanted to say it, for it would show him to be on the same side as Leslie Stephen – the ending to the novel is hopelessly vitiated, made slackly and romantically tragic, because

Stephen Guest (apart, of course, from the insufficient strength of moral fibre betrayed under the strain of temptation – and it is to Maggie he succumbs) is not worthy of her spiritual and idealistic nature. There is no hint that, if Fate had allowed them to come together innocently, she wouldn't have found him a pretty satisfactory soul-mate.[28]

The fact that George Eliot, the writer and moralist these critics greatly admire, is telling them that Maggie Tulliver longs to make love with Stephen Guest, that her predicament is that she desires a man she is not able altogether to trust, goes unheard. It is wrong of George Eliot to let *their* lovely Maggie so forget herself as to desire the body of a rich and handsome young man, who would nonetheless be just as much a *persona non grata* in Trinity Fellows' Garden as Maggie would herself. The tone is self-congratulatory, as of a fatherly appreciation of a good girl, who is 'touching and attractive' and should not have bothered with a provincial bounder. She could, after all, have turned to more serious men, who would have let her type their manuscripts, read their proofs. They could have dedicated their books to her, 'without whose devoted . . .etc.' With George Eliot's prompting they are able to see that Casaubon will not do. He never gets his book written anyway. There are men who are exasperated with Dorothea for not suspecting at once that Casaubon never would get that book finished, though George Eliot's triumph is to have made Dorothea's absolute inability to see through Casaubon all too believable as a consequence of her nature, her upbringing and her experience. Virginia Woolf, who was the daughter of Leslie Stephen, after all, was nearer the mark about Maggie and Stephen; though, as so often, she is hampered by her wish to be read and admired by men like her father:

First Philip Wakem is produced, and later Stephen Guest. The weakness of the one and the coarseness of the other have often been pointed out; but both, in their weakness and coarseness, illustrate not so much George Eliot's inability to draw the portrait of a man, as the uncertainty, the infirmity, and the fumbling which shook her hand when she had to conceive a fit mate for a heroine.[29]

So women, it seems, know what they like but not what is best for them. A drawing of G. H. Lewes in 1841 by Anne Gliddon[30] shows a slim, wavy-haired young man, who might have modelled for Stephen Guest. George Eliot seems to have got what she wanted. When she lets her heroine fall in love with a beautiful and responsive young man she is not heard. Maggie's struggle at the end of the novel is meaningless if sexual feeling is removed from it. Her attraction is to a young man who feels as strongly as she does and is able to recognise what sort of woman she is. That, for women, is essential. The trouble, of course, is that women have learned all too thoroughly what is good for them. Their novels are likely to confront the problem of meeting men's requirements of them as women and as writers; and those requirements will extend to the men women write into their novels as worthy mates for their heroines. Katherine Mansfield was a writer who married a man who was 'worthy of her' and a writer, John Middleton Murry. Two entries in her diary, five years apart, suggest that she was not as fortunate as George Eliot and that she often longed for the love, the admiration and the vitality of a man who was not so 'worthy of her':

J would really think me important if I brought him £.s.d. He thinks he is far and away the first fiddle. How he'd love to boast of what I got out of a play. That's why I am going to start one to-day. I'll sweat my guts out till I bring it off, too. A hideous day.[31]

and

I *do* lament that he is not warm, ardent, eager, full of quick response, careless, spendthrift of himself, vividly alive, *high-spirited*. But it makes no difference to my love.[32]

If it is hard to deal with accusations of 'romantic haze', 'soulfulness', a 'schoolgirl's hero' when their target is George Eliot, how are we to deal with the idea of 'romance' when it is used disparagingly to mean sentimentality, fantasy, evasion more generally, and as descriptive of women's sexual needs and nature and of the stories they tell themselves about sex? 'Romance' has been allowed to place women reductively, whether they are objects of it, producers of it or addicted and cheated consumers of it. At its simplest it might be said that 'romance' offers women an alternative to the parts they are asked to play in that other kind of fantasy, pornography. Romance is a consolatory delusion of power for women in much the same way that pornography is a consolatory delusion of power for men. It would be wrong, obviously, to suggest that these are delusions with equivalent potential for damage. Some people have even wanted to attribute these discrepant fantasies to the anatomical differences between women and men. So that a girl's adolescent sexual stirrings, experienced as unspecific and expressed with reticence, correspond to the invisibility of her genitals; while the manifestness of a boy's explains his celebratory enthusiasm for putting them to use as soon as possible.[33] Quite different kinds of story might be told about those differences. For instance, that men's fear of women's sexuality (and its potential for casting doubt on their paternity) obliges men to control it; and that might derive from the exposed vulnerability of their genitals compared with the inscrutably secure and hidden nature of women's. All anatomical explanations fail to account for the fact that there are cultures in which womanly reticence is not encouraged (it is much less so in Western societies nowadays than it once was, after all). Yet it is also true that most societies have thought it essential to contain young women's sexuality, and if their ways of doing so have differed they may well have shared a belief that female sexuality was not only precociously active but potentially disruptive. Having asserted a need to tame it, its 'tamed' character could come to seem its 'nature', for as Shirley Ardener has pointed out, 'there is often a close correlation between what is thought *fitting* for people to do and what they are thought to be *capable* of doing, and the doers may implicitly concur.'[34]

In her discussion of *Shirley*, Rachel Harrison makes connections between what she calls 'the ideology of romance' and 'the relations of reproduction' and suggests that romantic love mediates the contradictions for women of selling their legal existence and their financial independence to men in exchange for love:

For this reason *Shirley* is both an exemplary text, and a cry from the heart. On the one hand, it is part of a range of literature, ideologically orchestrated by the publishing bourgeoisie, on the other, it is an indication of the way that this work of inculcation of female dependency provoked a resistance to the contradictions it set up.[35]

Such an analysis can make Charlotte Brontë seem both a poor sociologist and a duped novelist, but it does at least hint at the way in which romance may be a consciously manipulated response to social contradictions for women.

It may be that romance *is* an evasion. It is also often a conscious subterfuge. Whether the romantic dream is George Eliot's or glorified in *Woman*, it always holds the possibility of subverting men's peace of mind. For most of the time Jane Austen may well be thought to be concurring with men's views of women's sexual natures and at any rate recommending a workable compromise. Doing so makes it safe for her to tell us something else as well: that Elinor in *Sense and Sensibility* is excited by Willoughby, that Henry Crawford in *Mansfield Park* is sexually alive in a way that Edmund is not. George Eliot can be more open. Donnithorne, who seduces Hetty in *Adam Bede*, is far more sexually aware and awake than Adam Bede, for all his sterling qualities and weight-lifting build. It is easy to feel that George Eliot knew perfectly well that the palpable sexual excitement of Maggie's response to Stephen Guest in *The Mill on the Floss* ran the risk of being dismissed as romantic nonsense, and even that romantic nonsense is intentionally subversive. It is subversive because it appears to take on trust men's accounts of women as creatures preoccupied with love, while announcing that in that case men too are bound to sacrifice everything for love, as women are asked to do, absolving themselves from responsibility for the world, for work, for the maintaining of law and order. Interestingly, Shirley Ardener also quotes a study of sexual relations in Islamic society, where romantic love is perceived as dangerously disruptive:

What is feared is the growth of the involvement between a man and a woman into an all-encompassing love, satisfying the sexual, emotional and intellectual needs of both partners (which could constitute) a direct threat to the man's allegiance to Allah.[36]

Romance does constitute a threat, if only a phantom threat, to men's lifetime objectives, and women who share such objectives have joined men in condemning stories about young people in love which allow sexual passion to transcend the ordinary demands of life and adults' responsibilities for relationships and activities other than sexual ones. Most women come to recognise romantic love as an illusion, which has allowed them to dream of men joining them voluntarily in their captivity, a state of affairs which might satisfactorily undermine men without freeing women. It might be said that pornography, with its celebration of men's sexual power and mastery over women, performs a similar function for men. It asserts, as romance does, an idealised union, in which the will and wishes of one partner are justified by the temporary suspension of all resistance in the other. They are both forms of consolation and myth-making, and part of the social realities which constrain and dictate sexual relations between men and women.

Angela Carter demonstrates with her usual incendiary precision in *The Sadeian Woman* that we are all lost if we take either romance or pornography literally for what they tell us about women's sexuality. She superbly sets out for us the Marquis de Sade's imagined sisters, Justine and Juliette,[37] one the bruised victim, still frigidly virtuous because ungiven after a thousand rapes, the other a vampiric fury, who leaps at the power men wish to exert over her and uses it for her own purposes. Justine's virtue becomes meaningless in a world which systematically rapes it.

Juliette becomes the object of the rhetoric about women she denies by being no more than its antithesis. Neither Justine (who is all heart and no analysis), nor Juliette (who is all rationality and no heart) will do, for both are defeated by their terror of love, and 'it is in this holy terror of love that we find, in both men and women themselves, the source of all opposition to the emancipation of women.'[38]

Romance also has in common with pornography the faceless-ness of the sexual partner, the infinitely generalisable lover, divested of the particular and the real. Different organs of the body are employed for 'knowing' that partner: the heart in the first, the genitals in the second. Yet the fantasies they spell out are finally quite different. If neither mirrors reality exactly, both work with the kinds of realities they are also intended to disguise, and both determine to a considerable extent the discourses available to us when we contemplate, imagine or engage in sexual relations. Romance soothes women and mediates for them the painful ambivalence they internalise about men's power over them in the world by proposing to reduce men to their level, inducing de-pendence in a man on a woman, a dependence viewed by other men as grovelling and abject. Pornography, on the other hand, reasserts for men images of conquest and control, desperate consolation for childhood losses and adult defeats.

I have wanted to dwell on the nature of 'romance' in novels because it may help us to understand why men have jibbed at aspects of the novels I have been discussing, and because these same novels have been read by women as explorations of the ambiguity for women of loving men. Men have sometimes re-sponded to women's accounts of such love as evasive and sen-timental rather than as necessarily tactical and concealed. For romance has been necessary to women, to sugar the pill and to mediate contradictions. In wanting to celebrate the heroisms of women – which are not to be measured solely in terms of achievements won in spite of being a woman – women writers have needed to focus on what women could actually know and say about their own feelings and possibilities. It will be necessary for men to see romance as something other than wilful evasion of the truth. It can also be the discourse of the dependant, holding conflicting messages of mutiny and love. It might also be said to stand for women's longing for men stripped of their stern swords and pens, men who could read Anna Akhmatova's lines as a woman might:

At the given signal
He'll come out of his lair,
Wild as a woodsprite,
Gentler than a sister.[39]

6

Another Story

In order to avoid total annihilation, to escape man's habitual urge to colonize, she must conserve some space for herself, a sort of *no man's land*, which constitutes precisely what men fail to understand of her and often attribute to stupidity because she cannot express its substances in her inevitably alienated language.

Claudine Herrmann[1]

'Be a feminine George Eliot. Try your hand.'

Dorothy Richardson[2]

Jane Austen, the Brontës, George Eliot were telling their readers that women were not only as men see them, that they were more than wives or sisters or mothers, more than the creatures of myth or romance or pornography, more than female bodies imbued, in a few cases, with a leavening of intelligence, which was male. More than that, they were demonstrating that for women the world and men look different from men's accounts of them. Yet each was impeded as a messenger of such news by the form of the novel and by the impersonations required of them as they entered that form and its language.

Dorothy Richardson was born in 1873, so that she was seven when George Eliot died. She was born a Victorian and lived until 1957. She began the sequence of novels which is called *Pilgrimage* in 1913, and the last of the thirteen was published in 1938. Virago's new edition[3] of it comes with its volumes adorned and strangely illuminated by four of Gwen John's series of nine

paintings called 'The Convalescent'.[4] There is no evidence that
the two women knew of each other, though they were contemporaries and had a good deal in common. Both lived alone for much
of their lives, in small city rooms which frame and are part of their
portraits of women: portraits which are also self-portraits, revealing of their makers and of themselves, intensely concerned with
their own composition, fiercely contained, even restricted in
scope, yet assertive and alive with qualities of energy and concentration. If the work of both women has been seen as especially
'feminine' I shall want to argue that this was, first, no more than a
description of their lives, and second, much truer of Dorothy
Richardson than of Gwen John, in that the writer's work has been
explicitly carved out of the confusions and multiplicities which the
word 'feminine' has come to contain.

Miriam Henderson is seventeen at the beginning of *Pilgrimage*
and nearly forty at the end. The handling of time and of aging, as
the quality of human experience, makes this a pilgrimage rather
than a quest. Miriam is expelled from a happy suburban childhood in South London when her father's always dubious, and
aspirant, financial dealings fail. She is sent off to Germany to
teach in a girls' school, and returns to a cramped and dingy school
in North London which she leaves to become a governess before
taking a job as a dentist's receptionist at £1 a week. On this she
lives, lodging in Bloomsbury and enjoying her liberty. There are
few novels which enter so well into the intricacies and comedy of a
particular job and the evenings and weekends her working only
just pays for. She is solitary and free in Bloomsbury, able to
explore several worlds and belong to none of them. An old
schoolfriend has married a famous writer and lives in Surrey.
Hypo Wilson (famously based on H. G. Wells), with whom
Miriam has an awkward love affair, urges her to write 'middles'
for magazines; another friend proposes 'the confessions of a
modern woman':[5] suggestions which she scorns, though Dorothy
Richardson was to take them up. Yet another friend is the Russian
Jew, Michael Shatov, who wants to marry her. Then there are
women, ones who smoke and joke and chat into the night, others

who whine and batten, others still who marry, as two of her three sisters do, unhappily, so that at the end of the novel Miriam is able to congratulate herself on having evaded 'the convention that kept urbane women alert at the front gates of consciousness to guard the ease of men waiting to be set going on their topics':[6] woman as greyhound handler!

Miriam attends lectures and meetings, she reads and talks and bicycles and listens and looks; and slowly, with much argument and back-tracking, she finds her own topic and life and becomes a writer. Her topic could be said to be her own life, and the events of her life are very like the events of Dorothy Richardson's life. Yet Miriam is also an imagined character, watched and watching, remembered and remembering. The novel is shaped by acts of remembering and by their trophies, brightly lit moments and fragments which wait, like rooms, to be occupied.

The novel does not deal in the habitual or the repeated, but moves through moments, each one exceptional, and the living of them. Books, conversations, faces, lectures, glimpses from windows and through them, meetings, noises, clothes are experienced, sensed, known, and never passively, so that Miriam quarrels with books, mimics voices, marvels at what she reads in newspapers, despairs of a blouse. New ideas and people and places assault her as she assaults them, and she is changed by them. Memory alights on those moments which nudge her into fresh insight and knowledge, and for this to happen the moments themselves must be inhabited again. Here, for instance, is the first paragraph of her third novel, *Honeycomb*:

When Miriam got out of the train into the darkness she knew that there were woods all about her. The moist air was rich with the smell of trees – wet bark and branches – moss and lichen, damp dead leaves. She stood on the dark platform snuffing the rich air. It was the end of her journey. Anything that might follow would be unreal compared to this moment. Little bulbs of yellow light further up the platform told her where she must turn to find the things she must go to meet. 'How lovely the air is here.' . . . The phrase repeated itself again and again, going with her up the platform towards the group of lights. It was all she could summon to meet the new situation. It satisfied her; it made her happy. It was enough; but no one would think it was enough.[7]

A real moment is caught with the mind's words, which both hold the moment and create it, yet 'no one would think it was enough'. Consciousness is continuous, but it fluctuates, and memory retrieves and resolves the past into moments which are more important than other moments, not because such moments have acquired in retrospect a historical significance, but because they contain thought, feeling and their verbal expression, met in such a way that both time and the self are moved on by them.

Intellectual growth and personal discovery are not easy for her. Learning happens unpredictably and with struggle. Miriam can never simply be taught, but must learn and relearn, on her own, painfully and resistingly. She liked her own school because 'it had not gone against the things she found in herself'.[8] Learning is never so simple again, and she is conscious of having a lot to learn. In this as in much else she is like all the most interesting of women's heroines: Jane Eyre, Lucy Snowe, Dorothea Brooke, whose education continues into adulthood. The reader is not cajoled into either sympathy or agreement with this extraordinary woman, whose candours are often contradictory and provisional. The novel's effect is to rock its reader into the same kinds of assertion, resistance and uncertainty that Miriam goes through herself. To read *Pilgrimage* is to know, minutely and sometimes uncomfortably, the rhythms of another consciousness.

Memory can turn the past into history, providing what is recalled with a spurious or partial significance, which Miriam dreads as subversive of the reality she comes to think of as 'current existence, the ultimate astonisher'.[9] Plots, endings, even opinions develop purposes and plans of their own, which may reduce the confusions of life without really explaining them; and it is the 'man's hilarious expostulating narrative voice'[10] – the voice of men and of novels, of sequence and of logic, a voice which Dorothy Richardson responded to and knew how to use – which she also set out to avoid. Memory regurgitates the past in a discontinuous way as a rule, and that discontinuity may fight with the time sequence implied by narrative. It was characteristic of Dorothy Richardson to jib at the word 'stream' when May Sinclair, writing of her novels in 1918,[11] used William James's 'stream of consciousness' to describe them. 'Pool', she thought, would have done better.[12] She began writing her novel, it should be remembered, in 1913, the year when *The White Peacock* and the first volume of *Du Côté de chez Swann* came out and a year before *Dubliners*. Her fiction has always been seen as experimental, and it still is, in the best possible sense. It is also of its time, in its feminist and its Fabian socialist politics and in what it owes to early film-making. What Dorothy Richardson particularly shares with Proust and with Joyce is the incorporation into her novel of its own history and creation. More than that. *Pilgrimage* is not just a novel about a woman's life, even a woman writer's life. It is a novel which lives out a developing rationale for a new language and a new form to express how a woman experiences herself and her life in ways which cannot be adequately represented by the traditions of narrative and the novel.

Miriam will eventually write the novel she occupies, like the rooms she creates and lovingly describes. She is a passionate reader, quick to see what is best in a writer, excitable, greedy for ideas, but always finally dismayed. So that Henry James, who is present and parodied in *Pilgrimage* as the writer who 'had achieved the first completely satisfying way of writing a novel',[13] becomes for Dorothy Richardson 'a venerable gentleman, a charmed and charming high priest of nearly all the orthodoxies, inhabiting a softly lit enclosure he mistook, until 1914, for the universe'.[14] The dismay is not just with James or Conrad or Gissing, or even with Shakespeare, whose women had 'no reality' because they were 'women as men see them',[15] but with the alternative they forced her towards: the terrifying need to create a kind of fiction and a language which would reflect and contain what was peculiar to women's experience and women's minds. She began to see this as 'what is left out' of most novels.

In *Dawn's Left Hand*, Hypo Wilson, blithely encouraging, tells her that 'Women ought to be good novelists. But they write best about their own experiences. Love-affairs and so forth. They lack creative imagination.' 'Ah,' replies Miriam, 'imagination. Lies.'[16] She is beginning to match what she misses in men's novels with what she might do herself:

Even as you read about Waymarsh and his 'sombre glow' and his 'attitude of prolonged impermanence' as he sits on the edge of the bed talking to Strether, and revel in all the ways James uses to reveal the process of civilizing Chad, you are distracted from your utter joy by fury over all he is unaware of. And even Conrad. The self-satisfied, complacent, know-all condescendingness of their handling of their material. Wells seems to have more awareness. But all his books are witty exploitations of ideas. The torment of *all* novels is what is left out. The moment you are aware of it, there is torment in them. Bang, bang, bang, on they go, these men's books, like an L.C.C. tram, yet unable to make you forget them, the authors, for a moment. It worries me to think of novels. And yet I'm thrilled to the marrow when I hear of a new novelist.[17]

What *is* peculiar to women's experience and women's minds? Miriam finds this no easier to grapple with than any of the rest of us, not least because she often feels herself to be 'mannish', or anyway 'some sort of bad unsimple woman',[18] who is as ambivalent about men and women as she is about herself. 'How utterly detestable mannishness is; so mighty and strong and comforting when you have been mewed up with women all your life.'[19] She has love affairs and friendships with men and with women. A woman she uneasily shares a flat with for a time accuses her of failing, as she would never have done with a man, to keep a promise she'd made to her. Miriam is superbly indignant and privately ashamed. It is true. She can say disparagingly of a fat woman she sees at a concert that she is 'two-thirds of the way through a life that had been a ceaseless stream of events set in a ceaseless stream of inadequate commentary without and within'.[20] Yet men are taxed with 'talking *about* people and things and never being or knowing anything.'[21] Assertions and contradictions characterise Miriam's sense of the dilemma and her tackling of it. It is out of the duality of her own nature that the language of the novel will emerge, and it is a duality which is expressed as a quality of language itself. Language and languages and ways of speaking are sometimes her element, there for sport, for mimicry and invention, for catching and lighting up what is precious and uniquely hers. She is an excellent linguist, with an ear for idiom and idiosyncracy. While translating some dry academic French, she discovers that, in their failure to meet and match, the words of two languages can produce meanings beyond either: yet 'each was expressive, before its meaning appeared.'[22] If language can generate the meaning and be made to mean, it can also evade or wither meaning: 'If you can speak of a thing, it is past . . . Speaking makes it glow with a life that is not its own.'[23]

The language Miriam works for, so that ultimately she will describe the 'years falling into words, dropping like fruit',[24] will be one which approximates to the language of impression and thought: dense, flexible, playful, reflexive. The abbreviations of inner language, sentences reduced to their predicates because their subjects and even verbs are too obvious to the thinker, or too painful, to need articulating, will, in detail and throughout the novel, work to ensure that the reader enters the text on terms which make it necessary to query and doubt and reread. For instance: Dorothy Richardson's mother spent many years in a state of torturing depression, and was taken by Dorothy at the end of her life to a hotel by the sea. The mother's condition deteriorated as her dependence increased, and one day, when her daughter had gone out to get help from a doctor, she killed herself. This episode is made part of Miriam's story at the end of *Honeycomb*. Yet we are not quite told that this is what happened, only that Miriam came back to a horror, whose effect on her is alluded to several times in her later life, and whose cause remains unsayable. Miriam will muse and speculate about someone before introducing them or describing her meeting with them. She will wonder how another friend might view this new acquaintance, imagine them together, make comparisons and predictions, rehearse idiosyncracies of speech or dress or behaviour. The reader, initially bludgeoned and bemused by such treatment, comes to recognise its truth to the way we respond to new people, circling them with our hypotheses as we attempt to interpret them, as mysterious possessors of faces and voices and gestures first, as owners of names and histories only afterwards.

Between 1927 and 1933, Dorothy Richardson wrote film reviews for Bryher's magazine *Close-Up*.[25] *Pilgrimage* is importantly affected by her understanding of the possibilities of the film camera and, paradoxically, by her sense that the arrival of 'talkies' would be a threat to these possibilities. 'Vocal sound, always a barrier to intimacy, is destructive of the balance between what is seen and the silently perceiving, co-operating onlooker.'[26] The paradox was not lost on her; indeed, the kind of loquaciousness she developed to replace the camera contained its own wariness of everything in language which works to categorise and therefore tempts the writer to go for what is clinching, summarising. It was the eye behind the camera which should have supremacy. In a review of *Finnegan's Wake*, she quoted Goethe; 'the novelist's business is to keep his hero always and everywhere onlooker rather than participant and, "by one device or another" to slow up the events of the story so that they may be seen through his eyes and modified by his thought.'[27] The notion that language might be what it represents, rather than simply mediating individuals' accounts of reality, is Miriam's goal. Dorothy Richardson developed a prose in which rhythm, intonation, sentence structure and punctuation[28] contribute to a representation of the movement of attention rather than to the sequencing of narrative or logic.

Maturity in the last four novels is expressed as a new confidence in what Miriam uniquely is. She is no longer freakish to herself, no longer divided, but a person in whom variety and contradiction are recognised and productive. She is drawn to the Fabians and later to the Quakers by what both groups have to say about sharing and collaboration, about the individual conscience and its relation to common experience. Writing will make possible a merger or treaty between those aspects of her life which have seemed polarised: male and female, speech and silence, ideas and impressions, thinking and feeling. Literature, and what she will write, is, Miriam finds out, communicative after all.

Dorothy Richardson made duality the starting point for her exploration of a woman's experiencing. Miriam's recognition of her own bisexuality begins from her relationship with her father and develops, as a troubling and organising principle of the novel, into something like a theory of perception and realism. In all her encounters with men, her father, her sisters' husbands, employers, friends, strangers and writers, she is working out for herself, 'what is left out'? In the foreword to the 1938 edition of *Pilgrimage* she wrote:

Since all these novelists happened to be men, the present writer, proposing at this moment to write a novel and looking round for a contemporary pattern, was faced with the choice between following one of her regiments and attempting to produce a feminine equivalent of the current masculine realism.[29]

As the third of four sisters she delighted in her father's alliance with her, his treating her as a son, and drew back from the implications of that. At the beginning of the novel Miriam wakes up on the day she is to leave for Germany with the thought that,

Pater knew how hateful all the world of women were and despised them.
He never included her with them; or only sometimes when she pretended, or he didn't understand . . .[30]

He accompanies her to Germany, gallantly and yet mer-etriciously, and as they are introduced to her new employers at the school,

She glanced at him. There could be no doubt that he was playing the role of the English gentleman. Poor dear. It was what he had always wanted to be. He had sacrificed everything to the idea of being a 'person of leisure and cultivation'. Well, after all, it was true in a way. He was – and he had, she knew, always wanted her to be the same . . .[31]

Loving her father, identifying with him, constantly beady and suspicious, of his snobbery, his idleness, his hedonism; and aware that her mother's recurrent crises of depression are largely to be attributed to him, Miriam's love and disapproval of him become self-regard as well as self-distrust. She will delight in her father, boast of his superiority, and yet disapprove of her own, womanly, indulgence of him:

He used to come home from the City and the Constitutional Club and sometimes instead of reading *The Times* or the *Globe* or the *Proceedings of the British Association* or Herbert Spencer, play Pope Joan or Jacoby with them all, or table billiards and laugh and be 'silly' and take his turn at being 'bumped' by Timmy going the round of the long dining-room table, tail in the air; he had taken Sarah and Eve to see *Don Giovanni* and *Winter's Tale* and the new piece, *Lohengrin*. No one at the tennis-club had seen that. He had good taste. No one else had been to Madame Schumann's Farewell . . . sitting at the piano with her curtains of hair and her dreamy smile . . . and the Philharmonic Concerts. No one else knew about the lectures at the Royal Institution, beginning at nine on Fridays. . . . No one else's father went with a party of scientific men 'for the advancement of science' to Norway or America, seeing the Falls and the Yosemite Valley. No one else took his children as far as Dawlish for the holidays, travelling all day, from eight until seven . . . no esplanade, the old stone jetty and coves and cowrie shells . . .[32]

Men are beguiling for their knowledge, their mysterious lives, from which they return to tell stories, and for their playful eruptions and unpredictability. When she stands for the first time in the small local German church, looking at strangers, she is aware of having a kind of knowledge of women and an ignorance of men which prompts questions:

Then as she watched their faces as they sang she felt that she knew all these women, the way, with little personal differences, they would talk, the way they would smile and take things for granted.

   And the men, standing there in their overcoats. . . . Why were they there? What were they doing? What were their thoughts?[33]

As the sermon proceeds her own thoughts swirl with exasperation and conflict; 'those men's sermons were worse than women's smiles . . . just as insincere at any rate . . . and you could get away from the smiles, make it plain you did not agree and that things were not simple and settled ... but you could not stop a sermon.'[34]

Her stay in Germany is liberating and illuminating. She has discovered some facts about herself. She is a woman, she is English, she has a personality, sometimes found abrasive and chilly by others, but which is not confined to the one her family casts her in. She realises as she learns German that language and languages are both private and public, that she is constituted differently to herself and in the world when she talks family slang, the jokes and abbreviated communications of her childhood rather than the opaque discourse into which she enters amongst strangers. At this stage she is experiencing language as the sounds of speech, noise and music, responding emotionally, barely concerned to penetrate, differentiate or agree to meanings. She delights in the equivalences and the divergencies of English and German, marvels at the capacity of particular languages to contain and reflect different histories, ways of life, outlooks. She is playful and inventive with words, which can be changed, newly used. 'Frugal' seems to her ideal to describe a poor, pinched French girl and is echoed nearly a hundred pages later when the same girl is given a 'mouth ... frugally compressed'.[35] An awful blouse inspires the invented 'flountery',[36] which is taken up later in the 'flounter-*crack* of a raincloak smartly shaken out'.[37] Gazing at the sick, white face of a German woman Miriam feels that 'Fräulein seemed cancelled.'[38] The word is substantiated by memories of her grandmother's death from cancer and the pots of calceolarias she associates with the house where her grandmother died.

Even before Miriam has arrived to be governess of the Corries' children in *Honeycomb*, she has developed the beginnings of a theory about women's and men's language. Conversations between women are seen as only the surface aspect of their communication. Women attend to the sub-text, which exists simultaneously with the sounds it both underpins and undermines. Miriam hears a voice singing Solveig's song from *Peer Gynt*. The words work mysteriously against the music, need to be separated from it.[39]

She registers the effect on her of codes and accent and emphasis, learns to mimic. Her meeting with the upper-class Mrs Corrie, whose children Miriam will teach, is made comical by the woman's idiosyncratic habits of speech:

'The kiddies were 'riffickly 'cited. Wanted to stay up. I hope you're strict, very strict, eh?'

'I believe I'm supposed to understand discipline,' said Miriam stiffly, gazing with weary eyes at the bars of the grate.

'We were in an awful fix before we heard about you. Poor old Bunnikin breakin' down. She adored them – they're angels. But she hadn't the tiniest bit of a hold over them. Used to cry when they were naughty. *You* know. Poor old kiddies. Want them to be awfully clever. Work like a house afire. I know you're clever. P'raps you won't stay with my little heathens. Do try and stay. I can see you've got just what they want. Strong-minded, eh? I'm an imbecile. So was poor old Bunnikin. D'you like kiddies?'

'Oh, I'm very fond of children,' said Miriam despairingly.[40]

This is more than a clever imitation of the speech of an upper-class mother, who is not quite as vacuous as she seems. The registering of the speech and Miriam's replies contain Miriam's responding to it. Incompatibility of outlook, character, use of language will colour the relationship between the two of them. There is no backing away to commentary on Mrs Corrie or to Miriam's view of her. All must be kept within Miriam's visual and auditory field. Miriam's sense of language is optimistic here, playful and expansive. She plays with meanings, invents words, gives solid correspondence to the sounds of voices. Mrs Corrie has a 'laughing, wavering chalky voice'. Entering a new language, whether German or an upper-class English dialect, reveals new connections between language and thought and sensation, exposing social norms and deviations from them as arbitrary and yet binding. She is fascinated by translation and by what is possible and not possible in it. Then there is translation between the different languages of individuals, of classes, of nations and of the sexes.

Miriam is intrigued by Mr Corrie, a busy London lawyer,

whose rare presences and distance give him glamour. There is a dinner party for his friends:

The men of the party were devouring their food with the air of people just about to separate to fulfil urgent engagements. They bent and gobbled busily and cast smouldering glances about the table, as if with their eyes they would suggest important mysteries brooding above their animated muzzles.

Miriam's stricken eyes sought their foreheads for relief. Smooth brows and neatly brushed hair above; but the smooth motionless brows were ramparts of hate; pure murderous hate. That's men, she said, with a sudden flash of certainty, that's men as they are, when they are opposed, when they are real. All the rest is pretence. Her thoughts flashed forward to a final clear issue of opposition, with a husband. Just a cold blank hating forehead and neatly brushed hair above it. If a man doesn't understand or doesn't agree he's just a blank bony conceitedly thinking, absolutely condemning forehead, a face below, going on eating – and going off somewhere. Men are all hard angry bones; always thinking something, only one thing at a time and unless that is agreed to, they murder. My husband shan't kill me. . . . I'll shatter his conceited brow – *make* him see . . . two sides to every question . . . a million sides . . . no questions, only sides . . . always changing. Men argue, think they prove things; their foreheads recover – cool and calm. Damn them all – all men.[41]

Miriam is always implicated as she delivers such diatribes, for she is excited by men, seduced by their talk, their ideas, their promises, their exclusion of women, their occasional inclusion of her. When her mother dies at the end of this novel Miriam is as guilty as her father and as guilty as the voracious and insensible men at the dinner party. She has wondered whether Mr Corrie 'was not quite conscious of his thoughts', as though he has let language, and his effortless using of it, replace thought for him. It seems to her that men's logic, their sequential ordering of time, experience and hierarchies of significance, mean that they take the systematic nature of language literally, equating logic with language (as most people have, of course). Women, in contrast, dislocated by exclusion, seem to her to move anarchically through the system of language, rupturing it and critically investigating its limitations and opportunities even as they speak and listen. Logic and linguistic structure, reflections of men's minds and lives and novels, threaten her as denials of the disturbed continuities of individual experience and the uneven, saccadic rhythms of thinking and sensing.

In some ways Miriam's questions about narrative are like E. M. Forster's, when he describes a similar confrontation between two kinds of time in the events and the experiencing of them which a novel needs to account for:

Daily life is also full of the time sense. We think one event occurs after or before another, the thought is often in our minds, and much of our talk and action proceeds on the assumption. Much of our talk and action, but not all; there seems something else in life besides time, something which may conveniently be called 'value', something which is measured not by minutes or hours, but by intensity, so that when we look at our past it does not stretch back evenly but piles up into a few notable pinnacles, and when we look at the future it seems sometimes a wall, sometimes a cloud, sometimes a sun, but never a chronological chart.[42]

Frank Kermode, in his *The Sense of an Ending*,[43] makes narrative – its sequence, its beginnings and endings, its organisation of time, its essential reliance on patterns of cause and effect – a universal structuring of experience and a consolation for chaos, which informs all myth, religion and literature and is embedded in language itself. He too is moved to focus on that other kind of time, when it stands still, leaps, stops, delivering new and different meanings. He pictures it as the space between the 'toc' and the 'tic' of the clock. Both Forster and Kermode examine these expressions of time as a kind of discordance, which corresponds to the individual's inner, or even double, life, and to the peculiar timelessness we occupy as readers. For literature always carries those gaps or lapses of time, between an historical time outside the text, to which the text refers, and the time taken to read of it. Richardson went further in proposing that historical time and narrative's simulations of it were both false to women's experience. She has been echoed in this by Julia Kristeva, who has taken

Bakhtin's dialogic or polyphonous voices within texts and Lacan's principle of the unconscious being structured like a language to be particularly relevant to women. 'Now in the polyphonic text,' she has written, 'the ideologies are shaped by the discourse of the divided speaker: they are fragmented and spread through the inter-textual space.'[44] Kristeva's own idiolect, a matter of post-structuralist jargon and space-age poetry, deliberately mirrors one form of female duality. Its 'divided speaker', fragmented, duplicitous, becomes subterraneously subversive of the discourses she wrestles with. Elsewhere, Kristeva can sound less of a polyglot, more of an immigrant; 'Estranged from language, women are visionaries, dancers who suffer as they speak.'[45] Miriam Henderson, polyglot and immigrant, dances with rage.

In speech with a man a woman is at a disadvantage – because they speak different languages. She may understand his. Hers he will never speak nor understand. In pity, or from other motives, she must therefore, stammeringly, speak his. He listens and is flattered and thinks he has her mental measure when he has not touched even the fringe of her consciousness.[46]

In the fourth and fifth novels, *The Tunnel* and *Interim*, Miriam is a working woman living in Bloomsbury alone. The novels have a wonderful vigour and exuberance. A young woman is exploring ideas and people and the city. Her job with a family practice of dentists in Harley Street exasperates and fascinates her. Her reading does too. Then halfway through *The Tunnel* she expresses desperation with her lot as a woman, with men's contempt for women and their almost scientific scrutiny of them as a minor species:

And the modern men were the worst . . . 'We can now, with all the facts in our hands, sit down and examine her at our leisure.' There was no getting away from the scientific facts . . . *inferior*, mentally, morally, intellectually, and physically . . . her development arrested in the interest of her special functions . . . reverting later towards the male type . . . old women with deep voices and hair on their faces . . . leaving off where boys of eighteen began. If that is true everything is as clear as daylight. 'Woman is not undeveloped man but diverse' falls to pieces.

Woman is undeveloped man . . . if one could die of the loathsome visions . . . I *must* die. I can't go on living in it . . . the whole world full of *creatures*; half-human. And I am one of the half-human ones, or shall be, if I don't stop now.

Boys and girls were much the same . . . women stopped being people and went off into hideous processes. What for? What was it all for? Development. The wonders of science. The wonders of science for women are nothing but gynaecology – all those frightful operations in the *British Medical Journal* and those jokes – the hundred golden rules. . . . Sacred functions . . . highest possibilities . . . sacred for what? The hand that rocks the cradle rules the world? The Future of the Race? What world? What race? Men. . . . Nothing but men; for ever. . . .

It will all go on as long as women are stupid enough to go on bringing men into the world . . . even if civilized women stop the colonials and primitive races would go on. It is a nightmare.

They invent a legend to put the blame for the existence of humanity on woman and, if she wants to stop it, they talk about the wonders of civilization and the sacred responsibilities of motherhood. They can't have it both ways. They also say women are not logical.

They despise women and they want to go on living – to reproduce – themselves. None of their achievements, no 'civilization,' no art, no science can redeem that. There is no pardon possible for man. The only answer to them is suicide; all women ought to agree to commit suicide.[47]

For a time Miriam is in despair. 'There was nothing to turn to. Books were poisoned. Art. All the achievements of men were poisoned at the root. The beauty of nature was tricky femininity.'[48] She becomes involved with the tricky Miss Dear, marvellously winning and mendacious, and with her fellow lodgers and her landlady. *Interim* is written with a Balzacian relish for the bizarre relationships of solitary people in a city, their speech, their secrets and their thoughts about each other. Miriam herself is slippery too, particularly with men. As they threaten her identity and autonomy in books, so does their interest in her life. She is becoming as resistant to the culture and the intellectual traditions of men, from which she has been excluded as a woman, as to their offers of conciliation and love.

The three novels in Volume 3 of *Pilgrimage*, *Deadlock*, *Revolving Lights* and *The Trap*, are woven out of two love relationshps with men and her first beginnings as a writer. Michael Shatov, a Russian Jewish intellectual, and Hypo Wilson, a version of the H. G. Wells Richardson knew, differently love her and encourage her. Yet her experience with both men persuades her finally that she cannot be what men want her to be and be herself. As Gillian E. Hanscombe puts it, 'Miriam can neither enter the world of men as the female type they have invented and understand, nor can she enter it as one of their brethren'.[49] Shatov is 'Miriam's most ardent challenger in her personal battle of the sexes'[50] precisely because he loves her as a woman and believes, as a Jew and a Russian, heir to Tolstoy and Turgenev, that he is 'also perhaps not so undiscriminating as are some men'.[51] He would be a good husband, would love her, make a mother of her, respect her intelligence sufficiently to take her literary education in hand and believe that he knew her and allowed for who she was. Women who can be wives seem to Miriam to accept 'an impossible idea; the idea of a man being consciously attracted and won by universal physiological facts, rather than by individuals themselves'.[52]

Shatov and marriage are easier for Miriam to reject than the friendship and the adulterous affair which Hypo Wilson lingeringly offers her, maddening her with his expert's love of her as a woman. He becomes for her the male intellect at its most falsely 'scientific', rational and determinist, both appealing and repellent, as her father was for her. His mind, his success, his need for women, stand as intolerable temptations. Masculinity, buttressed by the educational and literary institutions from which she and all women are excluded and by which they are reductively defined, lures her through Wilson. He is sexually drawn to intelligent, mutinous women, and it is because of their minds that he wants their bodies. His conquest of them provides evidence of his own superiority, of men's superiority. Her mutiny is partly subdued by his need to prove himself superior, and to do so by encroaching on a woman's individuality, his making capital of her ambivalence for his own security. His long, spasmodic wooing is interrupted. She even considers marriage with Densley, a flattering escort, whose warm-hearted worldliness misleadingly fastens on her unworldliness and her 'man's mind'.[53] The prospect he offers, of sophisticated sociability, is rejected. It would tame and control her integrity by admitting it as charming eccentricity.

Miriam watches herself allowing Hypo Wilson to pursue his seduction of her. It produces a kind of submission in her, not to him, but to her compassion for his weakness and need:

He was two people. A man achieving, becoming, driving forward to unpredictable becomings, delighting in the process, devoting himself, compelling himself, whom so frankly he criticized and so genuinely deplored, to a ceaseless becoming, ceaseless assimilating of anything that promised to serve the interests of a ceaseless becoming for life as he saw it. And also a man seeming uncreated, without any existence worth the name.[54]

Even before they have stiffly removed their clothes and confronted each other she is disarmed by her pity for him:

With a flash of insight that freed her for ever, she felt, of jealousy of his relationships past, present, and future, she saw how very slight, how restricted and perpetually baffled must always be the communication between him and anything that bore the name of woman. Saw the price each one had paid with whom he had been intimate either in love or friendship, in being obliged to shut off, in order to meet him in his world, his shaped world, rationalized according to whatever scheme of thought was appealing to him at the moment, three-fourths of their being.[55]

And then,

His body was not beautiful. She could find nothing to adore, no ground for response to his lightly spoken tribute. The manly structure, the smooth, satiny sheen in place of her own velvety glow was interesting as partner and foil, but not desirable. It had no power to stir her as often she had been stirred by the sudden sight of him walking down a garden or entering a room. With the familiar clothes, something of his essential self seemed to have departed.

Leaving him pathetic.[56]

She is moved to rock and cradle him like a child, touched by his incapacity to meet her or move her. They dress and go to a café, talk about writing and then about Amabel, the woman Miriam has recently met and loves. Hypo wants to know what is so lovable about Amabel, and Miriam tells him how her friend elicits love from everyone who knows her:

By loving them. She has the most real rare love for the essential human being. Even for the people she sees through. And a deep, unusual respect and solicitude. For what to you is nothing or next to nothing: the personal life in everybody.[57]

Miriam's bleak, detached mating with Hypo Wilson is honestly watched. For Wilson it has been a kind of experiment, one he repeats and repeats for assurances that he is the man he aspires to be, is thought in the world to be. The affair is relegated next day to its place, well below work and his domestic routine. To her surprise and relief Miriam feels that 'Within her was something that stood apart, unpossessed.'[58] She is disappointed and exhilarated by her discovery that sex with a man will not of itself create a unity of her inner contradictions. The love she feels and receives from Amabel, which is not explicitly or straightforwardly sexual, is something she recognises as respectful and solicitous of individual integrity, the quality she cherishes in herself as a writer. At the end of *Dawn's Left Hand* Miriam has discovered 'a calm delightful sense of power'. We leave her 'full of inward song and wishing for congratulations'.[59]

In *Clear Horizon* she finds that she is 'booked for maternity'[60] as Wilson maddeningly puts it. She introduces Amabel to him and recoils from his condescension towards her, implicitly towards Miriam as well. Her bringing together of Amabel and Michael Shatov and their marriage is Miriam's act of generosity, for she loves Amabel and is guilty that she doesn't love Michael enough to marry him herself. Yet it suggests a new, and perhaps a novelist's, ruthlessness. Miriam miscarries and recuperates with a Quaker family in *Dimple Hill*, half falls in love with the son of the family and gathers strength. In the final novel, *March Moonlight*, Miriam sometimes takes over her own narration, becomes 'I' as she embarks on her novel. Amabel is married, domesticated, reminding Miriam of her own solitude, difference. She finds herself 'rooted in the doorway reduced to the status of a man, a useless alien'.[61] Yet Amabel and Michael are unhappy: 'Marriage is awful'.[62] Miriam knows the value of her solitude as she begins to go back to the past, to write. 'Why say distance *lends* enchantment? Each vista demands, for portrayal, absence from current life, contemplation, a long journey.'[63] She wonders whether she is denying her life's faith in 'current existence, the ultimate astonisher'.[64] For

To write is to forsake life. Every time I know this, in advance. Yet whenever something comes that sets the tips of my fingers tingling to record it, I forget the price, eagerly face the strange journey down and down to the centre of being.[65]

An elegantly tattered figure appears at her lodging-house, and becomes a kind of talisman for her and for her writing. He is also an ironic comment on the husband and the wedding which have ended a thousand novels about women. Dorothy Richardson began writing her novel when she was thirty-eight, at just about the age she leaves Miriam writing hers. The tattered stranger recalls Alan Odle, a painter much younger than herself, whom Dorothy Richardson married, believing that he would die early of TB and alcoholism. They were happy for many years, and were so, Gloria Fromm suggests,[66] for conspiring to maintain mutual and intended misunderstandings. He allowed her to believe that he was more of a childlike incompetent than he was so that she could rely on his dependence. We leave Miriam writing:

While I write, everything vanishes but what I contemplate. The whole of what is called 'the past' is with me, seen anew, vividly. No, Schiller, the past does not stand 'being still.' It moves, growing with one's growth. Contemplation is adventure into discovery; reality. What is called 'creation' imaginative transformation, fantasy, invention, is only based upon reality.[67]

So is this a woman's novel, a feminine, even a feminist novel? I
have been conscious as I quoted from *Pilgrimage* and traced its
heroine's development that I have made the novel sound like an
elaborate argument rather than a work of fiction. This novel is
unusual in having as its heroine an argumentative intellectual.
There had certainly been intelligent and serious, well-read and
well-informed heroines in novels before this. Dorothy Richardson makes Miriam Henderson a novelist, a reader and a critic, a
thinker and a theorist, who inhabits a woman's body and lives her
life as a woman. It would be possible to redefine Miriam's
personal sense of duality, and even Dorothy Richardson's purpose in writing a new kind of novel, as less a struggle between the
male and female in her, and in novels generally, than an argument
about polarities in language and culture and literature, and the
psychological development of an individual who is tugged and
buffeted by those polarities. Possible, but quite misleading, I
think. Yet Dorothy Richardson was far too intelligent to imagine
that something called a woman's novel could just emerge and be
recognised as that simply because it was by a woman, about a
woman and claimed for itself some very general feminine, as
opposed to masculine, character. The characteristics of a
woman's consciousness and a woman's novel could not be adum-
brated beforehand or *in vacuo*. Both would have painstakingly to
be pieced together out of what she as a woman found 'left out' of
the novels by men which she read. Dorothy Richardson is
emphatically not speaking for all women. Indeed, her difference
from all the women she writes about is as significant as her
difference from the men she writes about. Notions of a woman's
consciousness, a woman's way of experiencing her life, are proposed initially as a hypothesis which might be helpful in dis-
tinguishing between different kinds of drive and emphasis in her
own nature, many aspects of which felt contradictory and therefore fragmenting of her in her own life.

John Cowper Powys became a friend of Dorothy Richardson,
and she dedicated *Dimple Hill* to him. The essay he wrote about
her work, which had originally been intended by them both as an

introduction to one of the novels, and was finally published in 1931[68] on its own, became, as Gloria Fromm[69] points out, an embarrassment to her. It is an effusion, often acute and intelligent. Yet it takes the 'femininity' of *Pilgrimage* as unproblematically its quality and its virtue. It is praised for being unlike the work of George Eliot and Virginia Woolf, who 'betray their deepest instincts by using, as their medium of research, not these instincts but the rationalistic methods of men.'[70] It is also praised for dodging mere feminine cleverness and feminine charm. One passage in the essay seems particularly likely to have made Dorothy Richardson writhe:

She is, in fact, the modern priestess of a strange and exciting Renaissance of certain lost illuminations which must have originated the unknown ritual of the Great Mother's 'Mysteries' at Eleusis. One of her most devoted feminine disciples has pointed out to me only recently that it must be remembered that the planet we live upon is essentially a *feminine* planet. No mythology has ever dared to make the earth masculine.[71]

With a friend like that, one might say, what woman needs enemies? If, however, we are to give Powys the benefit of the doubt and allow his use of 'feminine' to describe the learned strategies of behaviour, of thought and of feeling which women have developed surreptitiously and in opposition to male culture, then it is interesting to consider what he found new about the novels and what he thought of as distinctively feminine about them. He identifies as feminine, for instance, a dogged survivor's courage, a capacious and accepting (perhaps maternal) unfastidiousness, an ability to see pleasure as more than an orgasmic and final achievement, but as importantly chancy, intermittent, diverse. He also singles out as feminine Dorothy Richardson's sense of women necessarily creating their environment, however unpromising or exiguous. Spaces are for being in and also for making and remaking, for spending time on as well as in.

Other men have written about Dorothy Richardson. John Rosenberg's biography[72] is principally concerned to match events of Richardson's own life with those she uses as part of Miriam's,

and C. R. Blake discusses her technique in terms of stylistic innovation rather than as language intendedly subversive. The more recent biography by Gloria Fromm is thorough and sympathetic, focusing more on the woman who described herself as 'burly' but was also able to rise in her fifties 'from her deck chair in the garden to twirl about in a dance she had invented herself'[73] than on the author of *Pilgrimage*. Like many other writers about Richardson Fromm tends to discuss Miriam's assertions, about men and women and novels, for instance, without considering how Miriam uses assertiveness as one of a number of strategies for locating herself during a tortuous journey towards the stability which might enable her to write her own novel. Tentativeness, self-mockery, a registering of change and fluctuation, even denial of her own intuitions, are at least as characteristic of Miriam as is her use of extreme points of view, often mutually contradictory, to suggest the movement of her essentially solitary mental life and the interplay of reflection with mood and sensation. The novels which emerge from Gloria Fromm's 'Life' can seem dull. This is Leslie Fiedler's charge. He does more than invoke 'the peculiar nature of the dulness [sic] which characterizes Miss Richardson's 2,000 page novel'; he puts it into perspective. If the 'boredom' in the novel generally is 'one source of its authority, a warranty of its commitment to truth and the dull reality we all inhabit... It is the fate of Dorothy Richardson to be quite as baffling and unorthodox as any of her more flamboyant opposite numbers but to be so palely, *dully*. Hers is the least acceptable of dulnesses, the sort of *avant-garde* dulness inevitable once one has abandoned the expected delights attendant on the fully articulated plot: the suspense, the reversal and recognition – and has refused to replace them.'[74]

In a diary entry for the beginning of 1920, Virginia Woolf excitedly contemplates the 'idea of a new form for a new novel'. 'One thing should open out of another', she writes, and there will be 'no scaffolding; scarcely a brick to be seen; all crepuscular, but the heart, the passion, humour, everything as bright as fire in the mist. Then I'll find room for so much – a gaiety – an inconse-

quence – a light spirited stepping at my sweet will ... What the
unity shall be I have yet to discover; the theme is a blank to me.'
Her novel will be light, dancing, where Richardson's is burly.
Virginia Woolf was wary of the work of her most innovative
contemporaries:

I suppose the danger is the damned egotistical self; which ruins Joyce
and Richardson to my mind: is one pliant and rich enough to provide a
wall for the book from oneself without its becoming, as in Joyce and
Richardson, narrowing and restricting?[75]

More recently, writers like Elaine Showalter and Gillian E.
Hanscombe discuss *Pilgrimage* as a novel which evolves as an idea
of 'feminist consciousness' through its inner oppositions to men
and masculinity. Showalter is inclined to see Richardson's com-
pulsion to work for a female aesthetic as ultimately destructive of
the novel:

Pilgrimage can be read as the artistic equivalent of a screen, a way of
hiding and containing and disarming the raw energy of a rampaging
past. Richardson devised an aesthetic strategy that protected her
enough from the confrontation with her own violence, rage, grief, and
sexuality that she could work. The female aesthetic was meant for
survival, and one cannot deny that Richardson was able to produce an
enormous novel, or that Virginia Woolf wrote several, under its shelter.
But ultimately, how much better it would have been if they could have
forgiven themselves, if they could have faced the anger instead of
denying it, could have translated the consciousness of their own
darkness into confrontation instead of struggling to transcend it. For
when the books were finished, the darkness was still with them, as
dangerous and as inviting as it had always been, and they were helpless
to fight it.[76]

It is easy to feel reproved in one's enthusiasm for the novel by this
intelligent and positive reminder that neither Dorothy Richardson's own life, nor the life of women generally, have been much
improved by the elaboration of theories which might account for
women's duality. Yet it seems necessary to say too that Dorothy
Richardson can hardly be faulted for not confronting her rage and
that she is unhelpfully linked to Virginia Woolf in that respect.

The difficulty is still there for women that in wishing to isolate, define and insist upon their own experience as valid and unheard they are forced into oppositional and negative postures, which do less to unite women in a recognition of that experience as peculiarly theirs than alert them to their need to seek security and protection within male accounts of what women are. Gillian Hanscombe, who has written the most sensitive critique of *Pilgrimage*, is prepared to admire it for what it is and for what Dorothy Richardson did:

... she is one of the very few to attempt the very complex task of explicating a feminist world-view at the same time as developing a feminist aesthetic in a work of imaginative literature. The attempt may be thought misguided, even offensive, but that *Pilgrimage* enacts such an attempt is fundamental to its stature.[77]

Leslie Fiedler was right to remark on the absence of plot in *Pilgrimage*. Plot, with its sequencing, its patterns of cause and effect, its structuring of significance, of human growth and morality, its assumption of order, has gone. The continuity of the novel is the continuousness of one person's being alive and experiencing herself as alive. Memory controls the sequence of events and articulates their selection. Elision, caesura, juxta-position, extrapolation are dictated by the activities of memory and of remembering. Remembering is either guided by the Miriam who writes about her past at the end of the novel, a process of concentration and searching, or it is involuntary, induced accidentally, as it were, as Proust's is, by the madeleine: a starting point erupting unexpectedly to illuminate hitherto hidden territories. What is produced by remembering is significant for being remembered and for the process of thought which has enacted the remembering. And Miriam is remembered re-membering, just as she is remembered wondering about the future:

Turning at last from her window, Miriam glanced at her sisters and let her thoughts drop into the flowing tide. Harry, sitting there sharp and upright in the fading light, coming in to them with her future life

streaming out behind her, spreading and shining and rippling, herself
the radiant point of that wonderful life, actually there, neatly enthroned
amongst them, one of them, drawing them all with her out towards its
easy security . . .[78]

The two verbs 'glanced', 'let drop' are signals from Miriam the
writer, the rememberer and the participant in the scene she is
remembering. Her own thoughts carry her, and the reader, with
their present participles and continuous forms, into the sights
which are seen, the seeing of them, the experience and the
recording of it on paper. It is a characteristic passage, and might
be thought characteristic of Woolf's dreaded 'egotistical self'.
Alternatively, it is possible to respond to the directions of the
remembering writer as to a guide or courier, who is showing us
how to look at these sights so that we may understand the
meanings they can have only for the person who already knows
them, for whom they are already a part of history. The novel
teaches us how to read it. Nor are these kinds of representation of
memory simply visual. Far from it. 'People,' as Miriam observes,
'talked incessantly because in silence they were ghosts.'[79] In
Pilgrimage we hear the words that Miriam hears and we hear her
hearing. Speech is not paraphrased, nor are people's natures and
histories inferred from their speech. Miriam's speculations about
other people will always revolve round their actual speech.

It could well be argued that tactics like these are just tactics, that
other writers have used them (though it is hard to think who used
them earlier than Dorothy Richardson), that men particularly
have used them since and that there is nothing intrinsically
feminine about them. But then Dorothy Richardson was never
claiming anything as 'intrinsically' feminine. Rather, she was
posing different kinds of writing and different modes of thought,
behaviour, looking and hearing and speaking, which in their
difference exposed conventions of narrative as both arbitrary and
historically deriving from men's points of view. Men have not
always been as scrupulous as Dorothy Richardson was in refusing
to speak for her sex. Some men have claimed as universal habits of
perception and thought which belong to particular histories and

cultures and indeed gather their strength from that embedded-ness and exclusiveness. What might be said to be 'feminine' or indeed 'feminist' about Dorothy Richardson's writing lies in its capacity to undermine and to reveal the exclusions inherent in forms which have been claimed as universal, though historically they have developed as expressions of men's accounts of men's lives.

The image of Eve being created out of Adam's (presumably redundant) rib is one of the most insidiously potent metaphors of Christian cultures. The lines which account for God's superbly economical use of resources are followed in *Genesis* by,

And the rib, which the Lord God had taken from man, made he a woman, and brought her unto the man.

And Adam said, This is now bone of my bones, and flesh of my flesh: she shall be called Woman, because she was taken out of Man.

More significant even than the fact that God made women after men and for men is the idea that women are made *out of* men. There is a correspondence between that metaphor and the ways in which English (and, differently, all languages) mark the female of the species. I am referring not simply to those wonderful absurdities of the 'Man is a mammal who suckles his young' variety, nor to women's uncertainty as to whether they are present within male pronouns or not. I am more concerned with the struggle going on in all language between its apparently generalised meanings and its particular historical meanings. Speaker and context will alert most of us to the particular inclusions and exclusions intended by a phrase like 'The British People'. Similarly, 'men' may include 'women', unless otherwise stated, though 'women' specifically excludes 'men'. The issue is not solved by proposing new pronouns or coining new ungendered names for people. More radically, we need to understand the effect on any group of people who must live with uncertainty as to their inclusion or exclusion and to show how power is thereby made available to those who control or even manipulate that uncertainty.

In an absolutely idealised sense, words like doctor, prime minister, thinker, writer could be said to have included women, though in practice they have not been used in that inclusive way, because most users of the language had no reason to think of those words as being at all likely to refer to women. These are not, of course, original thoughts about language. They are, indeed, what 'every schoolboy knows'. The difficulty for women writers, and it was one which Dorothy Richardson made the subject of her novel, issues from this sense of being both included in men and excluded by them. The way in which the possibility of Mrs Thatcher lurked within the capacities of the term 'prime minister' to include her before she was prime minister is like the unspecified rib of Adam, the one God appropriated before he 'closed up the flesh instead thereof'. So long as the potential for there being a woman prime minister remained unrealised that word was inclusive of women in only the most ghostly, negative way.

By the time Dorothy Richardson considered becoming a writer, 'writer' was beginning to include the idea of a woman who was a writer, though it was, as it still is, customary to mark such a person as a 'woman writer'. Ideally we would breathe new, differentiated meanings into language in advance of historical change. In practice language follows only moderately fast foot upon change. This has been a digression; a necessary one, which I have needed to make on behalf of the kinds of assertion I am making about Dorothy Richardson and about other women writers. Language, novels, narrative, time are as available to women as to men as concepts and as practice. Yet women have wanted and needed to wrench out of the meanings they can seem to share with men meanings of their own.

I want to return particularly to Leslie Fiedler's charges,[80] to his regretting in *Pilgrimage* its 'dulness', its boredom, its absence of plot. 'Uneventfulness' as a description of a life does not literally mean that it contains no events. It is a word which has meaning for people only in relation to its opposite, and then it becomes a question of which events are thought most generally to interest and be valued by which people. The 'boredom' Leslie Fiedler invokes can only be understood in that way too. Dorothy Richardson does not write about people feeling bored (as Jane Austen does, for instance), but she does, and insistently, write about a life which many readers of novels would, as she knew, regard as boring. She is showing us the events of a woman's life, which are not at all boring to her, though they are often exasperating, and demonstrating how utterly different they are from the events in novels which people have come to expect and find interesting; and, more bizarrely, have come to see as true to life.

A novel which undertakes to account for the way in which a woman finds and makes her life interesting is bound to conflict with conventions deriving from the ways men have devised to make their lives sound interesting. Needless to say, these differences are not based on biological ones but on the real possibilities of people's lives. A novel about being a dentist's receptionist could not be interesting, perhaps, to a reader looking for tumultuous social change or individual acts of daring. *Pilgrimage* is not proposing that all we need to do is learn to find the life of a dentist's receptionist as interesting as the life of a great leader or thinker (that would be like supposing that by using 'chairperson' we have changed the social relations which make 'chairman' the more generally appropriate term). What Dorothy Richardson is able to remind us of is that so long as certain lives are privileged as against other lives, those other lives are impoverished, because they are denied the capacity in all individuals to imbue their own experience with value and interest. The novelty of *Pilgrimage* is that it questions from a woman's point of view fundamental assumptions about power, and its determining of value, by revealing the ways in which novels appear, or pretend, to reflect reality.

Time is lived and known differently by each of us, though clocks and calendars, at the very least, suggest that we make some common assumptions about it. We date events and measure duration according to what most matters to us. It is a commonplace that women who have had children date events in the past in relation to their children's births and measure periods of time in relation to the experiencing of nine months of pregnancy. Many women mark out and use the time in their days in relation to when people must be fed, sent off, received home, provided with clean clothes and clean spaces. Such organisation of time is different from a man's and often dependent on a man's. Longer periods of education, apprenticeship or training, the now somewhat threatened notion of young men embarking on jobs or careers with promotions, increased wages and pensions as predictable landmarks, measure time differently for men. Even though a majority of women in this country does paid work outside the home, a majority of those women may regard this work as part-time, temporary or secondary to the work they do that is unpaid. This affects their using of time, the value they put on it and even the amount of it they feel to be at their disposal. It is possible to see that unemployment develops new time scales for people too: weekly or fortnightly 'signing on', uneasily synchronised with the arrival of giro cheques or with replies to letters applying for jobs.

Dorothy Richardson's time is her life from eighteen to nearly forty. The pilgrimage takes her back in time (to the novel's present) and her heroine forward to Dorothy Richardson's present, so that Miriam will start the novel just as Dorothy Richardson is finishing hers. This looping and weaving is effected by the operation of the memory, which works not only by rearranging or distorting chronology, by selecting and foreshortening and eliminating, but by providing its own emphases. These emphases are neither precisely those accorded to particular moments or stretches of time as they were in progress, nor are they a historian's emphases: on turning points or moments which have acquired moral or emotional significance in retrospect. Quite other considerations may determine the moments which memory chooses for the novel.[81] They may be moments of peculiar self-consciousness or self-awareness. They may, on the contrary, be moments exceptional for their absence of self-awareness. Sometimes they are moments which stand as epitomes of many very similar moments; at other times they are moments which disturb or subtly change what is ordinary, habitual, customary. Fiedler's 'dull' representation of 'the dull reality we all inhabit' is not in itself any more or any less like dull reality than an exciting representation might be. If it is in fact an exciting representation of that reality for some of us that may be because we recognise it as a reality, and a representation of it, which has not been thought the stuff of fiction before. Time is known and spent differently in Dorothy Richardson's novel, as it is known and spent differently by each of us; and novels are, after all, about spending time. If *Pilgrimage* proposes a new way of spending time and of describing how that time is spent it does so within a literary tradition which has reinforced, for both men and women, a historical habit of regarding the way men spend it as more valuable, in every sense, than the way women spend it.

Norman Mailer doubts 'if there will be a really exciting woman writer until the first whore becomes a call girl and tells her tale'.[82] Lionel Trilling remarks the absence in women 'of the moral life that self-love bestows'.[83] Views of that kind have not simply glanced off women. Something which might be called a woman's novel, even a feminist one, is likely to require robustness and a good deal of Virginia Woolf's dreaded and 'damned egotistical self'[84] if it is to survive and be read as a woman's vision of the world. *Pilgrimage* is read, though not enough. It can still be turned to as an early and an outstanding attempt to show that what is peculiar to women's experience may be missed or marginalised if it is read as no more than what survives after its translation into a recognisable version of a male narrative.

There are ways in which the novels of the five twentieth-century writers I discuss in the next chapter are less radical than Dorothy Richardson's. Though I want to characterise them all as 'feminist' novels, they are that in very different ways. Yet collectively, and cumulatively, they do represent a growth in confidence and a shifting perspective in women's writing. New questions become askable, new resistances imaginable as the challenge is more and more openly made to the notion that men have the measure of women, or indeed of themselves. It will, I think, help me to make this point if I start from some men's accounts of their marriages and their wives.

7

Resisting the Bullies

The fact is that no one could come back from an ethnographic study of 'the X', having talked only *to* women and *about* men, without professional comment and some self-doubt. The reverse can and does happen constantly.

Edwin Ardener[1]

Two weeks after the death of his second wife, Julia, in May 1895, Leslie Stephen, from whom we have already heard, began to write what came to be known in his family as *The Mausoleum Book*.[2] As its editor, Alan Bell,[3] points out, this short account of his two marriages is directed to his children and to his wife's children by an earlier marriage and is couched, with some elaborateness, in the intimate language of a private testimony to his widower's desolation. Yet it is also the confident work of a man of letters; its grief controlled by its style and by the transparent need to make of his life as a husband and a father the sort of 'success' which he often appears to have felt had eluded him as a writer and a thinker. The work has obvious antecedents in Carlyle's reminiscences of his wife and John Stuart Mill's of his.[4] Indeed, Stephen's memoir can seem intent on outdoing Mill, in terms of sensibility and indebtedness, and also as a catalogue of those wifely virtues bestowed on him by an incomparable woman. It is worth listening to these competitive sages, I think, as they offer up their dead wives as items of their own *curricula vitae* in a contest for the prizes of distinction, greatness. Here is Mill:

To be admitted into any degree of mental intercourse with a being of these qualities, could not but have a most beneficial influence on my development; though the effect was only gradual, and many years elapsed before her mental progress and mine went forward in the complete companionship they at last attained. The benefit I received was far greater than any which I could hope to give; though to her, who had at first reached her opinions by the moral intuition of a character of strong feeling, there was doubtless help as well as encouragement to be derived from one who had arrived at many of the same results by study and reasoning: and in the rapidity of her intellectual growth, her mental activity, which converted everything into knowledge, doubtless drew from me, as it did from other sources, many of its materials. What I owe, even intellectually, to her, is, in its detail, almost infinite; of its general character, a few words will give some, though a very imperfect, idea.[5]

The encomium rises like a monumental member, and collapses into a relaxed contemplation of the qualities in his own work for which praise has been given and deserved. Leslie Stephen was less naïve. He had children in whom he may have already detected some capacity for irony about their parents' perfect marriage. He is also better than Mill at covering his tracks:

My darling says in one of her early letters that my love of her is as great a miracle to her as any of the miracles in which I declined to believe. Such a sentiment is of course not uncommon, and if I replied, as I could with perfect truth, that her love of me is to me quite as marvellous, you might think that we were both indulging in lovers' commonplaces. It is in fact difficult, I suspect, for a woman to understand the feelings with which a man regards her and the converse is equally true. I can not doubt, without impugning her judgement, that there must be somewhere something lovable in me. I will not ask what. But the sentiment came naturally to her: for humility, in the sense of unconsciousness of her own charms, was one of her obvious characteristics. She thought no more of her beauty to all appearance than if she had been as plain as – I need not particularize. And she was equally unaware of the inner beauty of soul. I have quoted what she said of her having a 'lower standard' than mine; and I have given the reply which it suggested to me. This, I will add here, was in fact the natural diffidence with which a person who acts from instinct regards the person who acts by logic – or professes to be so guided. You, it seems to such a one, have a theory and a rule and therefore you must have higher principles than I. There is a fallacy in that upon which I need not dwell. Her instincts were far more to be trusted than my ratiocinations.[6]

It would not be fair to regard these two men's accounts of their wives and their marriages with them as powered by vanity alone. It is possible to detect anxiety too. Both had, in fact, to contend with ghostly earlier husbands – Harriet and Julia had been married before – and both Mill and Stephen put in some spade-work on their predecessors, heavily and honourably assessing them as stalwart gentlemen, who were unlikely, nonetheless, to have provided the spiritual and intellectual succour their wives were lucky enough to receive as a consequence of their timely deaths. It is easy enough too to recognise in these ponderous accounts the other side of those hopes for a mentor expressed by the heroines of some women's novels both men had most certainly read. We have heard Leslie Stephen deploring the unworthiness of Stephen Guest as a mate for *his* Maggie in *The Mill on the Floss*. He appears generally to have found husbands unworthy of their wives – given, like Mr Ramsey in his daughter's *To the Lighthouse*, to thinking 'the girl is much too good for that young man'[7] – and where husbands stood in any relation to him which might seem to invite comparison, he is unable to control his anxious, perhaps questioning, contempt for them. Of his father-in-law he wrote:

He was not a man of any great mark: and I may tell you that I was rather puzzled, especially in the early years of my acquaintance with the Jacksons, by his position in the family. Somehow he did not seem to count – as fathers generally count in their families.[8]

A brother-in-law is compared to Carlyle in his treatment of his wife and found 'even in one respect less excusable, for Mrs Carlyle must have been more capable of taking her own part than was poor Adeline.'[9] Stephen is asking his children for reassurance.

There is, then, a good deal of sentimentality as well as self-importance in all this praise of wives who were at once 'adored' and patronised. Elizabeth Hardwick, in a book which discusses the role of those women who were powerfully the wives or sisters or daughters of famous men of letters, wants to insist on what such women get and have always got out of their situation. 'Women desire to have mastery over their husbands',[10] she writes, and the suggestion is that in gaining mastery over powerful and talented men they may themselves achieve a kind of heroism.

A sense that her mother had been beguiled by some such hope, and that she had also been worn out and diminished by it, certainly emerges from Virginia Woolf's expressed accounts of her parents' marriage. She was thirteen when her mother, Julia Stephen, died. *To the Lighthouse*, which has often been thought her best novel, was published in 1927. She had been married herself for fifteen years to Leonard Woolf when she wrote this novel about a marriage: her parents' marriage. Her diary glories in the ease she found in writing it. While the story was still simmering she wrote, 'But the centre is father's character, sitting in a boat, reciting. We perished, each alone, while he crushes a dying mackerel.'[11] Just over a year later, when she had finished the first part of the novel, she could ask herself, 'Why am I so flown with words and apparently free to do exactly what I like?'[12] In the year after *To the Lighthouse* was published there is an entry in her diary:

Father's birthday. He would have been 96, 96, yes, today; and
could have been 96, like other people one has known:
but mercifully was not. His life would have entirely   1928
ended mine. What would have happened? No writing,   1832
no books; – inconceivable.

I used to think of him and mother daily; but writing the *Lighthouse*
laid them in my mind. And now he comes back sometimes, but
differently. (I believe this to be true – that I was obsessed by them both,
unhealthily; and writing of them was a necessary act.) He comes back
now more as a contemporary. I must read him some day.[13]

There is no question that in this novel, which she thought of as 'the most difficult abstract piece of writing',[14] she was able to explore her own duality through a return to her childhood (in which she is both the child, Cam, and the painter, Lily Briscoe) and to her parents' relationship, which is watched as it simultaneously includes their children and excludes them. The question the novel seems to have set itself is the one many women who read it must ask: How could Mrs Ramsey bear it?

I want in this chapter to explore *To the Lighthouse* alongside novels by Rosamond Lehmann, Jean Rhys, Christina Stead and Doris Lessing, and I want to suggest that all these writers were feminist writers, though 'feminist' will have meant very different things to each of them. The novels I shall consider represent varieties of women's resistance. For Virginia Woolf and for Rosamond Lehmann the battleground was family life and its brutalities within the upper-middle-class and English world they grew up in. The enemy are fathers and husbands, lovers and brothers, and the web in which women struggle is marriage and the sexual roles it reinforces. For Jean Rhys, Christina Stead and Doris Lessing, sexual exploitation is understood within the injustices and the exploitation they recognised in English society from their growing up in the West Indies, Australia and Africa. Exploitation is about money in the novels of Jean Rhys and it is about capitalism and imperialism in those of Christina Stead and Doris Lessing. So that feminism becomes, for the last two of these writers, an urgent commitment to change, lived and expressed by women who see their interests and their struggle as shared with all those who are exploited and unheard. In order to appreciate the significance of this shift it will be necessary to recapitulate, to chart the development of a women's resistance which is held back by its limiting insistence on the inequalities between men and women of the same class to a feminism which proposes kinds of alliance and analysis which are socialist.

In the first half of *To the Lighthouse* Mr and Mrs Ramsey are in their holiday house in Scotland with their eight children and an odd collection of Mr Ramsey's disciples. Mrs Ramsey, beautiful, inscrutable and endlessly and yet invisibly busy, is watched by her children and by Lily Briscoe, who is in her thirties and unlikely, Mrs Ramsey pityingly surmises, to marry. The watchers are both exasperated and amazed by her:

Apart from the habit of exaggeration which they had from her, and from the implication (which was true) that she asked too many people to stay, and had to lodge some in the town, she could not bear incivility to her guests, to young men in particular, who were poor as church mice, 'exceptionally able', her husband said, his great admirers, and come there for a holiday. Indeed, she had the whole of the other sex under her protection; for reasons she could not explain, for their chivalry and valour, for the fact that they negotiated treaties, ruled India, controlled finance; finally for an attitude towards herself which no woman could fail to feel or to find agreeable, something trustful, childlike, reverential; which an old woman could take from a young man without loss of dignity, and woe betide the girl – pray Heaven it was none of her daughters! – who did not feel the worth of it, and all that it implied, to the marrow of her bones.[15]

Her daughters silently 'sport with infidel ideas which they had brewed for themselves of a life different from hers; in Paris, perhaps; a wilder life; not always taking care of some man or other.'[16]

The family is still seen broadly here, from a distance and publicly. The view is a counter at this stage to Stephen's funerary monument to his marriage, its achievement and finality: the argument a daughter might want to put to a dead father she could not quite argue with in his lifetime. Mr Ramsay's daughters' rebellious thoughts, his youngest son's pure and murderous hatred of him, are seen to be inadequate and unfair, not just to the parents but to the feelings of the children. The novel begins and ends with the question of a trip to the lighthouse. James, the six-year-old youngest of the Ramseys, longs to go. His mother encourages the idea, the father douses it. At the end of the novel, ten years after Mrs Ramsey's death, old Mr Ramsey bullyingly insists on the trip, taking his adolescent children, James and Cam. The visit is a sentimental pilgrimage on the father's terms, utterly unable to meet or fulfil either the child's dream or his mother's sympathy for it. For James, the trip returns him to his childhood and to that earlier moment of murderous hatred:

Had there been an axe handy, a poker, or any weapon that would have gashed a hole in his father's breast and killed him, there and then,

James would have seized it. Such were the extremes of emotion that Mr Ramsay excited in his children's breasts by his mere presence; standing, as now, lean as a knife, narrow as the blade of one, grinning sarcastically, not only with the pleasure of disillusioning his son and casting ridicule upon his wife, who was ten thousand times better in every way than he was (James thought), but also with some secret conceit at his own accuracy of judgement.[17]

This is male feeling, straightforwardly Oedipal, a proper response to a father's magisterial authority. He watches with hatred and horror as his father demands his mother's sympathy, rehearsing his old doubt that 'he was a failure'. Mrs Ramsey responds, suddenly suffused with energy, attention, 'delicious fecundity',[18] as she pours herself into reassuring her husband. Mr Ramsey moves off, apparently consoled, to his duties as father and as sage, and his young son watches his mother shrink, depleted, exhausted by what she has given to her husband, drained and ashamed that her husband, so much 'more important' than she, should reveal his dependence on her to other people. It is an ugly scene, small, intense and carrying one version of the ambiguity of the marriage. The son cannot forgive his father. The poet, Archibald Carmichael, who has watched it too, is never quite able to like or trust Mrs Ramsey.

That vision of the marriage, though, is not quite Virginia Woolf's, nor quite the one she allows to either Lily Briscoe or Cam, the youngest Ramsey daughter. Lily Briscoe is trying to paint in the garden as she ponders this marriage. She sees Mr Ramsey as the father to whom his wife 'gave him what he asked too easily', as the grand visionary and intellectual, tickled by and also above the adulation of his disciples, reduced by them and reductive of them and of his family. 'How strangely he was venerable and laughable at one and the same time',[19] she thinks.

Lily is not comforted by seeing what is ridiculous in Mr Ramsey. The reverence accorded Mrs Ramsey, for her beauty and her maternity, is tempting, and momentarily Lily 'took shelter from the reverence which covered all women; she felt herself praised.'[20] Even as she does so she steals a look at the picture she is painting and finds it 'infinitely bad'. She cannot manage both, her painting and the temptations of wifehood and motherhood. Mrs Ramsey is loved and admired by impressive men because she preferred 'boobies to clever men',[21] because 'she pitied men always as if they lacked something'.[22] This is her power for men: her compassion enables her to be heroically supportive of them, self-denyingly intent on maintaining their delusions, disguising their vulnerabilities for them. That is not possible for Lily Briscoe the painter and it is not possible for Cam.

In the boat with her father and her brother and the boatman on their trip to the lighthouse long after Mrs Ramsey's death Cam can see and feel her brother's hatred of her father, even revel in it. But she cannot share it. In the end Virginia Woolf did not make Mr Ramsey crush a dying mackerel, but intently read a book, bound and speckled like a plover's egg. His attention to the book is crushing, excluding of his son's hatred, his daughter's ambivalence, Lily's double focus on her painting and the tiny boat moving with its cargo beyond her vision. Mr Ramsey 'had always his work to fall back on',[23] and yet the tension in the boat, in which they are marooned together and isolated from each other, allows us to feel his concentrated attention to his book as an inability to confront feeling (his own and other people's), a vulnerability to the half-known truth about himself and his place in the family. It was Leslie Stephen, after all, who raised the question of how 'fathers generally count in their families'. He is also enviable for his capacity to concentrate, live in the head, even for being able to deny the reality and importance of other people's heads. Cam envies her brother his hatred and his determination to resist the father's tyranny. 'You're not exposed to it, to this pressure and division of feeling, this extraordinary temptation',[24] she thinks.

The last thoughts of the novel are Lily's, the adult artist's. Mr Ramsey has had his way. He has made his pilgrimage in his own time and for his own reasons. Lily turns from her thoughts of the boat reaching its destination to look at her painting. She accepts that its destiny is to 'be hung in the attics', even to be destroyed.

But 'It was done; it was finished. Yes, she thought, laying down her brush in extreme fatigue. I have had my vision.'[25]

The vision is the astigmatic vision of a woman who can neither simply 'shelter' in men's reverence nor straightforwardly seek consolation in work, as a man can. Nor can she quite bring herself to vandalise her father's mausoleum, dismiss its maker and its occupant. The mausoleum, a magnificent monument to death and to marriage, to men's destinies and women's role in promoting them, still stands, confident of its structure and its eternity. Women cannot argue with it. At best, they can carefully explain to the fathers and husbands and brothers and sons in their lives that there was a different view to be had of it all and hope that the builders of mausoleums will recognise that that is true for them too.

For most of this century women writers have been writing of women's lives as in transition. For Dorothy Richardson and for Virginia Woolf this required new forms of writing and of language to express what, in Dorothy Richardson's words, had been 'left out' of men's novels: new ways of seeing and understanding, new treatment of time and memory, more flexible and fragmented approaches to narrative and to its shaping of experience and establishing of significance. Novelists like Rosamond Lehmann, Jean Rhys and Christina Stead, a younger generation, start from the ways in which life has actually changed for women since the end of the First World War, particularly in terms of the possibilities for different relations with men.

At the end of *The Echoing Grove*, a novel Rosamond Lehmann wrote in the early fifties, two sisters, Dinah and Madeleine, are reconciled after the war and a long separation. Dinah had for years had a love affair with her brother-in-law, Madeleine's husband Rickie. He has died, and the sisters are contemplating a loveless middle age after the turbulences of their youth. Dinah, who has been a bohemian waif and a socialist, makes a speech which is not altogether characteristic of her as she has been in the novel but which Rosamond Lehmann herself seemed bent on making:

'I can't help thinking it's particularly difficult to be a woman just at present. One feels so transitional and fluctuating . . . so I suppose do men. I believe we *are* all in flux – that the difference between our grandmothers and us is far deeper than we realize – much more fundamental than the obvious social economic one. Our so-called emancipation may be a symptom, not a cause. Sometimes I think it's more than the development of a new attitude towards sex: that a new gender may be evolving – psychically new – a sort of hybrid. Or else it's just beginning to be uncovered how much woman there is in man and vice versa.'[26]

From her first novel, *Dusty Answer*, which was published in 1927, Rosamond Lehmann's heroines recoil from, when they are not rejected by, a 'fundamental masculine apartness'.[27] Even Cambridge, where Judith, *Dusty Answer*'s heroine, spends three years as an exemplary student at Girton, 'had disliked and distrusted her and all other females'.[28] She has been loved by men, but the man she has loved since childhood, and finally made love with, Roddy, is primarily homosexual and certainly intent on reminding her, as other men remind women in the novels, that he is 'never to be taken seriously'.[29] Judith is also in love with a woman in the novel, though that, significantly, is less openly admitted to. Homosexuality is not just a fact about some people but a new term in women's understanding of their relations with men. Rosamond Lehmann's heroines are thin, boyish, clever and independent. Their more matronly sisters opt for marriage and children, for continuities between their private and their public lives, for security, having enough money. Both kinds of women look to a man for love and recognition, and both kinds are finally disappointed. Judith, Olivia, Dinah are women whose sympathy for men and search for independence attract men. They seem free, capable, even like men. Yet they are secretly as possessive in love as their sisters are. Judith is appalled by her capacity to threaten and even to destroy in a man she loves exactly those

qualities which attract her in him and which she is partly inclined
to emulate:

Supposing she were to take Roddy from Tony, from all his friends and
lovers, from all his idle Parisian and English life, and attach him to
herself, tie him and possess him: that would mean giving him cares,
responsibilities, it might mean changing him from his free and secret
self into something ordinary, domesticated, resentful. Perhaps his
lovers and friends would be well advised to gather round him jealously
and guard him from the female. She saw herself for one moment as a
creature of evil design, dangerous to him, and took her hand away from
his that held it lightly.[30]

Rollo, who becomes Olivia's lover in *The Weather in the Streets*,
is 'sketchy', like his letters. An older, upper-class man she had
longingly watched in the earlier *Invitation to the Waltz*, he is
unhappily married now and looking for a mistress when she meets
him again after her own unsatisfactory marriage has ended. His
sexual appeal is established through his public and man-of-the-
world confidence:

Here came something in a different style – a tall prosperous-looking
male figure in a tweed overcoat, carrying a dog under his arm, stooping
broad shoulders in at the entrance. With a beam and a flourish the fat
steward conducted him to the seat opposite Olivia. He hesitated, then
took off his coat, folded it, put the dog on it, patted it, sat down beside
it, picked up the card, ordered sausages, scrambled eggs, coffee, toast
and marmalade, and opened *The Times*.[31]

His charm is that he is a husband, though not hers. His love and
his virility are secretive and two-faced. He needs Olivia to be
independent of him, convincingly separate, and he needs his wife
to depend on him. Where women long for their lives to be all of a
piece, unified, men, it seems, can only operate from splits and
division. Olivia sells the ugly, expensive emerald ring he gives her,
to pay for an abortion. His 'delicate' wife delights him and his
family by becoming pregnant. He is punished by a car crash.
When Olivia and Rollo agree to part at the end of the novel he
reminds her that 'I always told you I wasn't any good, didn't I? I

told you I'd let you down.'[32] The new and liberated woman has to know that, know that she will be sacrificed to the wife in the end, that a flaunting of her emancipation has signalled her willingness to be treated badly. Rollo is not delicious, a mysterious siren, as the young men in *Dusty Answer* were. He is a solid English gentleman, easier to imagine dressed than undressed, likely to become rather red in the face with paternity. He too is precious as well as disappointing, yet no more in the end, it might be said, than a feather in the cap. The promise he offers, as do other men in Rosamond Lehmann's novels, whether as a husband or as a lover, is one which women invent and which men can neither quite understand nor adequately deliver. 'A new attitude to sex', the evolving of 'a new gender' are painful prospects for women and for men in the novels, for neither sex can quite relinquish their traditional expectations for themselves and each other.

Rosamond Lehmann has said in an interview that 'It looks now as if I was writing specifically about the predicament of women, though I was not conscious of it at the time.'[33] Her admirers have usually wanted to praise her particularly for her insight into women's feelings when they are in love with men. It is not easy to form very strong impressions of the Roddies and Rollos and Rickies who are loved by her heroines. Their natures are shifting as well as shifty, and though they are all endowed with a specifically masculine sexuality (a matter of necks and torsos and expensive habits and smells, for some of the time), they are evasive and evaded, and withered by the scorching passions of the women who cleave to them.

Rickie of the later *The Echoing Grove* is finally allowed to speak for himself out of his dazzling mysteriousness. It is not an articulate speech. He is sheltering from an air-raid with the wife of his best friend, with whom he has just made love. After making his speech he will stumble off into the night and die of a duodenal ulcer, produced, it is suggested, by the impossibility of meeting the demands women have made on him all his life. He recalls a meeting with a working-class man, when they talked about sex and women. Such a conversation with a man is exceptional, indeed unique for him. Men do not ordinarily discuss such things with each other. The other man confesses that sex with women and love have been 'terrifying', it 'took the virtue'[34] out of a man, revealed his incapacity to feel what he was required, supposed to feel. Rickie is survived by his wife and by her sister, his frailty set off against their resilience.

The anomalies of sex are interwoven with the anomalies of class and money and style here. Dinah's yearning for working-class men and for some kind of socialist commitment are finally made to seem dithering and escapist. Rosamond Lehmann's educated and independent young women are disconcerted to find that sexual freedom for them makes them outsiders in a rigidly class-bound world, which they still adhere to. What is possible for their brothers, young men of their class, is not possible for them. The women have desultory jobs, are short of money, envious of their sisters who are wives and opulently indulged, if not passionately loved. As mistresses they are déclassé, treated as actresses and demi-mondaines were in their mothers' day. They cannot afford to be feminists or angry any more than wives can, and most of them are ignominiously reduced to asking for handouts and loans from time to time. Lurking in the wings, dangerous and tempting, is a bohemian world, partly Bloomsbury, occasionally left-wing, but more often preoccupied by the evolving of new snobberies and alliances, where there are men and women who are artists, writers, many of them homosexual or, at any rate, sexually unconventional.

A recognition of the possibilities of 'a new gender' and of the problems for men and women of their holding to extremes and oppositions had not been canvassed in quite this way before, though versions of bisexuality are there, I have wanted to suggest, in many women's novels throughout the nineteenth century. The exasperation expressed by the women in Rosamond Lehmann's novels is not only with the difference, the remoteness, the unknowableness of the men they love. It is also an exasperation with the incompleteness of their own transformation. The suggestion that most men are covertly homosexual, unable to face up to oppositions in their nature, is made of women too. Older women in the novels have accepted that their femininity, which is their appeal as women for men, does not last and is not an aspect of themselves on which they can build their lives. Boyishness is not the answer, but some kind of sexlessness is. Glorious, glamorous men, heroes in the world and in bed, are women's fictions, shadowy, unreal, wished for. It may not be a revolutionary message that we are left with. Indeed, the wisest woman in *The Echoing Grove* is the widowed mother of the two sisters, who deplores the mess her daughters have made of love and sex and their relations with men. She has always known that men were weak and that she was strong; 'she could pity weakness if it was not, as so often it was nowadays, given a moral not to say mystic sanction: as if to play fast and loose with other people's lives took natural priority over duty and self-control.'[35] She is out of touch with the new dilemma her daughters are facing, but she is intact as they are not.

Rosamond Lehmann was registering an impasse reached by her more adventurous heroines. They begin to sense that they are held back by more than the inequities and imperfections of sexual attitudes and relations amongst upper-middle-class English people in the first half of the twentieth century. In *The Echoing Grove* Dinah's socialism, her affairs with working-class men, her involvement with the Spanish Civil War, are genuine for her in her youth, aspects of her personality and of her rebelliousness against her own class and its limiting view of women and of the poor and the oppressed. Yet she draws back in the end, admits that these moves were probably no more than a kind of flirtation, even slumming. By the end of the novel, she is approaching her middle age with 'common sense', invoking her mother's acceptance of a woman's strengths and weaknesses and proposing, a little windily, that what men and women need to heal their differences is 'a new gender', a blurring of sexual extremes.

This is an important moment. Novelists like Virginia Woolf and Rosamond Lehmann came close to seizing it, but drew back in horror, retreating into class solidarity and its consolations, asking only for equality with their brothers and a little time and space and money. It was becoming clear – and it had only been implicitly recognised until now – that it was no longer possible to consider sexual relations as separate from other social relations, as separate from class. The impasse reached by Rosamond Lehmann's heroines – and they come close to admitting it – is that they are asking for economic independence outside marriage but within the class into which they were born. What these women begin to recognise is that to defy marriage in that class is to defy the social relations that maintain that class. The revolutionary implications of that are terrifying for women whose security depends on their contiguous connections to the English class system. Defiance reminds them that their place within it is not as members. It took writers like Jean Rhys, Christina Stead and Doris Lessing, who had grown up as colonials and become immigrants, to see that their situation as women, and the possibilities of change, could not be addressed outside an understanding of the effects of a class society, imperialism and racism on all forms of human relations. It was becoming impossible simply to tinker with the relations between the sexes, to hope to modify marriage as an institution, with its particular economic history, without understanding that sex and marriage are ultimately connected with – some would say determined by – property, ownership, inheritance, conservatism, capitalism and class. To propose alternative ways for women to live their lives inevitably meant confronting class, race and economics.

Some of the strange history of Jean Rhys as a writer is known. I shall quote from a brief biography given by Francis Wyndham in his introduction to *Wide Sargasso Sea*:

Jean Rhys was born at Roseau, Dominica, one of the Windward Islands, and spent her childhood there. Her father was a Welsh doctor and her mother a Creole – that is, a white West Indian. At the age of sixteen she came to England, where she spent the First World War. Then she married a Dutch poet and for ten years lived a rootless, wandering life on the Continent, mainly in Paris and Vienna. This was during the 1920s, and the essence of the artist's life in Europe at that time is contained in her first book, *The Left Bank*.[36]

Thereafter she wrote four more novels and disappeared from public view until 1958, when she was 'rediscovered' and some of her work reprinted. In 1966, she published *Wide Sargasso Sea*, a novel which undertakes to explore the nature and sources of madness in the first Mrs Rochester, whom we meet as a terrifying and destructive fiend in *Jane Eyre*, a spectre for whom Jane Eyre herself feels some sympathy, when she says to Mr Rochester, 'you are inexorable for that unfortunate lady: you speak of her with hate – with vindictive antipathy. It is cruel – she cannot help being mad.'[37]

The heroines of the earlier Rhys novels were rootless waifs and victims, who could be beady and even sometimes pugilistic in their own defence, and always witty and able to take refuge in their thoughts and in words; so that, for instance, the lachrymose heroine of *Good Morning, Midnight* can, in a plaintive moment, remark, 'I don't belong anywhere'[38] and wonderfully think too, 'God, it's funny, being a woman!'[39] As a woman, she suffers particular kinds of exploitation. She is bought, sold, violated, rejected, tempted by men's love and terrorised by it. Yet in her degradation she is always joined by men, who are also diminished, trapped by poverty. They are gigolos, petty crooks, discarded, poor, misfits, scroungers, people who become hardened and wily from poverty and loneliness. Such a heroine is, as Francis Wyndham has written, 'a victim of men's incomprehension of women, a symptom of women's mistrust of men'.[40] Mistrust and incomprehension are also seen to characterise most relations in the world these women inhabit, for it is the consequence of the very real reasons there are for the rich and the poor to distrust one another. It might be possible to read the early novels and their weeping, drinking, accident-prone heroines with some exasperation, to feel that they get no more than they should expect if they hang around rich people and complain when they are exploited by them. Any such reading becomes an impossibility even in retrospect after *Wide Sargasso Sea*. In this novel, the blighting fear and confusions of Antoinette Cosway's growing up in Jamaica in the 1830s are not simply the terrors of a lonely girl at the mercy of men who momentarily desire her; they are made a part of the history of slavery in the West Indies and of the brutalities, the hatreds and the ineradicable suspicion and distrust woven into the life of a society in which white people have bought and sold Black people.

Antoinette's father had been a slave-owner, who had casually slept with Black women, producing half-caste children and ignoring most of them. He is already dead at the beginning of the novel. His daughter lives with her mother and her mentally defective small brother on the disintegrating family estate. She grows up unable to trust anyone, though she has affection for some of the few Black servants who have remained with the family. Such loyalty as they could ever have had to the family is corrupted by their history and position. They have a little power, now that their white masters have lost some of theirs, and they stay on because they were born there and there are still possibilities of making something out of this ruined white family. When Antoinette's mother marries rich Mr Mason their life is partially restored to its old grandeurs. It is too late, though. Furious Black people burn down the house. The small boy dies and the mother goes mad. After Mr Mason's death, his son by an earlier marriage gives Antoinette and her dowry to a young Englishman, intent as a second son on making his fortune and prepared to take on this bewildered and damaged girl for a price. The second half of the novel deals with this marriage, the one Mr Rochester tells Jane Eyre about.

The marriage is tainted, doomed, by the kind of transaction it represents. In a society based on the buying and selling of human beings marriage becomes another version of that exchange. Antoinette's ambiguously inherited insanity is ripened by the whisperings and hostility of the children of slaves and by the magic they have inherited to resist the white slave-owners. Neither Mr Rochester nor the other white characters in the novel are simply villains. They are heirs to a sickness, an insidious madness, as the Black people are too. Mr Rochester's inability to love Antoinette is continuous with his inability either to trust or be trusted by Black people. She is a stranger to him as they are: 'I felt very little tenderness for her, she was a stranger to me, a stranger who did not think or feel as I did.'[41] Antoinette's old nurse, Christophine, explains what it is that makes a loving marriage with his wife impossible:

'What you do with her money, eh?' Her voice was still quiet, but with a hiss in it when she said 'money'. I thought, of course, that is what all the rigmarole is about.[42]

Money is what all the rigmarole in the novels of Jean Rhys *is* about. Having money or not having money: this is what makes people strangers to each other, predators, suspect. Any relationship becomes a contest between strength and weakness, and so, inevitably, do relationships between men and women.

Francis Wyndham said in a recent interview:

Because the novels seem so autobiographical, you think of her as being always separate from a man and looking for another one. That wasn't so. She was married three times and always had a man. I wanted the letters to show that, to show how in essence the novels were about herself, a dreamy sort of person, having a think, going for walks, liking not being interfered with – but not the circumstances.[43]

This is helpful for a reading of Jean Rhys, illuminating of her heroines' vulnerabilities and their toughness. There is a characteristic conversation in *Good Morning, Midnight* between Sasha, the lost and aging heroine, and the gigolo, whom she is beginning to trust, about whether or not she is a 'cérébrale':

'What is a cérébrale, anyway? I don't know. Do you?'
'A cérébrale,' he says, seriously, 'is a woman who doesn't like men or need them.'
'Oh, is that it? I've often wondered. Well, there are quite a lot of those, and the ranks are daily increasing.'
'Ah, but a cérébrale doesn't like women either. Oh, no. The true cérébrale is a woman who likes nothing and nobody except herself and her own damned brain or what she thinks is her brain.'
So pleased with herself, like a little black boy in a top hat. . . .

'In fact, a monster.'

'Yes, a monster.'

'Well, after all that it's very comforting to know that you think I'm stupid. . . . Let's ask for the bill, shall we? Let's go.'[44]

A 'cérébrale' here is very like Wyndham's 'dreamy sort of person, having a think, going for walks, liking not being interfered with'. She is weak, poor, needy, but she has learned to keep a small part of herself in her head and her thoughts – a little black boy in a top-hat – which survives intact, knowing the worst about the world. Having sent the gigolo packing at the end of the novel, she regrets it, wants him back, realises that she can partly trust him because they have exposed their weakness to each other. She leaves her hotel room door open, hoping that he will return. A sinister figure takes advantage of this momentary dropping of her guard. But she knew that she was exposing herself to that possibility, and we feel that she could survive even what might happen next.

There has been a shift. A woman on her own, and a woman, Jean Rhys seems to be saying, is always alone if she depends on men, is an outsider, vulnerable and weakened as the immigrant, the foreigner, is vulnerable and weakened. But the oppression of women by men is part of, continuous with, the oppression of the weak by the strong, of the poor by the rich, of black people by white people. Jean Rhys can seem resigned to the hopelessness of looking for love and trust in such a world. At times she may appear to canvass the possibilities of an alliance between those who are powerless; at others she will sadly concede that even the powerless are so hopelessly corrupted by the power they have not got and want that, like the Black people in *Wide Sargasso Sea*, they themselves will turn on the weak because they can make no impression on those who are their real masters. The novels are pessimistic, sad and about sadness; they offer no political solutions, but they are also full of wit and resilience and a pugnacious attachment to privacy. Jean Rhys developed a lucid and inward style to stand for the outsider's experience, the watchful and distrustful onlooker of a world systematically organised to take advantage of her and people like her. Her heroines never win in the world, but their clear-sightedness, their wit and their capacity to live in their own heads make for a limited kind of triumph.

Christina Stead, born in Australia, has another outsider's view, wonderfully sharpened to perceive the distortions of character and stance produced by the parochialism of English and American society and their politics and literature. She left Australia in 1928, when she was twenty-six, for London and Paris, New York and California, and did not return to Australia until she was in her late seventies. Between 1934 and 1980 she wrote more than a dozen novels and volumes of stories. She wrote on an altogether more swashbuckling scale than Jean Rhys; was versatile, travelled, vigorous. Her novels deal with a huge variety of worlds, themes, characters, and they do so largely, carelessly, belligerently and unfastidiously. She shares with the younger writer, Doris Lessing, as I've said, a politics which enjoins a refusal to assume that women are simply victims of injustice and men the perpetrators. For this reason it will be necessary to focus on the bullies in her novels, whether they are men or women, and to consider her warnings to women as warnings to resist any easy or self-congratulatory belief in their own innocence. The last of her novels to be published before her death, *Cotters' England*, has at its centre a woman born into a working-class family in the north of England, now a journalist, who is a monster of egotism, self-indulgence and deludedness. Nellie is the product of the Depression and the Second World War, a creature of grandly destructive and self-destructive impulses, ardently committed to telling all truths but her own, who is superbly herself and utterly limited by the sentimentality of British society and the individualism it both spawns and neutralises. Monstrous egotists and individualists of different kinds are Christina Stead's forte. She watches them taking root, blossoming and luxuriantly going to seed in a world which encourages them as the fruits of its own decadence. They are richly disapproved of and adored and they become for Christina Stead the agents of her political critique, a warning against demagogues and all false consolations.

Eleanor in *Miss Herbert (The Suburban Wife)* is a writer and a rewriter, whose somewhat parasitical achievement it is to have turned a story by her father into a modest best-seller; a wry sort of apology, perhaps, for the wonderful novels – which have not been best-sellers – Christina Stead herself has written about oppressively exuberant fathers, but a judgement as well on those who live within borrowed scenarios. In earlier novels Christina Stead saw writers and children as those who are best able to resist bullies and take control of their own lives. Fourteen-year-old Louie is already a writer when she leaves her father in *The Man Who Loved Children*. Teresa, Louie's older incarnation in the later *For Love Alone*, escapes her father, and eventually his more ambiguous understudy, the autodidact Jonathan Crow, when she follows him to London from Australia and evades him to become a writer. Letty, in *Letty Fox: Her Luck*, records a life which threatens to dissipate itself in pursuit of a husband, and by telling her story gradually shapes and controls it.

Early in *Miss Herbert* Eleanor is struck by a story she reads by chance in a women's magazine, which 'had meaning for romantic women like herself who had been tempted by their own good looks'. Later 'she extracted the outline and rewrote the story a little.'[45] It is an episode characteristic of her: conformist, amoral, thrifty. Eleanor is one of Christina Stead's monstrous egotists, who boil with self-respect, and are superb and ridiculous in wishing only for the simplest things in life: things like love, happiness and scope for the free play of a benign will. The novel begins with and returns to – as *The Man Who Loved Children* did – something like a frozen group-portrait, which stands for a touched-up public version of youth and friendship or family happiness, and is allowed to develop as a notion, an increasingly hectoring and recriminatory one, of the 'good life', the real one, which has been so irresponsibly smudged by other people. *The Man Who Loved Children* alludes to a simpering arcadia, with all the prettified poverty of the TV Walton family, which is Sam

Pollitt's dream of the family life he deserves and can still, momentarily and almost convincingly, seem to create. When his wife's ferocious misery and their violent quarrels splinter the dream, we see that this conventional idyll is more than a delusion. It has become instrumental in creating the unhappiness it attempts to conceal, a deceiving generalisation, which must be held partly responsible for people's pains and frustrations and for their incompatibilities and their inadequacies in social and sexual relations.

Eleanor's health and beauty propose from the outset a glorious happiness as no more than she deserves. We see her first in the 1920s, glowing in the midst of a group of friends, young women graduates with characters and destinies. She is easier with and on women 'because she was much the handsomest of all'. Men are more difficult because 'she wanted to be taken seriously'[46] and must be on her guard. She has realistic and womanly plans for herself. She will write and then, having sampled men and love, will move richly into marriage and motherhood. There will be no triumphant culmination to it all (as there might be for a man), rather a life lived in decorous stages, each calculated to make use of her superior capacity to experience life's most valued offerings. Her love affairs seem tawdry and unfeeling to other people, but they are hers, and transformed by her capacity to distance herself from them. When she realises, more slowly than she might, that she has married a crass and petty tyrant, she consoles herself with making extravagant economies, and the discovery that 'all the commonplaces of her present life were delicious to her'.[47]

Desertion and divorce are also able to bring out the best in her, inspiring her even to take a little interest in other people, so long as they can discredit her husband and confirm her own magnanimity. Her plight uncovers new energies born of heroic indignation, and these enable her to hold the family together while she returns in her fifties, ignominiously but with poise, to the fringes of the literary world. Her strength lies in her ability to accommodate to the reductions of age, to see them as worthy challenges to her charm and ingenuity. It is a strength which also accounts for her disintegration; and she is English. There is no doubt that this proud disintegration is meant to be England's too, that England is under attack for its wearying buoyancy, its tinselly imperialism. The brave and sensible novels of women are under attack too, as are many of the accommodations women make to ensure themselves a place and some dignity in an unjust society.

Christina Stead is a writer for whom the promise as well as the vicissitudes of family life and sexual relations hold metaphors for society and the possibilities of oppression and collaboration within it. Eleanor is all too recognisable, an anachronism and a pirate rather than a partner, who has learned to smile dispassionately upon a world which has no place for her. Sam Pollitt, the man who loves children, is an embodiment of American idealism, the melting-pot kind, and of its rhetoric, which in extending its embrace to the world's children simultaneously adjures them to flee the contamination of the undecided and the sceptical. Once contaminated they will have to stand outside that melting-pot. It was easy enough to applaud Christina Stead's attack on America in *The Man Who Loved Children* and her insight into the traditions of individualism, which in Sam tip so effortlessly into tyranny and the divine right of patriarchs. It is too easy, for Christina Stead is constantly alert to other rhetorics, the ones, for instance, which allow varieties of debility to excuse an absence of idealism, defeated and vitiated energies, compensating vanities and self-regard. She is warning women that there is no excuse for collusion with fathers and bosses and bullies.

Eleanor's particular vanity is to have quite limited ambitions but to believe that she has an absolute right to their fulfilment. Her literary work, her friends, husband and children, are the tapes and records of an 'athletic' performance, which maintains its standards by diminishing, imperceptibly, the length of the course and the height of its hurdles. She asks and takes for herself special handicaps and then dissolves them if they threaten to diminish her achievements. What would be degrading for other people – grubbing for publishers' work, lending herself to an old man's pornographic fantasies, sacrificing her children to her marital tussles – she forgives herself, on the grounds that they provide occasions for displays of making do, rising above, staying young, absorbing shock. Rewriting, touching up, patchwork repairs are skills she comfortably develops. They are not seen as 'feminine' skills but as skills with a terrible temptation and danger for women.

Andrew Hawkins, the father of *For Love Alone*, reminds his grown-up daughters that he has been loved by women for being 'the good-looking, sincere young idealist'.[48] Teresa responds sceptically and scornfully. She will nurse her own idealism, shielding it from her father's rapacious assumptions, and she will run away to Europe. There are characters in all Christina Stead's novels who are asked to offer a nearly impossible resistance to nearly irresistible blandishments. Some of them, and most of them are young, manage this. Eleanor does not. She has been 'well, but vaguely educated',[49] and she has learned to keep her sights low and rely on good breeding and a university education to get her through. Poor judgement, failures of both spontaneity and concentration, an inability to keep as friends the women who gave edge and confidence to her youth, and, above all, a shrinking from men who are attractive to her and intelligent enough to rumble her emptiness: all this is soothed for her, lubricated, by vanity and snobbishness. It is a harsh indictment, one which an English reader, many English writers and a good many women amongst both, are meant to find hard to shrug off; especially as Eleanor herself refuses to be reduced by it. She does not know, as we are encouraged, even tempted to believe *we* do, that she might be seen in this way. That is another of her strengths: a conceit which transcends self-consciousness.

Christina Stead has little patience with victims. Children are watched for the growth in them of resistance and independence, and it is this which makes them amongst the best-understood of fictional children. Her monsters are incorrigible, but they can be denied and deflated. Once denied they are creatures of comedy as well as terror. The young and the oppressed are not helpless, because they still have choices, while oppressors reduce their options and stitch their own strait-jackets. Nor is marriage inevitably an invitation to battle or constraint. It is also allowed to provide opportunities for co-operation and freedom.

Miss Herbert (The Suburban Wife) and *Cotters' England* offer gloomier, more negative pictures than some of the earlier work. They have more of the sermon. *Miss Herbert* suffers from Eleanor's self-absorption, so that we have to rely on authorial sleights-of-hand for our focus on her. There are moments of bravura: a glum visit Eleanor makes to a patronised old friend who has disconcertingly made a success of her life as a doctor and a mother; another when Eleanor rampages through her ex-husband's files in search of damning evidence and discovers under 'Various' exactly the trite and repetitive love letters she expected. The volcanic rhythms of *The Man Who Loved Children* have become small spasms here as Eleanor moves from each failure to 'the next stage of life'.[50] She does slightly less damage than Sam does, and this is partly because he is as much the creation of his watched and watching children as their creator.

It would be possible, but misleading I think, to attribute the reduced scope and muteness of Eleanor's terrorisms to her being a woman. As a destroyer of all and sundry, Sam Pollitt could be said to meet his match in Nellie of *Cotter's England*, who presides over national tragedies and the tragedies of her family and friends like some demented party-giver receiving the gifts which are due to her. It may be significant, though, that Sam's flushing-out of his family's secrets and privacies, and his bending of them to his rituals, imprints itself on the stuff of their interwoven lives and on the individual futures of his children. Eleanor is a single, hieratic figure, on her own as she performs to a scattered and faceless congregation. She is out of touch, and the world she is out of touch with is less present in this novel than in earlier ones. Yet she stands memorably as a telling image of contemporary Britain and as a warning to women who cannot see that their position must be understood politically, that going it alone is self-defeating.

Christina Stead can be as angry with women as with men, for their collusion with bullies and for their aping of them. She offers a kind of warning, and it is one which more and more women writers have heeded in recent years. It is one which Doris Lessing, coming here from her childhood and youth in Southern Africa, offers too. Like Christina Stead, she can be impatient with a feminism which begins and ends with an analysis of the oppression of women and fails to see the causes and the nature of that oppression within a historical view of societies in which sexual relations are one – if a peculiar and a peculiarly constant, ubiquitous one – of the sites of human antagonism and estrangement. The power of both writers lies in their insistence on the centrality of women's experience and their accounts of it.

The Golden Notebook, which was published in 1962, breaks into Doris Lessing's five-novel sequence, which began with *Martha Quest* in 1952 and has been aptly described by Lorna Sage as 'a study in social, sexual and cultural vagrancy forged out of her own life-history'.[51] It breaks into that sequence in the sense of becoming a novel about them, about itself and its writing and its author, so that it was, mistakenly I think, thought by some readers at the time to be fashionably and self-consciously engaged in not much more than a writerly deconstruction of itself. It was also gently reproved in an early review for being 'not a creation but a document', a fascinating document, but one which 'never gets off the level of a natural experience, which is not the same as a fully human one'.[52] It was also, it should be said, taken very seriously, though not always in ways which the author herself could either recognise or accept.

The novel's outer, or containing, narrative holds the four notebooks kept by the writer Anna Wulf and moves ultimately into a final section called 'The Golden Notebook'. That outer narrative is entitled 'Free Women', a theme which is ironically addressed by Anna and her friend, Molly, to whom Anna, more or less rhetorically, puts the question: 'if we lead what is known as free lives, that is, lives like men, why shouldn't we use the same language?'[53] The novel is constructed to suggest the uneasy order and tidiness imposed on the parcelled-out, compartmentalised life of a woman who is a writer in the middle of the twentieth century. The topics and entries and modes of writing in her notebooks are separate and overlapping. They deal with her past in Africa, her early and current involvement in left-wing politics and her disillusionment with the Communist Party, her sexual relations with men and her life with her child, her friendships with women, her life as a writer and the stories she makes of her own life.

One persistent theme of the novel is a suspicion of literature and of the writer. It is reminiscent of Dorothy Richardson's fear that language and literary form might deny or reduce or destroy 'current existence, the ultimate astonisher'.[54] Anna Wulf's fear that 'Literature is analysis after the event'[55] holds some of that existential doubt as to literature's capacity to give the physical quality of life, the living of it, through an act of writing which might make nostalgia or history of it; but it is also a political doubt. In 'The Golden Notebook' at the end of the novel Anna and her lover Saul go mad. 'They "break down" into each other, into other people, break through the false patterns they have made of their pasts, the patterns and formulas they have made to shore up themselves and each other, dissolve.'[56] Each finally encourages the other to write by offering a story or a starting point. In the last pages of the outer narrative, however, Anna gives up writing to become a marriage counsellor, join the Labour Party and 'teach a night-class twice a week for delinquent kids'.[57] Those alternative endings stand for more than alternative lives and commitments available to a woman. They stand for two kinds of politics. The couple who 'break down' and swop stories, as it were, have changed themselves, their sexual relationship, and the world and the kind of writing about it which might be possible. In the other version Anna has settled for women's traditional role as repairer, healer, soother of delinquencies created by a society which self-fulfillingly defines them as that.

The writer, for Doris Lessing, is committed to change and to the telling and making real in personal experience what importantly connects that experience with a general and a social one. The novel's pessimism about sexual and social relations has allowed readers of quite different kinds to read it as a much more naturalistic account of women's situation than it can have been meant to be. Whether that account has been seen as depressing or as exhilarating, such a reading reduces it to a complacent review of those pressures on women which might be thought to produce fragmentation and to encourage the kind of tidying-up operation to which women are traditionally given. Anna's notebooks suggest both confusion and a tidy mind making sense of it all. This has exasperated men who had their ears pricked for a big women's novel which would tell them what women thought about it all. It has also allowed some feminists to refer to it mournfully as to a textbook for a study of their woes. In her preface to a later edition of *The Golden Notebook* Doris Lessing is determinedly reasserting the novel's commitment to criticism and to change:

Yet the essence of the book, the organisation of it, everything in it, says implicitly and explicitly, that we must not divide things off, must not compartmentalise.[58]

What makes Doris Lessing such an uncomfortable writer (as Christina Stead is) is that because she 'assumed that that filter which is a woman's way of looking at life has the same validity as the filter which is a man's way',[59] she did not expect that a novel of ideas, a political novel, which was written by a woman and about a woman's life, would be read as if it were no more than a repository of women's concerns and women's views. Her focus and her 'filter' is valid as a vagrant's or an immigrant's is valid. Her dismissing of George Eliot is unfair, but it is helpful to an understanding of what Doris Lessing has wanted to do and of the kinds of dismay and misappropriation with which she has needed to contend:

George Eliot is good as far as she goes. But I think the penalty she paid for being a Victorian woman was that she had to be shown to be a good woman even when she wasn't according to the hypocrisies of the time – there is a great deal she does not understand because she is moral.[60]

That carries a number of rebukes, and not all of them, of course, directed at George Eliot. It does imply, though, that George Eliot's not being truthful about herself vitiated her morality as a novelist and as a woman, so that in representing 'the intellectual and moral climate' of Britain in the second half of the nineteenth century she was cowardly, because she evaded the very realities which she knew from the position she occupied as a woman and a writer in that society. There is, of course, something in that, and it returns us to all kinds of old questions about the courage and the reliability of women writers who have sheltered, however diversely, within male protectiveness. It is interesting in this context for offering a way of hearing how Doris Lessing is asking to be read herself. That is, as a woman, whose view of the contemporary world is not only as valid as a man's would be, but is one which gathers its validity from its vantage point of being both an outsider's and shared. 'Writing about oneself, one is writing about others, since your problems, pains, pleasures, emotions – and your extraordinary and remarkable ideas – can't be yours alone.'[61] This is not writing *as* or *on behalf of* women or outsiders, but writing from that position out of a commitment to other people in the world, because they share the same world and are threatened by the same terrors.

This by no means returns us to androgyny – any more than it proposes a melting-pot – but emphasises the centrality of a woman's experience and perceptions for an understanding of history and change. It is a voice which both men and women have become used to hearing as freshly and interestingly delivering itself of news from the frontier, or more often from the edges or margins, which is here quite straightforwardly – if with a clear expectation of trouble – demanding to be heard as one amongst others and as essential and authoritative.

Homosexuality, in the work of Dorothy Richardson, Virginia Woolf and Rosamond Lehmann, is posed as more than a matter of individual predilections. It becomes a hypothesised solution to (and perhaps an explanation of) women's duality and alienation. For Doris Lessing, homosexuality becomes an evasion, a

comforting but dislikeable one, of the sexual relations between
a man and a woman. That relation exemplifies and pervades what
is seen in the novel as the crucially modern conflict between freedom and commitment, the problem of subjectivity: 'that shocking
business of being preoccupied with the tiny individual who is at the
same time caught up in such an explosion of terrible and marvellous possibilities'.[62] The sexual act itself punctuates the novel and
stands more schematically for dangerous contradictions and delusions as well as for a new idea of community.

At the point when Ella, the heroine of the novel which occupies
Anna Wulf's 'Yellow Notebook', senses from the changes in her
sexual responses to her lover Paul that the affair is coming to an
end, Anna takes over to explain:

> Sex. The difficulty of writing about sex, for women, is that sex is best
> when not thought about, not analysed. Women deliberately choose not
> to think about technical sex. They get irritable when men talk
> technically, it's out of self-preservation: they want to preserve the
> spontaneous emotion that is essential for their satisfaction.[63]

That satisfaction is for Ella, and for Anna, a 'vaginal orgasm', and
that for them is only possible when 'a man, from the whole of his
need and desire takes a woman and wants all her response'.[64]
Paul, according now to Anna's narrative, 'involuntarily frowned,
and remarked: "Do you know that there are eminent physiologists
who say women have no physical basis for vaginal orgasm?"'[65]
The meaning of that exchange spreads to infuse the whole novel
and returns us to Anna's original question, 'Why shouldn't we use
the same language?' Failure to meet sexually is a failure of feeling
between men and woman and a failure of language. The agreement Anna and Ella look for in the act of sex is disrupted and
circumscribed by the discourses, usually male and frequently
professional, which define that act in terms of physiology,
gynaecology, marriage or even sin. The real connections between
people have to be fitted into those discourses, and men are
prevented from addressing their own realities by that process as
women are. The novel's women are not, of course, 'free', though

they are not married, as most of the men are. Wives are imagined as limply, sadly at home. Stripped of energy and individuality, married women have allowed sexual feeling to be deformed by the constraints of the marriage contract. It was possible in the early sixties to read this treatment of wives as the contempt of 'free' women for the women who settled for marriage. It may be easier now to understand that the novel sees not just wives, but most people, as damaged by and implicated in the acceptance of any relationship which rests on lies and unexamined forms of injustice and inequality. The husbands who become, temporarily, the lovers of Doris Lessing's 'free women' are predators only because they are hungry, incomplete, damaged as their wives are. They are incapable of a commitment which dislodges them, makes life unsafe. Ella 'thinks for the hundredth time that in their emotional life all these intelligent men use a level so much lower than anything they use for work, that they might be different creatures'.[66] Men fragment their lives too: work, marriage, fatherhood, sex. They are as mutilated as women are by their 'filter', their modes of looking at life. The discourses which rationalise male control of sexual behaviour and assert the primacy of male needs and pleasure serve to deny male satisfaction by allowing accounts of the most intimate emotions and sensations of half the world to be stifled or discounted, unheard.

The source of Doris Lessing's analysis of sex is Marxist, because, as she has written, 'Marxism looks at things as a whole and in relation to each other – or tries to.'[67] Sexual failure is not in itself either a male failure or a female failure, nor is it simply sexual. It becomes, as the site of most people's central experience of pain and isolation, the consequence of a world in which people are destructively at odds and cut off from each other. Sex promises the most complete of unions and most sharply articulates the devastations of a failure to achieve it. In a more lucid moment of her affair with Saul at the end of the novel, Anna wryly puts to him what seems at least a hope:

in a society where not one man in ten thousand begins to understand the ways in which women are second-class citizens, we have to rely for company on the men who are at least not hypocrites.[68]

The world Doris Lessing wrote about in *The Golden Notebook* was different from Virginia Woolf's in significant ways, though not different enough. There have, though, been changes in women's lives and in the ways in which they could and have written about them. It has become possible and even more vitally necessary for women to insist on a hearing for themselves. They need to do so because the Western world has become trapped by the endlessly reiterated stories it consoles itself with. I have argued elsewhere[69] for the potentially explosive messages which have come to us from bilingual writers and from all writers who bring to literature in English their knowledge of another culture and their perspective on a second. I wrote then about writers like Conrad and Kafka, who were bilingual. There are others like Maxine Hong Kingston and Salman Rushdie and Anita Desai, whom we may read for their capacity to tell us what we ought to know out of their double vision. I have come to see that the same kinds of illumination can be found in women writers, who have learned to be bilingual and are outsiders,[70] even when they seem most confidently to be telling us that they are insiders we should read androgynously. Writing of Doris Lessing's recent books of 'speculative fiction',[71] Lorna Sage suggests that these later works 'finally confirmed her marginality. In a spirit of irony, of course, since for her it is on the margins of the culture, and of the psyche, that imaginative life survives.'[72] Let us turn finally to some writers in America who have lived with that irony and have given it imaginative life.

8

Women's Men

'When he was a child,' she continued, 'his father ran off with another woman, and one day when Richard and his mother went to ask him for money to buy food he laughingly rejected them. Richard, being very young, thought his father Godlike. Big, omnipotent, unpredictable, undependable and cruel. Entirely in control of his universe. Just like a god. But, many years later, after Wright had become a famous writer, he went down to Mississippi to visit his father. He found, instead of God, just an old watery-eyed field hand, bent from plowing, his teeth gone, smelling of manure. Richard realized that the most daring thing his "God" had done was run off with that other woman.'

Alice Walker[1]

Lying in purple and green grass on the edge of pinewoods in Georgia, USA, are two Black teenagers, Cholly and Darlene. They have just been to a funeral and they are now, excitedly and for the first time, making love. The moon is shining. At the moment of their most intense pleasure they are interrupted. Two white men are standing over them with lights and long guns. Jeering and sniggering, the huntsmen encourage Cholly to get on with it, finish what he is about. 'With a violence born of total helplessness' he does.[2] That scene, cruelly lit by the white men's lamps and their contempt, a vicious rupturing of a single moment of innocence and pleasure, is crucial to an understanding of Toni Morrison's extraordinary first novel, *The Bluest Eye*, and of insights about men, and women's relations with them, which are offered by women who have written novels out of experiences of multiple oppression, as women who are poor or Black or both. Cholly is marked by that moment, and it is also a moment which has been predicted for him:

> Sullen, irritable, he cultivated his hatred of Darlene. Never did he once consider directing his hatred toward the hunters. Such an emotion would have destroyed him. They were big, white, armed men. He was small, black, helpless.[3]

Left at four days old by his mother on a junk heap by the railroad, uncertain even of his father's name, brought up by the old woman who has just died, he flees from Darlene now as he imagines his father must have fled from his mother. The father he finds is an angry, balding and frightened man, who, 'in a vexed and whiny voice shouted at Cholly, "Tell that bitch she get her money. Now, get the fuck outta my face!"'[4]

For most of the novel we see with the eyes of Claudia, a small girl living with her sister and her mother and father in a poor, Black neighbourhood of Lorain, Ohio. Her sharp child's vision and questions are woven with the stories she might one day tell herself in answer to those questions, and both are punctuated by the progressively more jumbled words of a child's school reader as it adumbrates, with lunatic inadequacy, the essential features of the perfect white family living in mindless accord in its perfect green and white house. Until that return to Cholly's illuminated deflowering the novel is orchestrated from the sounds of women's anger: as little girls, as wives and mothers, as the three whores, who preside in mocking splendour over the antics of the families in the street. Claudia dismembers her dimpled white doll. Her mother croons arias of rage at the mess in her life and her house, which is hers to clean up. Down the road and at each other's throats are Cholly Breedlove and his wife (who is not, of course, Darlene) and their two children. Sammy has run away from home twenty-seven times and will soon leave for good. Pecola, pitied by Claudia and her sister, and cowed by her parents, her ugliness and her life, longs only for blue eyes and beauty. When her father rapes her she senses that he does so as a gesture of helpless love, for 'What could a burned-out black man say to the hunched back of his eleven-year-old daughter?'[5] Cholly flees again and dies. His daughter's baby by him is miscarried. Claudia and her sister have tried to intervene magically on behalf of the baby, and have failed. A self-deluding healer and paederast, the blanched and withered offspring of generations of collusion between slave-owners and slaves, writes confessionally to God:

We in this colony took as our own the most dramatic, and the most obvious, of our white master's characteristics, which were, of course, their worst. In retaining the identity of our race, we held fast to those characteristics most gratifying to sustain and least troublesome to maintain. Consequently we were not royal but snobbish, not aristocratic but class-conscious; we believed authority was cruelty to our inferiors, and education was being at school. We mistook violence for passion, indolence for leisure, and thought recklessness was freedom. We raised our children and reared our crops; we let infants grow, and property develop. Our manhood was defined by acquisitions. Our womanhood by acquiescence. And the smell of your fruit and the labor of your days we abhorred.[6]

The novel is neither simply condemnatory nor deterministic, nor is it self-pitying. The tragic circularity in the histories of the men and the women and the children in it is revealed by quite a different light from the bleak torches of the gloating white hunters. Claudia's intelligence and clarity are the author's, and so is her compassion. Both of them know that the real enemy is the one which binds these human beings to one another because it lurks somewhere outside themselves in a society which shirks responsibility for their miseries by invoking freedom for the individual. The ways in which Black people may be beguiled by White culture are understood here as lethally the product of relentless and pervasive white racism. Cholly's wife even welcomes her husband's villainies, for they provide her with the excuse she wants to redeem her life as the dependable servant of that perfect white family her daughter meets in her school reader. Claudia dismembers her doll, but she envies the neatly dressed and prettily whitish girl who is the most popular girl in the school.

Pecola dreams of blue eyes and goes mad from believing she has them. An exemplary Black family, light-skinned and stand-offish, do not become white, but they do become racist. The novel's tragedies are sexual, acts of sex which wound and divide and perpetuate weakness through violent aggression by men on women: acts of love truncated by pain. Women retaliate, with whorish vindictiveness, or with rejection or with a terrible tidiness:

While he moves inside her, she will wonder why they didn't put the necessary but private parts of the body in some more convenient place – like the armpit, for example, or the palm of the hand. Someplace one could get to easily, and quickly, without undressing. She stiffens when she feels one of her paper curlers coming undone from the activity of love; imprints in her mind which one it is that is coming loose so she can quickly secure it once he is through.[7]

Writers like Toni Morrison, Alice Walker, Tillie Olsen, Paule Marshall and Maxine Hong Kingston, all of whom are Americans, writing out of their lives within communities which are poor and powerless in a racist, capitalist and sexist society, are in a position to tell us essential things about that society. We cannot, in any simple way, suggest that Toni Morrison's relation to modern America or even to the small Black community where she grew up is equivalent to the position of Jane Austen within the English gentry of the early nineteenth century or of George Eliot to the professional world she moved in as an adult. As women they could be said to share only the very general knowledge that they are not men, and that not being men involves forms of dependence on men and ambivalence towards them, towards other women and towards themselves. That could be subsumed under a notion like 'patriarchy', but I have wanted to avoid that term, as a simplification, which can too easily propose ahistorical or even biological explanations of women's relations to men. I have, for different reasons, wanted to avoid giving primacy to an analysis based on class, for in important respects women are dislocated, excluded and reductively placed by most accounts of class which are structural and founded on economic relations. Yet any analysis of women's social and psychological situation which is feminist in its diagnosis and its proposals for change can ignore neither patriarchal explanations nor ones based on class struggle. It is also possible to say that Jane Austen and Toni Morrison testify to a doubleness in their view of men which is not caught by and must overflow even the most sophisticated understandings of those difficult abstractions. It is, of course, a truism that a feminist politics is bound to be different from other politics,[8] though it is one worth insisting on. One difficulty for feminist debate has been its reliance on models and alignments within male political traditions which cannot be reconciled.

Juliet Mitchell, for instance, mounts her powerful defence of Freud on the function of his theory for a feminist politics, which must start, in her view, from the reality of all social organisation as patriarchal:

Freud's analysis of the psychology of women takes place within a concept that it is neither socially nor biologically dualistic. It takes place within an analysis of patriarchy. His theories give us the beginnings of an explanation of the inferiorized and 'alternative' (second sex) psychology of women under patriarchy. Their concern is with how the human animal with a bisexual psychological disposition becomes the sexed social creature – the man or the woman.[9]

For Mitchell, 'psychoanalysis is not a recommendation *for* a patriarchal society, but an analysis *of* one',[10] and she proposes this in the interests of a Marxist feminism, which must go beyond economic explanations of women's position in relation to production, labour and class if it is to get the measure of the problem for all women in all kinds of society. For her as for Sheila Rowbotham the feminist enterprise is a socialist one, yet Sheila Rowbotham has sharply queried the usefulness of the term 'patriarchy' and the implications of resorting to it:

However, the word 'patriarchy' presents problems of its own. It implies a universal and historical form of oppression which returns us to biology – and thus it obscures the need to recognise not only biological difference, but also the multiplicity of ways in which societies have defined gender. By focusing upon the bearing and rearing of children ('patriarchy' = the power of the father) it suggests there is a single determining cause of women's subordination. This either produces a kind of feminist base-superstructure model to contend with the more blinkered versions of Marxism, or it rushes us off on the misty quest for the original moment of male supremacy. Moreover, the word leaves us with two separate systems in which a new male/female split is implied. We have patriarchy oppressing women and capitalism oppressing male workers. We have biological reproduction on the one hand and work on the other. We have the ideology of 'patriarchy' opposed to the mode of production, which is seen as a purely economic matter.[11]

A feminist politics must address the position of women in societies which are divisively organised in terms of class and race in the interests of a small minority. Women are separated from each other by those divisions, and are never unproblematically included within them, since women's structural relation to the means of production must include, besides their position as paid workers, the nature of their unpaid work and the character of their economic dependence on men. 'Patriarchy' could, like 'biological difference', serve as no more than a form of functional explanation, delivered *post hoc*, for women's oppression and exclusion and for the nature of their specific inclusions. The word also encourages forms of idealism, universalism, ahistorical approaches and a feminist politics given to deploring rather than to critical and utopian planning. It could also suggest that it is actual fathers who cause the trouble. Yet it is clear that we need a way of conceptualising the ubiquitous construction of the female as inferior. We need, for instance, the kind of explanation which can unravel the fact that women's experience of their bodies as changeable, because of their reproductive potential, should also mark them in societies like ours as 'unreliable' rather than as superbly and sensitively adaptable. 'Patriarchy' is a difficult abstraction, but as that it also measures out the terrain which is at issue. That terrain overlaps with women's exclusions and inclusions, with their historical and material oppression and with those social structures which characterise the way in which their oppression is both shared with men and different. If 'patriarchy' is allowed to stand for those powers which construe and confirm what is female as inferior then its very abstraction makes room for challenge and manoeuvre.

There can be a dangerous sentimentality in insisting on what women have in common, or in there being, beneath centuries of cultural accretion, something like a 'pure' unhampered woman, struggling to get out. Culture is not helpfully understood as accretion, anyway, least of all when we are considering the cultural learning of lack or negativity. We would be disappointed if we looked to Toni Morrison and Jane Austen for some common 'feminine' character which was independent of their social development as women, unless we saw 'feminine' simply as what is negatively perceived as that within patriarchy. For what we may learn from both writers is in fact something of what it has been to be a woman and to write as a woman within particular, historical versions of social arrangements which have differently defined them as being women. Those social arrangements will not be comprehensively presented or accounted for in their novels, of course. Yet in both cases we are confronted with the way in which a woman views her relation to a class or a community and to men, who have themselves developed their identity from the power exercised within the whole society by that class or community, or upon them.

We have heard from women who have expressed their own possibilities, or lack of them, in terms of their fathers or their brothers. We have seen how that kind of insight allowed them to develop broader understandings about society and about power and individual freedom. Harriet Martineau's most passionate attachment and regret were felt in relation to a younger brother, who could outstrip her, eclipse her and become alien to her. It is possible to see a connection between that lesson and her struggles on behalf of women and the abolition of slavery. The difficulty for white and, as it were, middle-class, women writers has often been that even where their position as women has made them dependent on men and restricted by men's plans for them, they have also been beguiled by what their particular men could offer them as protection, love and values. Resistance to fathers and to the class and to the social organisation for which those fathers stood would have involved them in a rejection of certainties about men, real and actual men, and therefore about themselves, which were too dangerous to contemplate. So that a good deal of what could be won by such women was to be won by cajolery and deceit. Dimly, out of the corner of one eye, they were able to see what happened to women who lost men's protection or had never had it, sometimes because their fathers had none to offer them or because they were dead. It is possible to see Emma's championing of Harriet as inspired by a sympathy of that kind, even if it is also a sympathy which is risky and unrealistic. It is certainly not surprising that a novelist like Jane Austen did not recommend that a young woman explore the possibilities of living outside men's protection.

In the last chapter we saw how women coming to British and American society from outside it, writers like Jean Rhys, Christina Stead and Doris Lessing, began to develop in their novels an analysis of women's position, which made connections between sexual and social relations within any society based on class and race inequality. If that kind of insight was unavailable to Jane Austen, another kind was possible for her. Her heroines negotiate the difficult passage between the imperfections of actual fathers and their own lifelong dependence on forms of social paternalism. If 'patriarchy' is to work for a feminist political analysis it will need to account for more than the individual father.

In a family or a community assaulted by a racism so violent that it threatens lives and livelihoods and becomes a determining influence on individual and communal self-identity, the father, as symbol of the whole society's patriarchal or paternalist organisation, is transformed in reality into a figure both more terrible and more pitiable to his daughters than any symbol of fatherhood. The fatherly authority, gathered and bolstered in principle from the father's position in the world outside the family, is grossly undermined. Humiliated by the men who have power over him and who may deny him the means of working to support himself and his family (a particular requirement of fathers in a capitalist economy, after all), goaded and likely to be defeated by male competitiveness in the outside world, he returns to his family and to women, and wreaks on them a kind of vengeance for their denial of the consolation his very fury makes it impossible for them to give him. It is not a situation easy to emerge from affirmatively or with optimism, whether for a man or for a woman.

Black women have traditionally occupied the lowest position, economically, socially and sexually, in any society organised by white people, and they are right to suspect the motives of any white person who congratulates them on the strength and the resilience which some of them have won for themselves in spite of that position. Many Black women writers do present such strength and resilience, however, even as they record the appalling human misery with which their mothers and grandmothers as well as they and their contemporaries have had to contend. Out of injustice and fear have come novels by women which, in their creative and analytical intelligence, are able to give life and reality to perceptions about sexual relations as inevitably linked to and embedded within historically institutionalised forms of violence and control.

The language of *The Bluest Eye* is tense, exact, exuberant; responsive to all that is seen and heard, tough and delicate about feelings which can seem raw and devastating. Shared meanings are spoken or sung in chorus, made to be more and less than individual communication. There *is* affirmation and optimism in the energy with which the author and her small heroine meet the demands made on them by the lives lived in the novel. In it, the first and immediate enemy for Black women are Black men, but it is that admission which releases the novel's sympathy for these men's vulnerability and its anger. It has not been easy to make that admission, for it could seem to suggest an alliance with racist explanations of Black men's treatment of Black women. It is hard to think of many white women writers who are able to express pity or love for the men who harm women and who are also able to move from that to an understanding of the predicament women share with men and which divides them so disastrously from them. That understanding is political, and some of the writers who show us how to make it share it as a basic tenet of political faith. In 1977, the National Black Feminist Organization delivered a statement about their work since their first meetings in 1974, which announced their primary difference from other women's groups in America. A significant passage runs:

> We reject the stance of lesbian separatism because it is not a viable political analysis or strategy for us. It leaves out far too much and far too many people, particularly black men, women, and children. We have a great deal of criticism and loathing for what men have been socialized to be in this society: what they support, how they act, and how they oppress. But we do not have the misguided notion that it is their maleness, per se – i.e., their biological maleness – that makes them what they are.[12]

That statement carries meanings which reverberate through several of the novels written by Black women since the fifties. It acknowledges Black women's desperation with Black men and places that desperation firmly within the effects of racism and poverty in a capitalist society. It sees women's lives as intimately connected with men and with children, with family and race solidarities, while recognising the need for women to consider their problems as women who are trapped equally by their position in society and by their position in the family, and who can expect, therefore, little support from men.

Selina sat beside the mother on the bride's side, surrounded by all the faces she saw at every wedding. Always, on these occasions, she loved them. The lavish gowns, the earrings, the small beaded purses made them like ordinary people who loved dressing up and being gay. She saw Iris Hurley, majestic in mauve satin, her wide nose taut with watchfulness, and Florrie Trotman with her abundant breasts constrained in red lace and Virgie Farnum sitting unperturbed amid her restive brood in an off-white satin gown which matched her skin.

Their husbands sat with them, and Selina tried to discern in those inscrutable faces some trace of the faults ascribed to them by their wives. She saw nothing. They simply looked solemn and harmless in the tuxedos. Only the mother was without her husband, and even though her head still rose and fell in that proud elaborate bow, Selina detected a masked but unutterable longing in her glance.[13]

This scene, from Paule Marshall's first novel, *Brown Girl, Brownstones*, which was published in 1959, catches a good deal of the novel's humour and texture as well as its heroine's predicament. Selina Boyce is a young girl who is watched growing up in Brooklyn before and during the Second World War in a family and a community of Barbadians, who had been arriving in America since 1900. She is wiry and tough-minded, bent on an independence which begins as resistance to her family – to the gentle dutifulness of her sister, Ina, for instance – and grows beyond family and community to take on the implications of being a Black woman in America in the middle of this century.

Initially, it is the characters of her father and mother which frame her perceptions of the world and her own dilemma. Her mother – always *the* mother in the novel – has often seemed invincibly antagonistic and even dangerous. When the adult Selina remembers her she sees 'the mother hacking a way through life like a man lost in the bush'.[14] Her father is evasive, elegant, charming, given to skimping on courses in accountancy or trumpet playing, which he takes up in the hope of making his fortune. Pride makes it impossible for him to confront the truth about America, as his wife courageously and yet damagingly does. He has inherited a small patch of land in Barbados, and this becomes his dream of a return home, of a proud, elegant, free life.

The marriage is already riven by defensiveness and distrust when the mother announces that she has sold the land in Barbados, behind her husband's back, and plans to invest the money in buying the brownstone house they rent. The father retaliates by blowing the money on expensive presents for them all, bought in the wonderland stores of Fifth Avenue. The scene when he returns from his shopping spree provides one of several astonishing moments in the novel when Selina finds herself locked into a parental battle which spells impossible oppositions for her: between men and women, between America and the West Indies, between dreams and reality and between freedom and discipline. Then the father is injured at work. He retreats into the dubious fold of a plump charlatan called Father Peace, who adjures him to forget his family for God (and Father Peace):

'God is your father, your mother, your sister, your brother, your wife, your child, and you will never have another! The mother of creation is the mother of defilement. The word *mother* is a filthy word. When a person reaches God he cannot permit an earthly wife or so-called children to lead him away. God is all!'[15]

The mother reports her absconded husband to the immigration authorities and he dies, by suicide or suicidal carelessness, on his journey of deportation back to Barbados. The mother thrives, buys her house, exploits her lodgers and becomes a founder member of the Association of Barbadian Homeowners, a group of aspirant Barbadians who set their faces against including other Black or immigrant groups and who complacently settle for the most comfortable imitation of white American life the white society allows them.

Paule Marshall superbly makes Selina's development and maturing a matter of understanding these contradictions as they are lived within the lives of real people. It is important that most of them are not only Black, but recent immigrants, and that their sense of America's possibilities for them are modelled on the Jews, for whom many of them work and whose houses in Brooklyn they have taken over. The temptations for Selina are gigantic and conflicting ones. The mother, bonded with her women friends, proposes a fierce struggle, the abandonment of love and the embracing of the dollar: the kinds of success which the melting-pot prescribes. She is magnificent and appalling, powerful and painfully muddled. Against such blandishments the frail sensuality and charm of the father is infinitely appealing. Selina has the energy and talent of her mother. She does well at university, manages her studies and a love affair with Clive, a painter, who has wanted to escape from a similar background and is defeated by his own cynicism and by his mother's imperious demands on him. Selina finally leaves him, when he insists once too often on answering his mother's cry for help:

For a moment she thought he hesitated, she thought she even glimpsed his hand start toward her, but the effort died in his eyes and a cry – wrested from the hollow of his despair, rising up the wall encrusted with his defeats and fear – beat through the room, driving her back, 'What in the hell am I supposed to do? I'm the one who has her walking the streets talking to herself and people laughing at her!'[16]

The struggle between men and women is also felt as a struggle between children and their parents. The men and women who grow rich and strong in the Barbadian community are rewarded by blank, complacent, tractable children, their parents' energy and effort transformed into obedience and inertia. Selina learns to be protective of men who cannot stand up to their women and to nourish in herself the free-floating enthusiasms of her father, his grand disparagement of the ignominies involved for someone like him in 'getting on'. She ducks her mother's arguments and dogmatism, and is as swept into admiration for her as the reader finally is, by the force of her speech and by the quality of her anger:

'For years now I been trying to put little ambition in that man but he ain interested in making a head-way. He's always half-studying some foolishness that don pan out. Years back it was the car. He was gon be all this mechanic till he lose interest. Then it was radio repairing and radio guts spill all over the house and he still cun fix one. Now he start up with figures . . . I tell you I getting so I can't bear the sight of him. I does get a bad feel when he come muching me up 'pon a night. Virgie,' she whispered, her eyes narrowing menacingly, 'I feel I could do cruel things to the man.'[17]

She does do cruel things to the man, whose incompetence injures him and whose daughter can wonder, 'Why was he the seduced follower and not the god . . . ?'[18] The novel ends as Selina begins to accept that there has been a logic to the responses of both her

parents to their lives as Black immigrants in America. Her own
adult life begins with an immigration too, an exploration and a
return to Barbados. She has not been deported; nor will she
commit suicide.

   Paule Marshall is like other Black American women writers in
seeking to write history, the history of her family, and to rewrite
that history which has omitted to mention her as a woman or as a
Black person.[19] That double invisibility powers her chronicling,
and visibility and audibility are what is most potently registered.
Speech, clothes, bodies, rooms, noises, faces fill Selina's head.
Her dilemma can never quite be articulated nor move to resolutions outside the physical presence of people who are enacting
their own roles in the world and pressingly demanding confirmation of them. Her mother buys houses and fills their rooms
with people. Her father delights in silk undershirts and a golden
trumpet. It is women, though, resplendent as they are at the
wedding or soaring as they can be in their conversations, who
overwhelm men. It is also women who mourn the inability of men
to love them and fight alongside them. Sexual longing and its
realisations are part of Selina's self-discovery, learned from her
scrutiny of older women. Their pride in their bodies and in their
capacities for love and work, for grace and birth, hold a mysterious
pain for her. Those bodies are also the sites of their hatedness and
self-hatred, the beauty and the blackness for which they are
clipped, reminded of their place.[20]

   Selina receives complicated messages about sex from the adults
she watches. She knows that her father dresses up at least once a
week to visit a woman her mother scathingly calls his 'concubine'.
The woman who lives at the top of her family's house receives
callers at the weekend, who do not pay her. Selina grows up
knowing that women find men beautiful, that they long for them
sexually, and that that longing must often be submerged or denied
in the name of survival. Respectability and increasing prosperity
stifle the exuberance and delight of sex by legitimating it. Selina
dreads the fate of her compliant contemporaries:

The sanctioned embrace two nights a week, the burgeoning stomach, the neat dark children, the modest home on Long Island, the piano lessons to the neighbors' children and church each Sunday.[21]

Sexual love, the sexual act itself, holds conflicting meanings for women who are poor. Just as Toni Morrison's aspiring Black family are characterised by their joyless sex, so in Paule Marshall's novel, sex is diluted and even avoided by women who are struggling to better themselves and their families. To control sex becomes a way of controlling men and beginning to have some control over your own life as a woman. For poor women too, whether they are Black or white, sex focuses the paradox of their lives. It offers possibilities of love and warmth and pleasure and companionship in a grim life, with few other delights and little freedom or comfort. It offers the security of marriage or a continuing relationship and a man's love and protection. Yet it also becomes the cause of too many children, too little money, little chance to earn more, back-breaking, underpaid and unpaid work and illness. That can erode all trust between a man and a woman, a trust difficult enough to maintain anyway in a world which treats them as no more than an inadequate economic unit, of value (or worthlessness) to the outside world in terms only of the man's labour. Rape, in marriage, outside it, frequently incestuous, is a reality for such women; not just a provocation for a rallying cry against men, but an act feared and committed on them by men they know. Such women respond angrily and despairingly and out of a terrible knowledge of what has been done to the men who perpetrate such furious violences on them.

The Color Purple, Alice Walker's most recent novel, is a story of women's rebellion, a regenerative and affirming turning of the tables on men, whose brutality towards women may be understood but must also be resisted. With characteristic irony, the author reminds us in this story told through the letters of two Black sisters, Celie and Nettie, of the tradition of epistolary novels, in which sensitive young ladies bare their hearts to one another out of a very different version of social and emotional constraints on what they can know and tell. Celie's first letter, addressed to God when she is fourteen, asks for 'a sign letting me know what is happening to me'[22] and announces that she has been raped by the man she thinks of as her father. Celie is raped again and again, in body and spirit. The two children she bears are, she believes, snatched from her and dead. She is married off to an exhausted and brutal widower, and she submits as glumly to his assaults on her as to her duties as stepmother to children as old as she is. Her redeemer is a woman, Shug Avery, the one love of her husband's life, rackety, exciting, glamorous and a singer, who arrives at her old lover's house mortally ill. Celie nurses her back to life and falls in love with her. Shug teaches her about sexual pleasure, about love and about standing up for yourself.

The novel is full of women. Sofia, one of a family of strong sisters, stands up to her husband and to the white mayor, who has her beaten up and put in jail. Celie's sister Nettie has been educated and become a missionary in Africa. She has also, it turns out, rescued and brought up Celie's two lost children. Shug is less a fighter than an artist, who falls in and out of love, replenishes herself, sings, rests, exists confidently in herself. She is unaware of her own power over people and astonished only that other women are not as she is. She takes Celie away from her husband, teachers her to laugh, to make love and, wonderfully, encourages her to make trousers of every size and shape and kind, and through them to support herself.

The scene which Celie describes in a letter to Nettie, when Shug and Squeak and Sofia and she announce to their men that they are going off, leaving them, carries both the way in which Alice Walker takes us into the speech and the life of the people she is telling us about, and the men's astonishment at what is finally happening to them:

Oh, hold on hell, I say. If you hadn't tried to rule over Sofia the white folks never would have caught her.

Sofia so surprise to hear me speak up she ain't chewed for ten minutes.

That's a lie, say Harpo.

A little truth in it, say Sofia.

Everybody look at her like they surprise she there. It like a voice speaking from the grave.

You was all rotten children, I say. You made my life a hell on earth. And your daddy here ain't dead horse's shit.

Mr. _____ reach over to slap me. I jab my case knife in his hand.

You bitch, he say. What will people say, you running off to Memphis like you don't have a house to look after?

Shug say, Albert. Try to think like you got some sense. Why any woman give a shit what people think is a mystery to me.

Well, say Grady, trying to bring light. A woman can't git a man if peoples talk.

Shug look at me and us giggle. Then us laugh sure nuff. Then Squeak start to laugh. Then Sofia. All us laugh and laugh.

Shug say, Ain't they something? Us say um *hum*, and slap the table, wipe the water from our eyes.

Harpo look at Squeak. Shut up Squeak, he say. It bad luck for women to laugh at men.

She say, Okay. She sit up straight, suck in her breath, try to press her face together.

He look at Sofia. She look at him and laugh in his face. I already had my bad luck, she say. I had enough to keep me laughing the rest of my life.[23]

The novel is full of miracles and capaciously diverse solutions to Black women's predicament. Religion, fisticuffs, the poetry of abuse and women's friendship are traditional ones. Laughter, lesbianism, creativity and self-help are others. At the end of the novel Celie is back with a chastened husband. They can even discuss Shug, whom they have both loved:

Mr. _____ ast me the other day what it is I love so much bout Shug. He say he love her style. He say to tell the truth, Shug act more manly that most men. I mean she upright, honest. Speak her mind and the devil take the hindmost, he say. You know Shug will fight, he say. Just like Sofia. She bound to live her life and be herself no matter what.

Mr. _____ think all this is stuff men do. But Harpo not like this, I tell him. You not like this. What Shug got is womanly it seem like to me. Specially since she and Sofia the ones got it.

Sofia and Shug not like men, he say, but they not like women either. You mean they not like you or me.

They hold they own, he say. And it's different.

What I love best bout Shug is what she been through, I say. When you look in Shug's eyes you know she been where she been, seen what she seen, did what she did. And now she know.[24]

There is a celebratory and almost ecstatic quality in the novel as it moves from the brutalities of Celie's childhood to an understanding of herself and of men – Shug's 'Ain't they something?' – which is subtly expressed through the increasing confidence of her letter writing, the shift from tentativeness to speculation, even as she accepts that none of her letters appears to have reached its destination. Sex is central to the novel. Even Celie's brutal husband can be loving and is a good lover for Shug. Celie's discovery of her lesbian feelings is entirely positive, the finding of new territories and forms for love. That comes out of Shug's lessons to her that sex is a pleasure and never a right, and that women do not depend on men for their own sexual pleasure. Once women understand that they may be in a position to help men to understand it too.

Alice Walker wrote about her own family in an essay:

I desperately needed my father and brothers to give me male models I could respect, because white men (for example; being particularly handy in this sort of comparison) – whether in films or in person – offered man as dominator, as killer, and always as hypocrite.

My father failed because he copied the hypocrisy. And my brothers – except for one – never understood they must represent half the world to me, as I must represent the other half to them.[25]

Significantly, Alice Walker adds a footnote to that piece: 'Since this essay was written, my brothers have offered their name, acknowledgment, and some support to all their children.'[26] In one of her stories a young Black painter 'found black men impossible to draw or to paint; she could not bear to trace defeat onto blank pages.'[27] Alice Walker has often drawn men, comically, lovingly, sadly and angrily. In *The Color Purple* she provides the possibility for a miraculous redemption for men, as a by-product of women's laughter, creativity and delight in themselves.

Any white woman is bound to feel hesitant in ascribing strengths to these Black women writers as they make out of their experience and out of Black experience generally novels which so exhilaratingly defy constraints on what they write and how. Yet it is worth considering as one reads them whether this sense of strength may not be connected with their freedom from the cajolery and deceit which, I have wanted to suggest, is the white woman's strategy for entering what she knows as a male tradition of narrative and of novels. These are women who are making their own tradition, with little or no cap-doffing to men.

Tillie Olsen is a white writer who comes, as she puts it, 'from generations of illiterate women'[28] and who makes the sexual relation between men and women the site of women's vulnerability and the focus of the damage perpetrated on generations of human beings by capitalism. In *Yonnondio: From the Thirties*, a novel written partly in her early twenties and retrieved by her later after years of bringing up children and working, which made writing almost impossible for her, a young couple and their five children straggle across America, from mining town to arid farmland and back to the slums of a big city, as Jim, the father, tries to find work.

For several weeks Jim Holbrook had been in an evil mood. The whole household walked in terror. He had nothing but heavy blows for the children, and he struck Anna too often to remember. Every payday he clumped home, washed, went to town, and returned hours later, dead drunk. Once Anna had questioned him timidly concerning his work; he struck her on the mouth with a bellow of 'Shut your damn trap.'

Anna too became bitter and brutal. If one of the children was in her way, if they did not obey her instantly, she would hit at them in a blind rage, as if it were some devil she was exorcising. Afterward, in the midst of her work, regret would cramp her heart at the memory of the tear-stained little faces. ' 'Twasn't them I was beatin up on. Somethin just seems to get into me when I have somethin to hit.'[29]

The marriage bed, which can still be a refuge from the harshness of their lives, an invitation to tenderness and affection, becomes the place where Jim brutally impregnates her with another child they cannot afford and whose birth makes her ill and destroys her youth and her optimism and energy. Jim is too undermined by the degradations of his own life and his responsibilities for his family's to realise what he is doing. Anna conceives again, and eventually the doctor is called when she miscarries:

'How old's the baby?' (Damn fools, they ought to sterilize the whole lot of them after the second kid.)
'Four months, mm. You remember how long your wife's been feeling sick?' Of course not. These animals never notice but when they're hungry or want a drink or a woman.
'Hmmmm. Yes.' She took the ergot down quietly, but moaned at the hypo. 'So it was intercourse before as well as the fall?' Pigsty, the way these people live. 'And she's been nursing all along? We'll have a look at the baby.' Rickets, thrush, dehydrated; don't blame it trying to die. 'Viosterol is what it needs – and a dextri-maltose formula.'[30]

Jim is reproved (as Anna is too); and rest, fresh fruit, even a private doctor are prescribed for his wife. The beatings, the drunkenness, the marital rapes, realities of Anna's appalling life and of her most intimate relationship and sense of herself, become paradoxically precious and private as they are exposed to the superior, uncomprehending doctor. Against him and his view of their lives Anna's loyalty is to her husband. The novel ends with a wry affirmation of this. The family, in their stinking, fetid rooms, is nearly extinguished by a heat wave. They survive, and Anna's last words to her husband are:

'Here, I'll help you. The air's changin, Jim. I see for it to end tomorrow, at least get tolerable. Come in and get freshened up.'[31]

In the title story of *Tell Me A Riddle* Tillie Olsen elaborates on that insight in her wonderful story about the last year in the lives of an old married couple, who have reached a complete deadlock in their marriage, though they still share a bed and hold on to each other in the night. The wife is ill and angrily and resentfully dying, clinging to her domestic duties out of anger and an obsession with order and cleanliness, which reminds us of *Yonnondio*'s disgusted doctor and his disapproval. Her husband is constantly rebuked by that obsession, and he tries to persuade her to move into an old people's home, where they would be looked after and she would be spared the housework. He ignores her need to cling to her duties as an expression of her bitterness and her need to hurt him. He and their children long to release her, now that they are no longer so poor, to show her that they have loved her and appreciated her. It is too late; not only because she is dying, but because too much was asked of her in her youth, too much taken, and now she is unable to forgive either her husband or her children. She recoils from a new grandchild, lovingly placed in her arms as a sure-fire mollifier:

It was not that she had not loved her babies, her children. The love – the passion of tending – had risen with the need like a torrent; and like a torrent drowned and immolated all else. But when the need was done – oh the power that was lost in the painful damming back and drying up of what still surged, but had nowhere to go. Only the thin pulsing left that could not quiet, suffering over lives one felt, but could no longer hold nor help.[32]

Her cry to her husband, 'Go, go. All your life you have gone without me'[33] is a cry of rage and frustration with men, and, heartbreakingly, with the man who is nearer to her than any other human being, whose bed and life she has made herself a part of, and who is now, belatedly, anxious to express his concern and love for her. Yet he is the enemy, the one who has drained her of herself, if unwittingly, weakly, and as the pawn in a network of social relations which reduces him to becoming the oppressor of his own wife. Her cry of rage is a cry out of the 'silence' required of her as a woman, a 'silence' which Tillie Olsen makes both the stifling and muffling of human creativity and speech, and the particular silence of women who speak, but cannot quite hear themselves or be heard by others. Only on her deathbed can the old woman emit the strange noises which express a life in which she has not been able to practise speaking her own language, speaking for herself.

The power of these writers comes in part from their determination to record the experiences of people who have been allowed to be invisible and inaudible and from the forms and the language they have found for doing so.[34] Yet it would be sentimental and irresponsible to read them solely as chroniclers of communities hanging precariously to the margins of a society whose accounts of itself have simply chosen to ignore them. They are four of the most vigorous and original artists alive. In an essay which grew out of an interview, Alice Walker writes about a course she taught on Black women writers. She lists the writers she included and adds, 'Also Kate Chopin and Virginia Woolf – not because they were black, obviously, but because they were women and wrote, as the black women did, on the condition of humankind from the perspective of women.'[35] That perspective has been enlarged and enriched, I believe, by women writing out of experiences in which class and race can make men, women's own men, their fathers and brothers and husbands and sons, their first and most dangerous enemy, as well as the first and most desired of allies.

Eva, the invincible matriarch of Toni Morrison's *Sula*, burns her beloved son to death. She can no longer bear his defeats and addictions,

'a big man can't be a baby all wrapped up inside his mamma no more; he suffocate. I done everything I could to make him leave me and go on and live and be a man but he wouldn't and I had to keep him out so I just thought of a way he could die like a man not all scrunched up inside my womb, but like a man.'[36]

It is the most horrifying and shocking expulsion of a man by a woman, of a son by his mother, yet it is also to be understood as the most courageous act of love by a woman in a world where her men are threatened and weakened and become threatening and weakening to women. It is an act which has been quite literally unthinkable for most women writers in the past, and it happens in a novel in which women's lives are connected in an absolutely direct way with economic and historical realities and within a community clinging for its life to a hillside, denied work or land or a voice in the society, where housing, the bearing of children, ill-health and a blank future make relations between men and women at once the most important and the most vulnerable aspect of their lives.

Morrison, Marshall and Walker share an ability to write about sex erotically, openly and honestly, without prurience and with humour and delight. They do so as women who recognise women's desire for men and can as easily contemplate women's desire for women. It is not that the tragedies they write about are simply explained in terms of race and poverty; but that human relations, and most particularly sexual ones, are seen as the site of conflict for women. That conflict is never simply the product of either a patriarchal order or a capitalist economy, though both contribute to make women the recipients of the impossible contradictions faced by men, who are cast in the larger society as fathers and breadwinners and must inevitably in such a society be bad fathers and inadequate breadwinners. Virginia Woolf's minimum requirement for a woman writer of five hundred pounds a year and a room of one's own is not invalidated by the testimony of a writer like Tillie Olsen, though it is revealed as the tip of the iceberg; for it ignores the contradictions set up by a society which forces 'the working-class family to shoulder responsibility for its dependants',[37] and to do so on a wage determined by profits rather than need.

Angela Carter is right to insist that a 'free-masonry exists because of certain basic similarities between the experience of all, or almost all, women *as* women. Indeed, anywhere I go in the world, I can, given a few basic words in common, have perfectly splendid conversations with other women about babies, cooking, sex, and what dolts men are.'[38] She is also right to remind us to beware of the dangerous implications of a feminism which starts from there, for 'The sense of an emotional bond is created by ignoring the disparate circumstances of social reality; and this is an improper use of language since social reality may only be perceived through, and is in part created by, language.'[39] It is not just to a solidarity amongst women that the novels I have discussed contribute, but to a respect for the multiplicity of women's lives and insights, to their energy and flexibility and ingenuity. Acknowledging multiplicity is a beginning, for it attacks those assumptions underlying oppositions and polarities which have so oversimplified and constrained women's life options and their sense of them.

I have also wanted to point to continuities; and 'what dolts men are' is a part of those. 'Dolts' is, after all, a friendly if critical term, hardly an injunction to massacre. What Jane Austen might be said to share with Toni Morrison and with other women writers is an urge to explore, within the limits of the worlds they knew, how a woman can be admirable, legitimately proud of herself and her life, confident and creative. They also share a knowledge that it is not in any simple way men who prevent them from being and seeing themselves as admirable, for as Juliet Mitchell puts it, 'Under patriarchal order women are oppressed in their very psychologies of femininity.'[40] Both Austen and Morrison make clear, though they express it with significant differences, that women's sexual lives, their capacity to give birth, the using and spending of their bodily energies, have always been intimately interwoven with economics. They both make it clear in their work that women are implicated in a historical collusion to explain their dependence on and inferiority to men as natural. Both of them have shown how, nonetheless, women have found, within the interstices of that socially affirmed and ambiguously conceded inferiority, areas of power for themselves, and both have shown that those areas (of influence over their children, for instance, or through their very desirability to men) are liable to extend and complicate the trap women already find themselves in.

Women have had power, and yet they have often felt that power as blighting. Moreover, they have learned that the power they are offered and have taken, in their families, their homes, occasionally at work, can be used against them. They have learned to see female power as men have seen it: as subversive, dangerous, even monstrous, and they have found that what began as a retreat into domesticity, into the control of space and time and sustenance in the home, becomes a rationale for their exclusion from the world outside and the world of men. We cannot begin to understand the workings of power in the actual lives of men and women and children if we stick to an account of its sources which is dictated by metaphors of God, the father, the Crown or even the stock exchange. We need, if we are to understand what women novelists have been telling us, a model of power and of the ways it is exercised and resisted which is less like a child's drawing of the sun, holding all light and heat in itself and sending down, straight and direct, rays to be received on earth. Such a model excludes multiplicity and movement and change, or it makes change impossible to contemplate outside the kind of mass movement which women's dislocated position in a male stratified society has made nearly inconceivable. Most theories of power and of resistance to power have left women in a posture of passivity – of gamely cutting the sandwiches – which is remote from the kinds of energy and insight I have wanted to account for in women writers.

How are we to understand how power has worked to marginalise women if we are also to preserve historical specificity and the quite different material effects of that power on particular women? Women's relation to class and to men has not on the whole been well served by Marxist models of domination or hegemony, which have subsumed women into the class of their fathers and husbands. Nor does Engels's analysis of marriage under capitalism becoming 'prostitution' amongst the bourgeoisie but egalitarian within the working class help us to understand the destructive impact of poverty on marriages such as those Tillie Olsen describes.[41] Most theoretical models have failed to include women's relation to any society organised to promote male work and male pleasure, to the economy and to the actual men through whom women are to expect forms of protection and pleasure for themselves. They have failed to or thought it unnecessary, on the grounds that such arrangements had already divided women from each other, on the assumption that their primary loyalty would always be to men.

At first sight Michel Foucault's theory of how power operates in a society has seemed to allow room for the kinds of experience of it which women have written about in their novels:

Power's condition of possibility, or in any case the viewpoint which permits one to understand its exercise, even in its more 'peripheral' effects, and which also makes it possible to use its mechanisms as a grid of intelligibility of the social order, must not be sought in the primary existence of a central point, in a unique source of sovereignty from which secondary and descendent forms would emanate; it is the moving substrate of force relations which, by virtue of their inequality, constantly engender states of power, but the latter are always local and unstable. The omnipresence of power: not because it has the privilege of consolidating everything under its invincible unity, but because it is produced from one moment to the next, at every point, or rather in every relation from one point to another. Power is everywhere; not because it embraces everything, but because it comes from everywhere.[42]

For all its abstraction as an account of how power actually works in people's lives this does come closer, I think, to the powers, resistances and possibilities for change which we meet in women's writing, than those simpler models of monolithic male oppression and women's writing as a series of more or less satisfactory escape routes from it, which some critics have proposed. It allows, first, for writing in itself being a powerful act and operation for change. It also helps us to understand the way in which women have written about women who are simultaneously claiming power and recoiling from the implications of doing so. It allows us to forgive ourselves as readers for reading *as if* we were men at times, and to forgive women writers for writing occasionally *as if* they were men. It makes it possible to connect Toni Morrison's murdering mother with the collision between stories by men which cast the mother as a murderer, and stories by women which accept that role and explain it completely differently.

Foucault makes power an endlessly diffused electricity, inescapably pervasive of social life, and carried in social discourses, ways of talking and writing about people or things or ideas or experiences, which are historically made and remade to bear and manipulate power relations between people. So that there are gaps and ruptures, in language and therefore of authority, between, for instance, the ways in which a group of mothers may talk about their babies, a conference of obstetricians, a written report on infant mortality and a biology lesson on the reproduction of the runner bean. A woman may be an authoritative expert in the first, a case study in the second, a statistic in the third and a qualified biologist or ghostly analogy in the fourth. The discourses of each situation are historically constituted, and in their turn those discourses constitute the same woman as having at different times different kinds of power and authority in relation to other people and to forms of knowledge. Foucault puts it like this:

Discourses are not once and for all subservient to power or raised up against it, any more than silences are. We must make allowance for the complex and unstable process whereby discourse can be both an instrument and an effect of power, but also a hindrance, a stumbling-block, a point of resistance and a starting point for an opposing strategy. Discourse transmits and produces power; it reinforces it, but also undermines and exposes it, renders it fragile and makes it possible to thwart it. In like manner, silence and secrecy are a shelter for power, anchoring its prohibitions; but they also loosen its holds and provide for relatively obscure areas of tolerance.[43]

If we were to decide that such a model of power and of the discourses which construct its manifestations is helpful for an understanding of women's accounts of their predicament now and in the past, we should do so with the usual reservations. These passages are taken from Foucault's *The History of Sexuality, Volume One. An Introduction*, in which he proposes that such a history must inevitably be of the discourses about sexual behaviour (rather than a chronicle of what people might be said to have got up to) which were available, acceptable or denied at different times and by different people. Yet the relevance to this of what women could think or know or tell about the subject is barely at issue. It would be characteristically paradoxical if women were to develop their own theory of power out of one proposed by a man, who is not exercised by women's relation to historically developed discourses about sex and sexuality. It might seem equally paradoxical to defend that theory against the sort of critique of it which asserts its quietistic and circular effect on political analysis or action, as Edward Said does, when he claims that Foucault makes no allowance for

emergent movements, and none for revolutions, counter-hegemony, or historical blocks. For in human history there is always something beyond the reach of dominating systems, no matter how deeply they saturate society, and this is obviously what makes change possible, limits power in Foucault's sense, and hobbles the theory of that power.[44]

And yet women have waited expectantly and in vain for those 'emergent movements' or 'historical blocks' and have too often found themselves submerged within causes with which they are bound to have sympathy, but whose rationales, analyses and proposals ignore their interests. Foucault was an historian of institutions and therefore of men, yet his theory of power may enable us to understand what it is that women have been telling us about their complicated manoeuvres of acquiescence *and* resistance, of seeing themselves as men see them and seeing men as men are not able to see themselves. It may help us to disentangle the anomalies there have been for women in entering the discourses of writing and of novels as themselves. It could begin to explain why some of them chose forms of anonymity or masculine disguise, while others accepted what could be a disfiguring role as sybil, gifted woman, speaking for other women, but in voices which men were tuned to understand. To say that a woman writes as a woman or reads as a woman is to do no more than insist that she does those things with the same body and the same mind and the same experience of life that she does all those other things which have been allowed, wrongly, to be so unproblematically female. Women are never unproblematically female, and their novels, their adventures, their language will continue to be mis-read and misunderstood if they are simply included as men or excluded as women.

Mama, the central character in several of Lorna Tracy's stories,[45] is a young woman remembering her earliest days at school:

Mama wasn't sure when all this business had started with her but it had been at a very early age. She seemed always to have felt this way. Perhaps, though, it had something to do with the popularity in her kindergarten of 'Farmer in the Dell' which was all to do with choosing and leaving out. Mama felt now – when she thought about it at all – that she had not often been chosen, that she had usually trudged with a few others round and round and round the growing crowd of her little elected peers who faced her smugly from inside the circle and this made Mama feel sad about herself. But Mama knew that, to be fair, she had felt queer and uncomfortable whenever she had been chosen to stand inside. She had wanted to be chosen, yet when she had been it was never really nice. If she was included she was ill at ease; if she was overlooked she might be sad, but at least she was easy. Nevertheless she went on wanting to be chosen.[46]

That story, with its shuffling of attitudes to experiences of inclusion and exclusion, echoes Virginia Woolf's response to what both beckoned and repelled her in Cambridge: 'I thought how unpleasant it is to be locked out; and I thought how it is worse perhaps to be locked in.'[47] It would be easy enough, of course, to make of those experiences paradigms of the general human condition. They are too fundamentally characteristic of the accounts women have given in their novels of their own position in relation to men to generalise from them in quite that way. Women have wanted to be let in and have been appalled both at what they might be let in *to*, and at the terms on which they were permitted to enter. They have rationalised their ambivalence in different ways and have increasingly taken their courage in both hands and demanded to be let in, but as women and on their own terms. Once in, they have discovered the justification for what had seemed, even to them, impudence or temerity. They discovered that they were inside anyway, half the world as it is, and that what they had to say about war and politics and literature was as significant as what they had been allowed to say about families and love. Once in, it has been possible for women to discount their disqualifications as no more than a function of that version of what women are which had excluded them in the first place.

It has not been a matter of women's ignorance about or detachment from war or politics or work, for instance, nor of their incapacity to talk about them. What has been at issue is their own learned doubt as to the validity of their knowledge and the appropriateness of their ways of communicating it in a world which has, as it were, determined what is valuable knowledge and acceptable ways of expressing it behind their backs. That is why women have needed to become bilingual and to wear men's clothes. It must be clear from the small sample of women's writing during the last two centuries which I have chosen to discuss that bilingualism and even male disguise are hardly to be seen as crippling drawbacks. Once they are understood for the strategies they are, we are able to gain from women's novels, and from the world seen by women which they offer us, the inestimable benefit of confronting multiplicity and subterfuge for what they are.

I am not the first person to have seen women's uses of language in terms of bilingualism,[48] though too often that analogy has seemed to allude to confusions, haltings and stutterings, speech which trips over itself rather than tripping along. Bilingualism has even been allowed to stand for *non*lingualism or silence. More than half the world's population regularly uses two or more languages (and I am not here referring particularly to the women amongst them). For that majority, bilingualism is not the problem, not the *cause* of the high probability that they will also be poor and unheard. I have also wanted to invoke experiences of immigration, of vagrancy and of the outsider to account for how women have understood their position, while conceding that the experience for Jane Austen of being 'outside' the English gentry in the early nineteenth century was significantly different from the way in which the granddaughter of slaves in America's south feels herself to be an 'outsider' in America today. To smudge those differences is unnecessary as well as unhelpful. For it has been exclusion alternating with conditional inclusion which women have written about, and it is forms of exclusion and ambiguous inclusion which women recognise in each other and which they are in a position to recognise as the common property of most people on earth, now and in the past. People who are excluded do not always want to be included, to join the élite, though they are often tempted to because the élite have, amongst other things, given themselves an excellent press. The strengths of women's writing have more and more grown out of a sense of what women share with each other and with all those people, most especially children, who are not carefully listened to. As the marginal becomes mainstream the sybil becomes representative. Adrienne Rich's women, 'wakened by a child's cry from their eternally unfinished dreams',[49] gather power from the meanings of that experience for most people in the world.

I shall end with two novels by Maxine Hong Kingston, *The Woman Warrior* and *China Men*, because they tell women's and men's stories and because they show how we learn who we are and what we may become through stories. Maxine Hong Kingston grew up in a Chinese community in California. Her confusions came to her through the stories her mother told her about China, the stories her father did not tell her and which she needed to reconstruct for herself, and through the worlds of Chinatown and Stockton, California, in which she grew up. She grew up a bilingual and finally 'stopped checking "bilingual" on job applications.'[50]

Whenever she had to warn us about life, my mother told stories that ran like this one, a story to grow up on. She tested our strength to establish realities. Those in the emigrant generations who could not reassert brute survival died young and far from home. Those of us in the first American generations have had to figure out how the invisible world the emigrants built around our childhoods fits in solid America.

The emigrants confused the gods by diverting their curses,

misleading them with crooked streets and false names. They must try to confuse their offspring as well, who, I suppose, threaten them in similar ways – always trying to get things straight, always trying to name the unspeakable. The Chinese I know hide their names; sojourners take new names when their lives change and guard their real names with silence.

Chinese-Americans, when you try to understand what things in you are Chinese, how do you separate what is peculiar to childhood, to poverty, insanities, one family, your mother who marked your growing with stories, from what is Chinese? What is Chinese tradition and what is the movies?[51]

In *The Woman Warrior* the mother goes in for talk-stories: tales and sagas which move between her past in China, a more distant past there, and the present world of ghosts, amongst whom Chinese people move invisibly and inaudibly. The stories are full of contradictions, of woman warriors and illustrations of the belief that it is 'better to raise geese than girls'. One story is about the suicide of an aunt, who threw herself in a well with her new-born baby, who was illegitimate. The mother tells her daughter:

'Don't tell anyone you had an aunt. Your father does not want to hear her name. She has never been born.' I have believed that sex was unspeakable and words so strong and fathers so frail that "aunt" would do my father mysterious harm. I have thought that my family, having settled among immigrants who had also been their neighbours in the ancestral land, needed to clean their name, and a wrong word would incite the kinspeople even here. But there is more to this silence: they want me to participate in her punishment. And I have.[52]

Through all the whirling, conflicting stories that the novel's nameless heroine hears, tells and participates in she is also constructing herself, and in two languages: 'And all the time I was having to turn myself American-feminine, or no dates.'[53] The pressure is on her to speak, to hear herself speak. She torments a Chinese girl at school who refuses to speak and she is tormented by her own silence, her whispered words, for 'Insane people were the ones who couldn't explain themselves.'[54]

The history of Chinese emigration to America is for the most part a story of men going to the 'Gold Mountain' for work and returning or sending for their wives and children. The story of the barbaric exploitation of Chinese men's labour, usually in order to build the railway, is one the men are too 'frail' or too bludgeoned to tell the girl. In *China Men*, Maxine Hong Kingston offers a parallel history to the one she has made of her own stories and her mother's. The prose changes. She works in libraries, ferrets out of history books what has usually been ignored by them, fills in the details imaginatively and ends the novel with an account of one of her brothers being sent to fight in Vietnam, though he has told her almost nothing about it. When he returns, ' "He's back," they said, typically talking about him in the third person.'[55] So little does she hear from men about their feelings and thoughts that she is obliged to invent for them, to save them from going mad. She even 'invented a plan to test my theory that males feel no pain; males don't feel.'[56] She invests them with 'our language a music that charms away common sense'[57] in order to understand whether they really mean the curses which she hears her father casually and terribly directing at women. She is not prepared to put up with men's silences and withdrawal, as her mother and older women generally have: 'once Ma Ma telephoned her brother after not having seen him for fifty years'.[58] She will not be one of those Chinese-Americans, 'the young men who listen'.[59] Only speech will break the spell of the white 'ghosts' and men's silence. In its surreptitious subversions the language of Maxine Hong Kingston's novels enacts Julia Kristeva's injunction to women writers to exploit their position in relation to language:

> If women have a role to play in this on-going process, it is only in assuming a *negative* function: reject everything finite, definite, structured, loaded with meaning, in the existing state of society.[60]

Maxine Hong Kingston demonstrates the power women have within their traditional discourses, sets that against men's and then invades English, literary English, history, education, American life, armed with brave new intelligences and secrets which she can be sure will be recognised by anyone who has known what it is to be stifled by their own silence.

Women have always had an appetite for each other's work, and gradually they have learned from each other to see their own oppression within larger oppressions and to be on their guard against all the temptations there are to collude with them. They begin to trust their own stories and adventures and their own ways of telling them, and need no longer be reduced to spinning yarns out of the only adventure they once had: the exiguous piece of ivory, the phantom escapade, which led to marriage to a man and saintly and obscured motherhood. Women writers have come a long way from those 'English women' Flora Tristan first met in 1826:

What a revolting contrast there is in England between the extreme servitude of women and the intellectual superiority of women authors! There is no evil, suffering, disorder, injustice or misery arising from the prejudices of society, from its organisation and its laws, that has escaped their observation. The writings of the English women who cast such a brilliant light upon the intellectual scene are a dazzling phenomenon – especially when one considers the absurd education they have had to undergo and the brutalising influence of the environment in which they have lived.[61]

We are not there yet. Three anecdotes remind us of that. A battle-scarred and successful writer, excitedly reporting from the front where, it seems, young people still read her books and clamour for her support as a feminist, can take a moment off to preach to them and to us:

I agreed that there are still many difficult changes to be made in most societies before women have an equal chance with men of fulfilling their potentialities, but, from my own experience none of the men with whom I have had a close relationship in my adult life have ever treated me as an inferior.[62]

A man, just young enough to know better and invited to interview a famous American feminist, can simultaneously marvel at the glossiness of her hair, her nails and her tactics, which involve nothing less than role-reversal. 'She puts the (white male) reader in a different racial or sexual circumstance – then asks how *he* likes it'.[63] It would indeed be marvellous if, after all these years, women were to be congratulated for that: their answer to the syllogism. Then a news item headed 'Bastion Falls' announces that the last Oxford college to accept women has decided to do so 'because they felt academic standards were declining and the college was becoming an easy option'.[64] We are still invited in only when men decide they cannot do without us. For all the gains which have been made in recognising women's right to equality with men, the material conditions of the world's population, and of most women amongst them, has not improved.

I have wanted to chart continuities as well as changes and progress in women's novels, and to do so by considering how women have written about men. Men in their lives and in their novels have stood for forms of power and authority, to which women have needed to attend and which they have also felt bound to resist. In transforming themselves from men's heroines into tellers of their own stories, women have expressed that transformation as a double vision of themselves and of the society which requires that double vision of them. They have written out of doubts and duplicities and they have focused on their exclusions and on the ambiguities of their inclusions. These contortions have been felt by both women and men as pathological, quite literally as forms of disease and abnormality. Yet in registering the need for such contortions women have been obliged to begin an analysis of social arrangements, to unpick those assumptions (and women have often shared them, after all) which allow the majority of the human race to be negatively defined.

Those who win authority or have it bestowed upon them are not as a rule well placed to understand the implications for other people of that authority, even when they would like to. Few people, it is true, have absolute authority in every aspect of their lives, and some women have wielded quite a lot of it. Yet women have in common the experience of standing in an ambiguous relation to most forms of authority and of having had to internalise the justice of their exclusion. This, I believe, has allowed them to know something, but not everything, about the reality of oppression (and some of the strategies for resisting it) which is the lot of most people in the world. If women have been sensitive to children, to the poor, to the unfortunate or to groups discriminated against for their beliefs or their colour or their class, it has not been out of some genetically transmitted tenderness of heart. Nor would it be reasonable to suggest that *all* women have been able to move from an understanding of their own position to the problems of other people's. Yet where they have been better at understanding the ways by which a society imprints individual and group psychology with its generalised contempt for them they have been so because they know what they are talking about, are able to write out of such experience. They have used their knowledge to develop a critique of marginalisation. Women who write possess a powerful instrument of resistance, a double-edged sword, which they have felt as dangerous and have sometimes kept sheathed.

Those men who have wanted to find themselves in women's novels, as their makers and heroes, have either deluded themselves into believing that that *was* what they found in them or expressed disappointment or even scorn when they did not. Women writers have seen themselves as rewriting, as telling familiar stories differently, as forging new forms and language out of the old. They needed the old forms because they were the forms which had told them who they were, which they had trusted and which they now had to remake. There is a feminist poetics evolving which marks out a women's tradition and traces its obliquities and its fluctuations in relation to that other tradition which has intended to subsume or subvert it. It is possible to see women's writing as central to an understanding of a world in which most human beings are coerced into agreement with a very small minority, prepared to promote its own interest as the general one and to consume miles and miles of gents' suiting as it does so.

Wise women can no longer be allowed as exceptions, eccentrics or witches, possessed of extra-human insight when they are possessed of any insight at all. Their rewriting of the human adventure is part of a necessary rewriting of history and of the future, which they will share with men. A politics which concerns itself with the future of the human race will need to refuse the blandishments of single or simple theories or solutions. It could do worse than begin from new readings of what women have said and written about a world organised to exclude them.

Notes

Introduction

1 Ralph Waldo Emerson, 'History' in *Essays*, Grant Richards, 1902, p. 2.
2 Angela Carter, *The Passion of New Eve*, Virago, 1982, p. 101.
3 Adrienne Rich, from 'Natural Resources' in *The Dream of a Common Language, Poems 1974–1977*, W. W. Norton & Co, 1978, p. 62.
4 Virginia Woolf, *A Room of One's Own*, Granada, 1977, p. 28.

Chapter 1: Men in their Wisdom

1 Dorothy Richardson, *Pilgrimage*, Virago, 1979, in 4 vols; Vol. 3, p. 68.
2 From a letter from Franz Kafka to Max Brod, June 1921. Quoted in Erich Heller, *Kafka*, Fontana Modern Masters, 1974, p. 14.
3 Virginia Woolf, *A Room of One's Own*, Granada, 1977, p. 72.
4 Elaine Showalter, 'Feminist Criticism in the Wilderness' in *Critical Inquiry*, Winter 1981, p. 179. In this most useful survey and discussion of traditions in feminist criticism, which she distinguishes under four headings: organic or biological criticism, linguistic and textual theories of women's writing, psychoanalytically oriented feminist criticism and 'a theory based on a model of women's culture', she ends with a defence of the last of her categories. 'One of the great advantages of the women's-culture model is that it shows how the female tradition can be a positive source of strength and solidarity as well as a negative source of powerlessness; it can generate its own experiences and symbols which are not simply the obverse of the male tradition.' p. 204.
5 Dorothy Richardson, *op. cit.*, Vol. 3, p. 276.
6 From a letter from Jane Austen to her brother, J. Edward Austen, dated Monday 16 December 1816. In Jane Austen, *Letters 1796–1817*, selected and edited by R. W. Chapman, Oxford University Press, 1981, p. 189.
7 Quoted in J. E. Austen-Leigh's *Memoir* of his aunt, which is included in the Penguin edition of *Persuasion*, edited by D. W. Harding, 1965, p. 370. Scott's remark is taken from an entry in his diary for 14 March 1826, in

which he praises Jane Austen for her 'talent for describing the involve-
ments and feelings and characters of ordinary life which is to me the most
wonderful I ever met with. The Big Bow-wow strain I can do myself like
any now going but the exquisite touch which renders ordinary commonplace things and characters interesting from the truth of the description
and the sentiment is denied to me. What a pity such a gifted creature died
so early!'

8 Lady Murasaki (or Murasaki Shikibu), *The Tale of Genji*, translated and
with an introduction by Edward G. Seidensticker, Penguin, 1981, p. 25.

9 F. W. H. Myers, 'George Eliot' in *Essays Modern*, Macmillan, 1897.

10 Ronald Blythe's Introduction to the Penguin edition of *Emma*, p. 14.

11 Annette Kolodny, 'Turning the Lens on "The Panther Captivity": A
Feminist Exercise in Practical Criticism' in *Critical Inquiry*, Winter 1981,
p. 329. This phrase occurs in the final paragraph of her excellent article
about feminist criticism: 'I have simply invested an already established
approach with two questions which, up until now, have been the
special concern of the feminist critic only: (1) How do contemporary
women's lives, women's concerns, or concerns about women constitute
part of the historical context for this work? and (2) What is the symbolic
significance of gender in this text?' (p. 345) I have found these questions
and this formulation of them very useful.

12 In Jane Miller, *Many Voices. Bilingualism, Culture and Education*, Routledge & Kegan Paul, 1983.

13 This subject is dealt with well in Elaine Showalter, *A Literature of Their
Own*, Virago, 1982. Trollope gives a glimpse of women's involvement in
publishing in his stories, *The Spotted Dog and Other Stories*, Alan Sutton,
1983.

14 This is part of Anthea Zeman's argument in her *Presumptuous Girls.
Women and their World in the Serious Woman's Novel*, Weidenfeld &
Nicolson, 1977. In Sandra M. Gilbert and Susan Gubar, *The Mad
woman in the Attic*, Yale University Press, 1979, p. 69, the authors suggest
some of the difficulties inherent in writing for women. 'If a female
novelist uses the *Pamela* plot, for instance, she is exploiting a story that
implies women cannot and should not do what she is herself accom-
plishing in writing her book. Ambitious to rise by her own literary
exertions, she is implicitly admonishing her female readers that they can
hope to rise only through male intervention. At the same time, as Joanna
Russ has pointed out, if a woman writer "abandon(s) female protagonists
altogether and stick(s) to male myths with male protagonists . . . she
falsifies herself and much of her own experience."' Joanna Russ is
quoted here from her 'What can a Heroine Do? Or Why Women Can't

Write' in Susan Koppelman Cornillon (ed.), *Images of Women in Fiction*, Bowling Green University Popular Press, 1972, p. 10. Joanna Russ is also the author of *How to Suppress Women's Writing*, The Women's Press, 1984.

15 I have deliberately plagiarised myself here in using a formulation I developed about second-language learners and the immigrant experience in Jane Miller, *op. cit.* It has been significant for me that a consideration of women and language should have so much in common with the testimonies of bilingual people. Helpful as the idea of bilingualism is in considering the language and the novels of women it would be a pity to discount the notion of multiplicity as Julia Kristeva has developed it in relation to women's language and Bakhtin's 'polyphonic' voices in narrative, in her 'The Ruin of a Poetics' in *Twentieth-Century Studies*, No. 7/8.

16 From a letter from Jane Austen to her sister Cassandra, dated 5 March 1814 in *Letters 1796–1817*, *op. cit.*, p. 156.

17 Sandra M. Gilbert and Susan Gubar, *op. cit.*, p. 76.

18 John Stuart Mill, *The Subjection of Women*, Virago, 1983, p. 46 and p. 132.

19 George Eliot, *Daniel Deronda*, Chap. 51.

20 *Ibid.*, Chap. 28.

21 *Ibid.*, Chap. 6.

22 F. R. Leavis, *The Great Tradition*, Chatto & Windus, 1948, Chap. 2. 'George Eliot', pp. 47–82.

23 Melanie Klein and Joan Riviere, *Love, Hate and Reparation. Two Lectures*, The Hogarth Press and the Institute of Psycho-Analysis, 1937, p. 32.

24 Angela Carter, *The Sadeian Woman*, Virago, 1979, p. 109.

25 John Stuart Mill, *op. cit.*, p. 76.

26 Wayne Booth, 'Freedom of Interpretation: Bakhtin and the Challenge of Feminist Criticism' in *Critical Inquiry 9*, September 1982.

27 Terry Eagleton, *Literary Theory*, Basil Blackwell, 1983, Chap. 5. In his 'Reading as a Woman' (*On Deconstruction*, Routledge & Kegan Paul, 1983, p. 43) Jonathan Culler offers 'reading as a woman' as a deconstructive strategy, available to men as to women. It is an attractive position, with its suggestion of the usefulness of feminist criticism to men. It is also full of dangers, since it ignores as experiences the forms of marginality, negativity and exclusion out of which feminist criticism has grown. Men have much to learn from feminist theory of all kinds, but this kind of appropriation denies the crucial relation between experience and reading and between individual development and culture.

28 Besides her book, referred to in note 13, and the essay referred to in note 4, Elaine Showalter's 'Towards a Feminist Poetics' is included in Mary Jacobus (ed.), *Women Writing and Writing about Women*, Croom Helm in

association with Oxford University Women's Studies Committee, 1979.

29 Mary Jacobus, 'The Buried Letter: Feminism and Romanticism in *Villette*', in *ibid.*, p. 59. Mary Jacobus is also the author of 'The Question of Language: Men of Maxims and *The Mill on the Floss*' in *Critical Inquiry*, Winter 1981, p. 207.

30 Viviane Forrester, 'What Women's Eyes See' in Elaine Marks and Isabelle de Courtivron (eds), *New French Feminisms*, Schocken Books, New York, 1981, p. 181.

31 George Eliot, *Middlemarch*, Chap. 10.

32 Edward W. Said, 'Secular Criticism' in *Raritan*, Winter 1983, p. 10.

33 Virginia Woolf, *op. cit.*, p. 65.

34 I am referring here to Suzanne Langer's theory of art as 'virtual experience' as she expounds it in her *Feeling and Form*, Routledge & Kegan Paul, 1953.

35 Adrienne Rich, 'When We Dead Awaken: Writing as Re-Vision' in her *On Lies, Secrets, Silence. Selected Prose 1966–1978*, Virago, 1980, p. 37.

36 Jane Austen, *Northanger Abbey*, Chap. 14.

37 *Ibid.*, Chap. 2.

38 *Ibid.*, Chap. 14.

39 Anthea Zeman, *op. cit.*, p. 2 and p. 10.

40 Charlotte Brontë, in a letter dated 4 August 1839, wrote, 'I am certainly doomed to be an old maid. Never mind. I made up my mind to that fate ever since I was twelve years old.' Quoted in Elizabeth Gaskell, *The Life of Charlotte Brontë*, Penguin, 1975, p. 192.

41 A letter from Charlotte Brontë to James Taylor, dated 1 March 1849, in Clement Shorter, *The Brontës: Life and Letters*, Vol. 2, Hodder & Stoughton, 1908, p. 30.

42 F. R. Leavis, *op. cit.*, pp. 79–87.

43 Frigga Haug, 'Morals Also Have Two Genders' in *New Left Review*, No. 143, Jan.–Feb. 1984, p. 64.

44 Jane Austen, *Emma*, Chap. 34.

45 Jane Austen, *Pride and Prejudice*, Chap. 42.

46 Marilyn Butler, *Jane Austen and the War of Ideas*, Clarendon Press, 1975, p. 215.

47 Jane Austen, in a letter dated 23 March 1977 to her niece, Fanny Knight. In *Letters 1796–1817*, *op. cit.*, p. 199.

48 Jane Austen did speculate about the future of her characters in *Pride and Prejudice*, and even, in a letter to her sister Cassandra, dated 24 May 1813, imagined Mrs Darcy and Mrs Bingley fashionably present at an exhibition where a portrait of Mrs Bingley had been hung. In *Letters 1796–1817*, *op. cit.*, p. 139.

49 John Stuart Mill, *op. cit.*, p. 38.
50 D. W. Harding, 'Regulated Hatred: An Aspect of the Work of Jane Austen' in *Scrutiny*, Vol. VIII, No. 4, March 1940, p. 355.
51 Selma James, *The Ladies and the Mammies. Jane Austen and Jean Rhys*, Falling Wall Press, 1983. Selma James argues with enthusiasm and commitment that Jane Austen was like Jean Rhys in being concerned to attack imperialism and class oppression. The case is an attractive one, though not, in the end, persuasive.

Chapter 2: Fathers and Gentlemen

1 Harriet Taylor Mill, *Enfranchisement of Women*, Virago, 1983, p. 4.
2 Marilyn Butler, *Romantics, Rebels and Reactionaries. English Literature and its Background 1760–1830*, Oxford University Press, 1981, p. 99.
3 Peter Laslett, *The World We Have Lost*, Methuen, 1979, p. 20.
4 Marilyn Butler, *op. cit.*, p. 98.
5 *Ibid.*, p. 106. Women writers for children like Charlotte Yonge and E. Nesbit were given to removing fathers to prison, the colonies or the grave, perhaps in order to enlarge the scope for their children's adventure.
6 Geoffrey Gorer, 'The Myth in Jane Austen' in Wilbur Scott (ed.), *Five Approaches of Literary Criticism*, Collier Books, New York, 1962, p. 92.
7 Lord Raglan, *Jocasta's Crime*, The Thinker's Library, 1940. An anthropologist's attempt to answer the question: Why has Jocasta's action in marrying her son been regarded as a crime which could be expiated only by her death? A critique of Freud and of traditional incest theories.
8 I shall take up this notion of the Oedipus story as consolation within a peculiarly male reading in Chap. 4.
9 Jane Austen, *Sense and Sensibility*, Chap. 7.
10 Jane Austen, *Emma*, Chap. 8.
11 Jane Austen, *Mansfield Park*, Chap. 2.
12 Jane Austen, *Pride and Prejudice*, Chap. 42.
13 Michèle Roberts, 'Outside My Father's House' in Ursula Owen (ed.), *Fathers. Reflections by Daughters*, Virago, 1983, p. 104.
14 *Mansfield Park*, Chap. 2.
15 *Ibid.*, Chap. 48.
16 D. W. Harding, Introduction to *Persuasion*, Penguin, 1965.
17 Jane Austen, *Persuasion*, Chap. 1.
18 *Emma*, Chap. 1.
19 *Mansfield Park*, Chap. 1.
20 *Ibid.*, Chap. 39.

21 Jane Austen, *Northanger Abbey*, Chap. 31.

22 *Loc. cit.*

23 *Mansfield Park*, Chap. 35.

24 Anthea Zeman, *op. cit.*, p. 151.

25 Marilyn Butler, *op. cit.*, p. 105.

26 Ursula Owen (ed.), *op. cit.*

27 D. W. Harding, 'Regulated Hatred: An Aspect of the Work of Jane Austen', *op. cit.*, p. 355.

28 Lawrence Stone, *The Family, Sex and Marriage in England 1500–1800*, Penguin (abridged edition), 1979, p. 164.

29 *Ibid.*, p. 217.

30 Rosalind Mitchison, 'The Numbers Game'. A review of Peter Laslett: *Family Life and Illicit Love in Earlier Generations*, Cambridge University Press, 1977, and Lawrence Stone, *op. cit.* in the *New Review*, Vol. 4, No. 47, February 1978, p. 43.

31 Jane Austen wrote in a letter to her sister Cassandra, dated 14 September 1804 (in *Letters 1796–1817*, *op. cit.*, p. 55) 'Like other young ladies she is considerably genteeler than her parents. Mrs. Armstrong sat darning a pair of stockings the whole of my visit. But I do not mention this at home, lest a warning should act as an example.' Marghanita Laski, in *Jane Austen and her World*, Thames & Hudson, 1969, takes this remark to suggest what must have been significant changes in what was thought fitting for women to concern themselves with in Jane Austen's mother's generation compared with Jane Austen's.

32 *Persuasion*, Chap. 23.

33 *Pride and Prejudice*, Chap. 61.

34 *Mansfield Park*, Chap. 48.

35 *Emma*, Chap. 10.

36 Jane Austen, in a letter to her niece Fanny Knight, dated 20 February 1817 in *Letters 1796–1817*, *op. cit.*, p. 190.

37 *Sense and Sensibility*, Chap. 45.

38 *Ibid.*, Chap. 3.

39 *Emma*, Chap. 38.

40 *Ibid.*, Chap. 5.

41 *Ibid.*, Chap. 12.

42 *Ibid.*, Chap. 53.

43 *Ibid.*, Chap. 10.

44 Marilyn Butler, *op. cit.*, p. 98.

45 D. W. Harding, *op. cit.*, p. 347.

46 Ivy Pinchbeck, *Women Workers and the Industrial Revolution 1750–1850*, Virago, 1981.

47 *Ibid.*, p. 315.

48 *Emma*, Chap. 22.

49 Marghanita Laski, *op. cit.*

50 G. M. Trevelyan, *Illustrated English Social History: 4*, Pelican, 1968, p. 51. See also footnote on same page. Christine Delphy in her *Close to Home*, Hutchinson, 1984, reserves some of her most withering scorn for male disapproval of 'bourgeois' women's 'idleness', when that has been 'bought' by a husband, just as another woman's heavy labour may have been. See her 'Our friends and ourselves', p. 119.

51 Ivy Pinchbeck, *op. cit.*, p. 302.

52 Ellen Moers, *Literary Women*, The Women's Press, 1978, p. 67.

53 *Pride and Prejudice*, Chap. 61.

54 In a letter from Charlotte Brontë (signed C. Bell) to G. H. Lewes, dated 12 January 1848. Quoted in Elizabeth Gaskell, *op. cit.*, p. 337.

Chapter 3: Brothers

1 From a letter written by Robert Southey in 1837 in response to one Charlotte Brontë wrote him on 29 December 1836. Elizabeth Gaskell, *op. cit.*, p. 172. It had been included in C. C. Southey's Life of his father.

2 Elizabeth Gaskell, *op. cit.*, p. 581. This remark by Southey is quoted from a letter written by him to Edward Quillinan, Wordsworth's son-in-law.

3 Letter from Thackeray to Lucy Baxter, dated 11 March 1853. In *The Letters and Private Papers of William Makepeace Thackeray*, collected and edited by Gordon N. Ray, Vol. 3, Oxford University Press, 1946, p. 232.

4 Charlotte Brontë, *Shirley*, Chap. 20.

5 Charlotte Brontë, *Jane Eyre*, Chap. 14.

6 *Ibid.*, Chap. 23.

7 *Ibid.*, Chap. 27.

8 *Loc. cit.*

9 *Ibid.*, Chap. 38.

10 Adrienne Rich, *op. cit.*, p. 90.

11 Elizabeth Gaskell, *op. cit.*, p. 464.

12 Winifred Gérin, *Emily Brontë*, Oxford University Press, 1979, Chap. 18.

13 Virginia Woolf, *op. cit.*, p. 88.

14 *Jane Eyre*, Chap. 34.

15 Elizabeth Gaskell, *op. cit.*, p. 183.

16 *Ibid.*, p. 254.

17 Charlotte Brontë, *The Professor*, Chap. 25.

18 See note 60.

19 The relevant passage of Harriet Martineau's review of *Villette* is included as a note in Elizabeth Gaskell, *op. cit.*, p. 619.

20 There is an interesting irony to Harriet Martineau's comment; for in her own novel, *Deerbrook*, she contrasts her sister heroines' steadfast and monogamous love with the shift in both her heroes from loving one woman to loving another. As one of these heroes points out, 'Men know nothing of morals till they know women' (p. 280 of Virago, 1983 edn). The sense of women's being more 'moral', naturally and perforce, provides an echo to Charlotte Brontë's ambivalence towards her own brother and the men in her novels who are, in a variety of ways, brothers as well as potential lovers. *Deerbrook*, incidentally, was published in 1839, fourteen years before *Villette*.

21 Charlotte Brontë, *Villette*, Chap. 7.

22 By, for instance, Karl Miller, in his *Cockburn's Millenium*, Duckworth, 1975, and in his *Doubles*, Oxford University Press, 1985.

23 Jeremy Hawthorn, *Multiple Personality and the Disintegration of Literary Character. From Oliver Goldsmith to Sylvia Plath*, Edward Arnold, 1983.

24 *Ibid.*, p. 73.

25 Kate Millett, *Sexual Politics*, Virago, 1977, p. 140.

26 *Ibid.*, p. 146.

27 *Villette*, Chap. 1.

28 *Ibid.*, Chap. 19.

29 *Ibid.*, Chap. 17.

30 Harriet Martineau. See note 19.

31 *Villette*, Chap. 14.

32 *Ibid.*, Chap. 29.

33 *Ibid.*, Chap. 28.

34 *Ibid.*, Chap. 27.

35 *Ibid.*, Chap. 30.

36 Jeremy Hawthorn, *op. cit.*, p. 80.

37 *Villette*, Chap. 31.

38 *Ibid.*, Chap. 7.

39 *Ibid.*, Chap. 30.

40 *Ibid.*, Chap. 19.

41 *Loc. cit.*

42 John Berger, *Ways of Seeing*, BBC and Penguin, 1972, p. 47.

43 *Villette*, Chap. 19.

44 *Loc. cit.*

45 *Ibid.*, Chap. 20.

46 *Ibid.*, Chap. 23.

47 John Stuart Mill, *op. cit.*, p. 135.

48 An imaginative critical treatment of this idea: that women are 'natural' and men 'civilised', is to be found in Susan Griffin, *Woman and Nature. The Roaring Inside Her*, The Women's Press, 1984.

49 George Eliot's 'great' artist is Daniel Deronda's mother, whom I shall discuss in the next chapter.

50 *Villette*, Chap. 23.

51 *Ibid.*, Chap. 25.

52 *Ibid.*, Chap. 28.

53 *Ibid.*, Chap. 31.

54 *Ibid.*, Chap. 41.

55 Kate Millett, *op. cit.*, p. 146.

56 *Villette*, Chap. 42.

57 In a letter, dated 6 November 1852, Charlotte Brontë wrote to W. S. Williams, 'As to the name of the heroine, I can hardly express what subtlety of thought made me decide upon giving her a cold name; but, at first, I called her "Lucy Snowe" (spelt with an "e"); which Snowe I afterwards changed to "Frost". Subsequently, I rather regretted the change, and wished it "Snowe" again. If not too late, I should like the alteration to be made now throughout the MS. A *cold* name she must have; partly, perhaps, on the "*lucus a non lucendo*" principle – partly on that of the "fitness of things", for she has about her an external coldness.' Quoted in Elizabeth Gaskell, *op. cit.*, p. 485.

58 This determination to separate the woman from the writer is characteristic of Elizabeth Gaskell's treatment of Charlotte Brontë. A typical passage in the biography (p. 334) runs: 'henceforward Charlotte Brontë's existence becomes divided into two parallel currents – her life as Currer Bell, the author, her life as Charlotte Brontë, the woman. There were separate duties belonging to each character – not opposing each other; not impossible, but difficult to be reconciled.' Mrs Gaskell pursues this theme, partly, it seems, out of a sense that Brontë might otherwise be thought to reveal too much about her inner life in her novels. Again, on p. 495, Gaskell reports a conversation with Brontë about a suggestion that 'in certain instances, authoresses had much outstepped the line which men felt to be proper in works of this kind.' Gaskell goes on to say, 'I do not deny for myself the existence of coarseness here and there in her works, otherwise so entirely noble.'

59 Elizabeth Gaskell, *op. cit.*, p. 509.

60 *Ibid.*, p. 386.

61 Quoted in Margaret Drabble's Introduction to the Everyman edition of *Villette*, 1983, p. xviii.

62 *Loc. cit.*

63 See note 1.
64 Harriet Martineau, *Autobiography*, Vol. 1, Virago, 1983, p. 99.
65 Virginia Woolf, in her *Three Guineas*, Penguin, 1978, begins her argu-
    ment from the disparity between the social and private relations between
    brothers and sisters, which are made intolerable finally by economic and
    educational inequalities: 'You shall not learn; you shall not earn, you
    shall not own; you shall not – such was the society relationship of brother
    to sister for many centuries.' (p. 120) The book ends interestingly with
    the suggestion that only now were her male contemporaries learning to
    understand the experience of exclusion: 'You are feeling in your own
    persons what your mothers felt when they were shut out, because they
    were women. Now you are being shut out. You are being shut up,
    because you are Jews, because you are democrats, because of race,
    because of religion.'

Chapter 4: Sons

1 From the review of Charlotte Brontë's *Shirley* by G. H. Lewes in
  Edinburgh Review, No. CLXXXIII, Jan. 1850, p. 155, entitled '*Shirley: a
  Tale*. By Currer Bell.'
2 George Eliot, *Felix Holt*, Chap. 2.
3 A fascinating discussion of the collision for women between actual
  experience as a mother and the literary or mythical accounts they grow up
  with is Alice Walker's essay, '*One* child of One's Own: A Meaningful
  Digression within the Work(s)' in her *In Search of Our Mothers' Gardens.
  Womanist Prose*, The Women's Press, 1984, p. 361.
4 For instance, Judith Arcana in her *Every Mother's Son*, The Women's
  Press, 1983; Adrienne Rich in *Of Woman Born. Motherhood as Experience
  and Institution*, Virago, 1977.
5 Robert Graves, *The Greek Myths* (2 vols), Penguin, 1977. Vol. 2, p. 15.
6 The translation of Sophocles' *Oedipus Rex* used here is, in fact, E. F.
  Watling's *King Oedipus*, Penguin, 1961, p. 25.
7 The account of Freud's Oedipus Complex which I use here is from his
  General Introduction to Psychoanalysis (1916), translated by Joan Riviere,
  George Allen & Unwin, 1963.
8 Claude Lévi-Strauss: 'The Structural Study of Myth' in A. K. Pugh, V. J.
  Lee and J. Swann (eds), *Language and Language Use*, Heinemann Edu-
  cational Books, 1980, p. 232.
9 Freud did not, of course, leave it at that, at a simple reversal of the
  Oedipus story as an explanation for the development of female identity.
  Indeed, in his *Some Psychical Consequences of the Anatomical Distinction*

between the Sexes (1925), published in the Penguin Sigmund Freud, Vol. 7. *On Sexuality*, he writes, 'In little girls the Oedipus complex raises one problem more than in boys. In both cases the mother is the original object; and there is no cause for surprise that boys retain that object in the Oedipus complex. But how does it happen that girls abandon it and instead take their father as an object?' p. 334. In her excellent account of Freud's theory, in its relation to both feminism and Marxism, Juliet Mitchell writes, 'It is because it is repressed that femininity is so hard to comprehend both within and without psychoanalytic investigation – it returns in symptoms, such as hysteria . . . The girl only acquires her secondary feminine identity within the law of patriarchy in her positive Oedipus complex when she is seduced/raped by, and/or seduces the father.' Juliet Mitchell, *Psychoanalysis and Feminism*, Penguin, 1975, p. 404.

I need to emphasise that I am not disputing Freud's theory as such, nor am I in serious disagreement with Juliet Mitchell's position (though many feminists are). Rather I am looking at the stories, usually men's about women, which women have learned to accept as true of them even as they recoil from and resist them. Most women have wanted, at the very least, to re-explain Freud's 'penis-envy' in those of his formulations which are like this one: 'Here what has been named the masculinity complex of women branches off. It may put great difficulties in the way of their regular development towards femininity, if it cannot be got over soon enough. The hope of some day obtaining a penis in spite of everything and so becoming like a man may persist to an incredibly late age and may become a motive for strange and otherwise unaccountable actions.' In Freud, *op. cit.*, p. 336

10 Sophocles, *op. cit.*, p. 66.
11 Elaine Showalter, in her 'Feminist Criticism in the Wilderness', *op. cit.*, makes the point that 'All feminist criticism is in some sense revisionist'. (p. 183) She has also written (in 'Towards a Feminist Poetics' in Mary Jacobus (ed.), *op. cit.*, p. 39), that 'the task of feminist critics is to find a new language, a new way of reading that can integrate our intelligence and our experience, our reason and our suffering, our scepticism and our vision.'
12 The term had been used by Jung and specifically rejected by Freud for seeking 'to emphasize the analogy between the attitude of the two sexes', in Freud, *op. cit.*, p. 375.
13 Tony Tanner, in his *Adultery in the Novel. Contract and Transgression*, Johns Hopkins University Press, 1979, writes that it is 'the unstable triangularity of adultery, rather than the static symmetry of marriage, that is the generative form of Western literature as we know it'. (p. 12) Yet, in

his fascinating book, which claims that 'adultery (is) essential to narrative (p. 377), he skirts the issue of how that has or might affect women's narratives. His claim that George Eliot 'wrote her way out of her condition (which was adulterous) by writing about, among other things, women who found no such options for themselves' ignores her adulteresses and shelves the interesting question of whether women have agreed with men that whereas an adulteress adulterates, an adulterer is simply a sportsman or health fanatic. An interesting novel to consider in this context is Kate Chopin's *The Awakening*, The Women's Press, 1978.

14 From Freud's 'The Oedipus Complex', see note 7.

15 Sophocles, *op. cit.*, p. 60.

16 *Loc. cit.*

17 Caren Greenberg, 'Reading Reading: Echo's Abduction of Language' in Sally McConnell-Ginet, Ruth Borker, Nelly Furman (eds), *Women and Language in Literature and Society*, Praeger, 1980, p. 303. Julia Kristeva also explores the Oedipus story in terms of narrative and of Jocasta's role in the story in her 'The Novel as Polylogue' in *Desire in Language. A Semiotic Approach to Literature and Art*, Blackwell, 1980, p. 190.

18 Lionel Trilling in his Introduction to *Emma*, Riverside, 1957, p. xxi.

19 Nancy Chodorow, *The Reproduction of Mothering. Psychoanalysis and the Sociology of Gender*, University of California Press, 1978, p. 214. See also Chodorow's 'Mothering, Male Dominance, and Capitalism' in Zillah R. Eisenstein (ed.), *Capitalist Patriarchy and the Case for Socialist Feminism*, Monthly Review Press, 1979, p. 83.

20 Tillie Olsen, *Silences*, Virago, 1980.

21 Judith Arcana, *op. cit.*

22 Jane Lazarre, *On Loving Men*, Virago, 1981.

23 Adrienne Rich, *op. cit.*

24 *Ibid.*, p. 220.

25 Louis J. McQuilland wrote this in *The Bookman*. It is quoted in Jane Marcus's Introduction to Rebecca West's *The Judge*, Virago, 1980. *The Judge* was first published in 1922.

26 James Douglas, also quoted in *ibid.*

27 Samuel Hynes, in his Introduction to *The Essential Rebecca West*, Penguin, 1983, p. xii.

28 Adrienne Rich, *op. cit.*, p. 112.

29 Rebecca West, *The Judge*, p. 190 (Page references are to the Virago edition.)

30 *Ibid.*, p. 28.

31 *Ibid.*, p. 85.

32 *Ibid.*, p. 87.

33 In Sophocles' *Electra* (translated by E. F. Watling, *Sophocles' Electra and Other Plays*, Penguin, 1971), p. 84.

34 This view of the novel's title sentence is Jane Marcus's in *op. cit.* It could only be thought to mean a 'life sentence' in terms of West's allowing the Oedipal curse to be transmitted to the unborn child signalled on the novel's last page.

35 *The Judge*, p. 430.

36 *Ibid.*, p. 317.

37 Rebecca West, *St. Augustine*, Peter Davies, 1933. Also now included in *The Essential Rebecca West, op. cit.* It is by now well known that West's son, Anthony West (whose father was H. G. Wells), has at least twice written versions of his relationship with his parents. He did so in his novel *Heritage* (reissued by Secker, 1984) and in *H. G. Wells: Aspects of a Life*, Hutchinson, 1984.

38 *St. Augustine*, pp. 33–4.

39 George Eliot, *Felix Holt*, Chap. 10.

40 F. R. Leavis, *op. cit.*, pp. 54 and 55.

41 Rosemary Ashton, *George Eliot*, Oxford University Press, 1983, p. 61.

42 *Felix Holt*, Chap. 1.

43 *Loc. cit.*

44 *Loc. cit.*

45 *Loc. cit.*

46 *Loc. cit.*

47 *Ibid.*, Chap. 2.

48 *Ibid.*, Chap. 1.

49 *Ibid.*, Chap. 34.

50 *Ibid.*, Chap. 8.

51 George Eliot, *Daniel Deronda*, Chap. 19.

52 *Ibid.*, Chap. 17.

53 *Ibid.*, Chap. 32.

54 *Ibid.*, Chap. 1.

55 *Ibid.*, Chap. 50.

56 *Ibid.*, Chap. 51.

57 *Loc. cit.*

58 *Ibid.*, Chap. 53.

59 *Loc. cit.*

60 Angela Carter, *op. cit.*, p. 106.

61 Carolyn Steedman, in her forthcoming *Landscape for a Good Woman. Childhood, Class and Subjectivity*, Virago, 1986, gives an account of her own mother as a working-class woman trapped by a maternity she resents, and which also represented her only exchangeable value and

down-payment on her future. Steedman's analysis of working-class motherhood is harsh and unsentimental. It also tackles in an original way the nearly unspeakable dilemma of the mother who has not wanted to be one.

Chapter 5: Heroes

1 Daisy and Angela Ashford, *Love and Marriage. Three Stories*, Oxford University Press, 1982, p. 24.
2 Jenni Calder, *Women and Marriage in Victorian Fiction*, Thames & Hudson, 1976.
3 Alexandra Kollontai, *A Great Love*, translated by Cathy Porter, Virago, 1981, p. 33.
4 This episode is quoted by Cathy Porter in her biography, *Alexandra Kollontai*, Virago, 1980, p. 277. It is taken from Leon Trotsky's *Stalin: An Appraisal*, edited and translated by Charles Malamuth, Harper, 1941.
5 George Eliot, *Middlemarch*, Chap. 10.
6 *Ibid.*, Chap. 5.
7 *Ibid.*, Chap. 6.
8 *Ibid.*, Chap. 5.
9 Antonia Byatt's Introduction to *The Mill on the Floss*, Penguin, 1979, p. 27.
10 Leslie Stephen, *George Eliot*, Macmillan, 1902, p. 186.
11 Elizabeth Gaskell, *op. cit.*, p. 115.
12 Judith Okely, 'Privileged, Schooled and Finished: Boarding Education for Girls' in Shirley Ardener (ed.), *Defining Females. The Nature of Women in Society*, Croom Helm in association with the Oxford University Women's Studies Committee, 1978, p. 109.
13 From a letter from Jane Austen to her niece Fanny Knight, dated 18 November 1814. In *Letters 1796–1817*, *op. cit.*, p. 172.
14 *Ibid.*, 30 November 1814, p. 178.
15 'Heroism' is a word coined, as far as I know, by Ellen Moers, in her *Literary Women*, *op. cit.* She defines it as 'literary feminism', p. 122.
16 George Eliot, *Daniel Deronda*, Chap. 6.
17 From a letter from G. H. Lewes to Edward Dowden in 1877 in G. S. Haight (ed.), *The George Eliot Letters* (9 vols), Oxford University Press, 1979, Vol. 6, pp. 336–7.
18 G. H. Lewes's review of *Shirley*, *op. cit.*, p. 163. See Chap. 4, note 1.
19 Charlotte Brontë, in her Author's Preface to *The Professor*, which was not published until 1856, after her death.
20 Henry James, *Daniel Deronda: A Conversation* is included in F. R. Leavis,

The Great Tradition, op. cit., p. 252. This is the piece to which Lewes was referring in his letter to Edward Dowden.

21 Robert L. Stevenson in a letter to A. Patchett Martin, December 1877, in *The Letters of Robert Louis Stevenson to his family and friends*, selected and edited, with Notes and Introduction by Sidney Colvin, 2 vols, Methuen, 1899, Vol. 1, p. 123. The whole passage about George Eliot reads: 'I agreed pretty well with all you said about George Eliot: a high, but, may we not add? – a rather dry lady. Did you – I forget – did you have a kick at the stern works of that melancholy puppy and humbug Daniel Deronda himself? – The Prince of Prigs; the literary abomination of desolation in the way of manhood; a type which is enough to make a man forswear the love of women, if that is how it must be gained. . . . Hats off all the same, you understand: a woman of genius.'

22 Leslie Stephen, *op. cit.*, p. 190.

23 *Ibid.*, p. 191.

24 F. W. H. Myers, *op. cit.*

25 Leslie Stephen, *op. cit.*, p. 191.

26 *Ibid.*, p. 104.

27 F. R. Leavis, *op. cit.*, p. 40.

28 *Ibid.*, p. 43.

29 Virginia Woolf, *The Common Reader*, First Series The Hogarth Press, 1984, p. 169.

30 Included in Winifred Gérin, *op. cit.*

31 John Middleton Murry (ed.), *Journal of Katherine Mansfield 1904–1922*, Constable, 1984, 29 March 1914, p. 57.

32 *Ibid.*, May 1919, p. 158.

33 For instance, Joan Riviere in Melanie Klein and Joan Riviere, *op. cit.*, pp. 31–6. One example of a very different approach to girls and their sexuality is to be found in Marjorie Shostak's remarkable *Nisa. The Life and Words of a! Kung Woman*, Vintage, 1983.

34 Shirley Ardener in her Introduction to *op. cit.*

35 Rachel Harrison, '*Shirley*: Relations of Reproduction and the Ideology of Romance' in Women's Studies Group, *Women Take Issue. Aspects of Women's Subordination*, Hutchinson and Centre for Contemporary Cultural Studies, 1978, p. 192.

36 Shirley Ardener, *op. cit.*, p. 30.

37 Marquis de Sade, *The Complete Justine, Philosophy in the Bedroom and other writings*, translated by Richard Seaver and Austryn Wainhouse, Grove Press, 1965; *Juliette*, Grove Press, 1968.

38 Angela Carter, *op. cit.*, p. 150.

39 Anna Akhmatova, *White Flock*, translated from the Russian and selected

by Geoffrey Thurley, Oasis Books, 1978, p. 53. From the poem beginning, 'The timbered bridge is bent and black.' Colette has always celebrated women's longing for men to be more like women. In her *The Pure and the Impure*, for instance (Penguin, 1980, p. 46), she writes of an aging roué, 'I wanted him to give way to anger, to make some kind of row that would prove him to be illogical, weak, and feminine – what every woman wants every man to be at least once in his life.'

Chapter 6: Another Story

1 Claudine Herrmann, 'Women in Space and Time' in Elaine Marks and Isabelle de Courtivron (eds), *op. cit.*, p. 169.
2 Dorothy Richardson, *Pilgrimage, op. cit.*, Vol. 4, p. 240. Hypo Wilson offers this advice to Miriam Henderson in the novel.
3 I shall refer in this chapter only to volume and page number of the Virago edition. The volumes contain the following novels:
   Vol. 1 *Pointed Roofs. Backwater. Honeycomb.*
   Vol. 2 *The Tunnel. Interim.*
   Vol. 3 *Deadlock. Revolving Lights. The Trap.*
   Vol. 4 *Oberland. Dawn's Left Hand. Clear Horizon. Dimple Hill. March Moonlight.*
4 Mary Taubman, author of the book, *Gwen John*, published by Scolar Press in 1985, has often discussed with me the similarities and differences between Dorothy Richardson and Gwen John. What they have in common is a kind of self-portraiture, involving the composed and the composing self within a single frame. The first novel, *Pointed Roofs*, wonderfully establishes this as its mode of experiencing and expression.
5 *Pilgrimage*, Vol. 4, p. 525.
6 *Ibid.*, Vol. 4, p. 158.
7 *Ibid.*, Vol. 1, p. 349.
8 *Ibid.*, Vol. 1, p. 82.
9 *Ibid.*, Vol. 4, p. 611.
10 *Ibid.*, Vol. 1, p. 215.
11 May Sinclair, in an essay in *Little Review*, April 1918.
12 Vincent Brome: 'A Last Meeting with Dorothy Richardson' in *London Magazine*, 6 June 1959, pp. 26–32. Brome writes here, 'Abruptly she came out of her reverie and said, "Stream of consciousness is a muddle-headed phrase. It's not a stream, it's a pool, a sea, an ocean. It has depth and greater depth and when you think you have reached its bottom there is nothing there, and when you give yourself up to one current you are suddenly possessed by another".'
13 *Pilgrimage*, Vol. 3, p. 410.

14 In Dorothy Richardson's Foreword to the 1938 edition of *Pilgrimage*, which is included in Vol. 1 of the Virago edition, p. 11.
15 *Pilgrimage*, Vol. 2, p. 188.
16 *Ibid.*, Vol. 4, p. 240.
17 *Ibid.*, Vol. 4, p. 239. The reference is to Henry James's *The Ambassadors*.
18 *Ibid.*, Vol. 1, p. 284.
19 *Ibid.*, Vol. 1, p. 423.
20 *Ibid.*, Vol. 4, p. 305.
21 *Ibid.*, Vol. 2, p. 373.
22 *Ibid.*, Vol. 4, p. 215.
23 *Ibid.*, Vol. 2, p. 317.
24 *Ibid.*, Vol. 3, p. 288.
25 Dorothy Richardson wrote a fairly regular monthly column for *Close-Up* about films called 'Continuous Performance' between 1927–1933.
26 From 'Continuous Performance' in *Close-Up*, 4 October 1927.
27 'Adventure for Readers', in *Life and Letters*, Vol. 22, No. 23, July 1939, p. 45.
28 In Dorothy Richardson's 1938 Foreword to *Pilgrimage* (Vol. 1, p. 12) she wrote, 'Feminine prose, as Charles Dickens and James Joyce have delightfully shown themselves to be aware, should properly be unpunctuated, moving from point to point without formal obstructions.' Richardson's punctuation has been discussed by Christian McEwen in an unpublished dissertation (Cambridge, 1979) and by C. R. Blake in *Dorothy Richardson*, University of Michigan Press, 1960. Richardson herself wrote 'About Punctuation' in *Adelphi*, Vol. 1, No. 11 (April 1924).
29 Foreword to 1938 edition of *Pilgrimage, op. cit.*, p. 9.
30 *Pilgrimage*, Vol. 1, p. 22.
31 *Ibid.*, Vol. 1, p. 28.
32 *Ibid.*, Vol. 1, p. 33.
33 *Ibid.*, Vol. 1, p. 70.
34 *Ibid.*, Vol. 1, p. 73.
35 *Ibid.*, Vol. 1, p. 111.
36 *Ibid.*, Vol. 1, p. 123.
37 *Ibid.*, Vol. 1, p. 247.
38 *Ibid.*, Vol. 1, p. 172.
39 *Ibid.*, Vol. 1, p. 142. Many women writers have characterised women's conversation in similar ways. Colette, for instance, in *The Pure and the Impure, op. cit.*, writes, 'who can imagine the number of subjects, the amount of words that are left out of the conversation of two women who can talk to each other with absolute freedom.' (p. 87)

40 *Ibid.*, Vol. 1, p. 358.
41 *Ibid.*, Vol. 1, p. 437.
42 E. M. Forster, *Aspects of the Novel*, Penguin, 1974, p. 36.
43 Frank Kermode, *The Sense of an Ending*, Oxford University Press, 1966.
44 Julia Kristeva, 'The Ruin of a Poetics' in *Twentieth-Century Studies*, No. ·7/8, p. 113. See also Jacques Lacan, *Ecrits. A Selection*, translated by Alan Sheridan, Tavistock, 1977; and M. Bakhtin, *The Dialogic Imagination*, edited by Michael Holquist, translated by Holquist and Caryl Emerson, University of Texas Slavic Series, No. 1, 1981.
45 Julia Kristeva in an interview with Xavière Gauthier in Elaine Marks and Isabelle de Courtivron (eds), *op. cit.*, p. 166.
46 *Pilgrimage*, Vol. 2, p. 210.
47 *Ibid.*, Vol. 2, p. 219.
48 *Ibid.*, Vol. 2, p. 222.
49 Gillian E. Hanscombe: *The Art of Life. Dorothy Richardson and the Development of Feminist Consciousness*, Peter Owen, 1982, p. 92.
50 *Ibid.*, p. 67.
51 *Pilgrimage*, Vol. 3, p. 303.
52 *Loc. cit.*
53 *Ibid.*, Vol. 3, p. 479.
54 *Ibid.*, Vol. 4, p. 220.
55 *Ibid.*, Vol. 4, p. 223.
56 *Ibid.*, Vol. 4, p. 231. Dorothy Richardson seems to have dwelled on this point. Vincent Brome, *op. cit.*, recalls her telling him, 'He was rather ugly without his clothes.' p. 29.
57 *Ibid.*, Vol. 4, p. 245.
58 *Ibid.*, Vol. 4, p. 258.
59 *Ibid.*, Vol. 4, p. 267.
60 *Ibid.*, Vol. 4, p. 324.
61 *Ibid.*, Vol. 4, p. 602.
62 *Ibid.*, Vol. 4, p. 604.
63 *Ibid.*, Vol. 4, p. 656.
64 *Ibid.*, Vol. 4, p. 611.
65 *Ibid.*, Vol. 4, p. 609.
66 Gloria G. Fromm, *Dorothy Richardson. A Biography*, University of Illinois Press, 1977, pp. 352–4.
67 *Pilgrimage*, Vol. 4, p. 657.
68 John Cowper Powys, *Dorothy Richardson*, Village Press, 1974.
69 Gloria G. Fromm, *op. cit.*, pp. 245–6.
70 John Cowper Powys, *op. cit.*, p. 7.
71 *Ibid.*, p. 18.

72 John Rosenberg, *Dorothy Richardson*, Duckworth, 1973.

73 Gloria Fromm, *op. cit.*, p. 224.

74 Leslie Fiedler, Foreword to C. R. Blake, *op. cit.*, p. vii.

75 Virginia Woolf, *A Writer's Diary*, Triad Granada, 1983, p. 31. It is interesting to consider Woolf's strictures in the light of John Bayley's superb critique of Woolf, in which he writes, 'In very few writers does there seem such a gap between the sensibility projected by the art and the atmosphere generated by the personality.' 'Superchild', a review of *The Diary of Virginia Woolf. Vol. V: 1936–1941*, edited by Anne Olivier Bell, assisted by Andrew McNeillie. In *London Review of Books*, Vol. 6, No. 16, September 1984, p. 9.

76 Elaine Showalter, *A Literature of Their Own*, *op. cit.*, p. 262.

77 Gillian E. Hanscombe, *op. cit.*, p. 166.

78 *Pilgrimage*, Vol. 1, p. 302.

79 *Ibid.*, Vol. 3, p. 128.

80 See p. 185.

81 G. Genette, in his *Narrative Discourse* (Blackwell, 1980) gives a superb account of the relation in Proust's writing between the use of times and tenses and the activities of the memory, which it would be valuable to consider in relation to Dorothy Richardson's writing.

82 Norman Mailer, 'Evaluations – Quick and Expensive Comments on the Talent in the Room' in *Advertisements for Myself*, Panther, 1968, p. 387.

83 Lionel Trilling, *op. cit.*

84 Virginia Woolf, *op. cit.*, p. 31.

Chapter 7: Resisting the Bullies

1 Edwin Ardener, quoted in Kirsten Hastrup, 'The Semantics of Biology: Virginity' in Shirley Ardener (ed.), *op. cit.*, p. 54.

2 *Sir Leslie Stephen's Mausoleum Book*, edited and with an Introduction by Alan Bell, Clarendon Press, 1977.

3 *Ibid.*, Introduction.

4 Thomas Carlyle, *Reminiscences*, edited by C. E. Norton, J. M. Dent, 1932, pp. 35–169 'Jane Welsh Carlyle'; John Stuart Mill, *Autobiography*, edited with an introduction and notes by Jack Stillinger, Oxford University Press, 1971, Chap. 6.

5 *Ibid.*, p. 113.

6 Leslie Stephen, *op. cit.*, p. 95.

7 Virginia Woolf, *To the Lighthouse*, Penguin, 1964, p. 141.

8 Leslie Stephen, *op. cit.*, p. 26.

9 *Ibid.*, p. 69.

10 Elizabeth Hardwick, *Seduction and Betrayal. Women and Literature*, Random House, 1974, p. 185.
11 Virginia Woolf, *A Writer's Diary, op. cit.*, p. 81.
12 *Ibid.*, p. 92.
13 *Ibid.*, p. 137.
14 *Ibid.*, p. 92.
15 *To the Lighthouse, op. cit.*, p. 8.
16 *Ibid.*, p. 9.
17 *Ibid.*, p. 6.
18 *Ibid.*, p. 44.
19 *Ibid.*, p. 53.
20 *Ibid.*, p. 56.
21 *Ibid.*, p. 64.
22 *Ibid.*, p. 98.
23 *Ibid.*, p. 69.
24 *Ibid.*, p. 192.
25 *Ibid.*, p. 237.
26 Rosamond Lehmann, *The Echoing Grove*, Penguin, 1981, p. 292.
27 Rosamond Lehmann, *Dusty Answer*, Penguin, 1981, p. 121.
28 *Ibid.*, p. 302.
29 *Ibid.*, p. 229.
30 *Ibid.*, p. 150.
31 Rosamond Lehmann, *The Weather in the Streets*, Virago, 1981, p. 11.
32 *Ibid.*, p. 340.
33 Quoted in Janet Watts's Introduction to *The Weather in the Streets*.
34 *The Echoing Grove, op. cit.*, p. 249.
35 *Ibid.*, p. 146.
36 Jean Rhys, *Wide Sargasso Sea*, Penguin, 1982. Introduction by Francis Wyndham, p. 5.
37 Charlotte Brontë, *Jane Eyre*, Chap. 27. See also Chap. 3 of this book.
38 Jean Rhys, *Good Morning, Midnight*, André Deutsch, 1967, p. 44.
39 *Ibid.*, p. 104.
40 Francis Wyndham's Introduction to *Wide Sargasso Sea, op. cit.*, p. 9.
41 *Wide Sargasso Sea*, p. 78.
42 *Ibid.*, p. 130.
43 Francis Wyndham in an interview in *The Times*, 21 May 1984, in which he discussed the edition of Jean Rhys' letters he edited with Diana Melly in 1984: *Jean Rhys Letters 1931–66*, Penguin, 1985.
44 *Good Morning, Midnight*, p. 162.
45 Christina Stead, *Miss Herbert (The Suburban Wife)*, Virago, 1979, p. 39.
46 *Ibid.*, p. 5.

47 *Ibid.*, p. 104.
48 Christina Stead, *For Love Alone*, Virago, 1978, p. 6.
49 *Miss Herbert (The Suburban Wife)*, p. 219.
50 *Ibid.*, p. 172.
51 Lorna Sage, *Doris Lessing*, Methuen, 1983, p. 30.
52 Robert Taubman, 'Free Women', a review of *The Golden Notebook* in *New Statesman*, 20 April 1962. Robert Taubman returned to Doris Lessing and this novel in 'Near Zero' in *New Statesman*, 8 November 1963. He is also the author of 'Doris Lessing and Nadine Gordimer' in Boris Ford (ed.), *The New Pelican Guide to Literature. Vol. 8. The Present*, Penguin, 1983, p. 233. Women writers are, incidentally, extremely thin on the ground in this volume, as subject-matter or as contributors.
53 Doris Lessing, *The Golden Notebook*, Granada, 1983, p. 63.
54 Dorothy Richardson, *Pilgrimage, op. cit.*, Vol. 4, p. 611.
55 *The Golden Notebook*, p. 231.
56 Author's Preface to *The Golden Notebook*, p. 7.
57 *The Golden Notebook*, p. 638.
58 Author's Preface to *The Golden Notebook*, p. 10.
59 *Ibid.*, p. 11.
60 *Loc. cit.*
61 *Ibid.*, p. 13.
62 *Loc. cit.*
63 *The Golden Notebook*, p. 219.
64 *Ibid.*, p. 220.
65 *Loc. cit.*
66 *Ibid.*, p. 445.
67 Author's Preface, *op. cit.*, p. 14.
68 *The Golden Notebook*, p. 583.
69 In Jane Miller, *op. cit.*, Chap. 9.
70 Virginia Woolf ends *Three Guineas, op. cit.*, with a kind of proposal, that the 'daughters of educated men' found 'the outsiders society' to oppose war. She does so on the principle that women's experience of exclusion should unite them with an unheard majority of people (p. 122).
71 This is Lorna Sage's phrase.
72 Lorna Sage, *op. cit.*, p. 85.

Chapter 8: Women's Men

1 Alice Walker, 'A Sudden Trip Home in the Spring' in *You Can't Keep a Good Woman Down*, The Women's Press, 1982, p. 128.
2 Toni Morrison, *The Bluest Eye*, Triad Granada, 1981, p. 137.

3 *Ibid.*, p. 139.

4 *Ibid.*, p. 144.

5 *Ibid.*, p. 149.

6 *Ibid.*, p. 163.

7 *Ibid.*, p. 79.

8 An original and radical materialist analysis of women's oppression is the economist Christine Delphy's *Close to Home*, translated and edited by Diana Leonard, Hutchinson, in association with the Explorations in Feminism Collective, 1984. Delphy firmly sites women's oppression within domestic work done unpaid 'for' men. For a Marxist feminist theory, in which women's oppression is sited within the family as it 'serves' capitalism, see Michèle Barrett, *Women's Oppression Today. Problems in Marxist Feminist Analysis*, Verso Editions, 1980. Johanna Brenner and Maria Ramas in their 'Rethinking Women's Oppression', (*New Left Review* 144, March–April 1984, p. 33), which is a critique of Barrett, have set off a debate amongst feminist historians, which considers working-class women's work and family arrangements here and in America and questions of ideology (see *New Left Review*, Nos. 148 and 149, for example). This discussion demonstrates the scope of current feminist historical inquiry and more recent discussion of the relation of feminism to socialism.

9 Juliet Mitchell, *Psychoanalysis and Feminism, op. cit.*, p. 402.

10 *Ibid.*, p. xv.

11 Sheila Rowbotham, *Dreams and Dilemmas. Collected Writings*, Virago, 1983, p. 209. An early and useful rejoinder to Rowbotham was Sally Alexander's and Barbara Taylor's 'In Defence of "Patriarchy"', 1979, (in Mary Evans (ed.): *The Woman Question*, Fontana, 1982) in which they look towards the transforming of 'the meaning of sexuality itself. We would need to learn new ways of being women and men. It is this project, not the annihilation of "biological male persons", which the theory of patriarchy points towards.' (p. 81)

12 'The Combahee River Collective. A Black Feminist Statement' in Zillah R. Eisenstein (ed.), *op. cit.*, p. 367. Michele Wallace's *Black Macho and the Myth of the Superwoman*, John Calder, 1979, is a brave, personal and well-argued polemic, which makes the kind of case I have read from writers like Morrison, Marshall and Walker.

13 Paule Marshall, *Brown Girl, Brownstones*, Virago, 1982, p. 136.

14 *Ibid.*, p. 307.

15 *Ibid.*, p. 168.

16 *Ibid.*, p. 296.

17 *Ibid.*, p. 32.

18 *Ibid.*, p. 169.
19 Another recent novel, Rosa Guy's *A Measure of Time* (Virago, 1984), is based on the real life of the author's step-mother, her childhood in the South and then as a magnificently successful 'booster' in the Harlem of pre-Depression days. The sense that novels like these are both history and about a Black women's history are partly responsible for their scope and power. In Toni Morrison's *Song of Solomon* (Granada, 1980) she could be said to be proposing a woman's history and a man's as alternative responses to racism. The magic woman, Pilate, holds history in her life, her memory and her values. Her brother, Macon Dead, lives by the white values which killed his father and menace with death all Black people. His son's flight to the South of his slave ancestors is also the 'flight' which sings through the novel as the idea of the creation of a Black independence and autonomy, envisaged only by those Black women who free themselves from white values and from those Black men who mimic them.
20 Paule Marshall's third novel, *Praisesong for the Widow*, Virago, 1983, allows the effects of racism and kinds of Black accommodation to it to be felt, above all, as a constraint on the body of a Black woman. In this novel, her husband's success encourages Avey Johnson to corset herself, tighten her lips, control her natural exuberance, to the point of sickness, which is relieved only by a visit to the West Indies, in her late middle age, and by a violent, and graphically physical, 'letting go'.
21 *Brown Girl, Brownstones*, p. 300.
22 Alice Walker, *The Color Purple*, The Women's Press, 1983, p. 3.
23 *Ibid.*, p. 170.
24 *Ibid.*, p. 228.
25 Alice Walker, 'Brothers and Sisters' in *In Search of Our Mothers' Gardens*, *op. cit.*, p. 330.
26 *Ibid.*, p. 331.
27 Alice Walker, 'A Sudden Trip Home in the Spring' in *You Can't Keep a Good Woman Down*, *op. cit.*, p. 126.
28 Tillie Olsen, *Silences*, *op. cit.*, p. 23.
29 Tillie Olsen, *Yonnondio: From the Thirties*, Virago, 1980, p. 9.
30 *Ibid.*, p. 110.
31 *Ibid.*, p. 191.
32 Tillie Olsen, *Tell Me A Riddle*, Dell Publishing Co., 1961, p. 92.
33 *Ibid.*, p. 83.
34 Tillie Olsen called her novel *Yonnondio* after Walt Whitman's poem of that name. It is intended to be the story of people who have not been heard. Two lines from the Whitman poem run:

'Race of the woods, the landscapes free, and the falls!
No picture, poem, statement, passing them to the future:'

35 'From an Interview' in Alice Walker, *In Search of Our Mothers' Gardens*, *op. cit.*, p. 260.

36 Toni Morrison, *Sula*, Triad Granada, 1982, p. 69.

37 Johanna Brenner and Maria Ramas, *op. cit.*

38 Angela Carter, 'The Language of Sisterhood' in Leonard Michaels and Christopher Ricks (eds), *The State of the Language*, University of California Press, 1980, p. 229.

39 *Ibid.*, p. 231.

40 Juliet Mitchell, *op. cit.*, p. 414.

41 For Christine Delphy, *op. cit.*, the oppression of women is a system, and 'patriarchy' a precise term for the exploitation by men of their wives' unpaid labour. This, in her view, puts married women outside economic and social categories of class. 'Since the benefits which wives receive have no relationship to the services which they provide, it is impossible for married women to improve their own standard of living by improving their services. The only solution for them is to provide the same services for a richer man. Thus the logical consequence of the non-value of women's family labour is the hunt for a good marriage.' (p. 70, 'The Main Enemy'). I have found Delphy's analysis very useful for its penetration of the difficulties of considering women's relation to class, and for its siting of women's oppression within the family. It may be that she pays too little attention to the ways by which women have been coerced into giving their labour for nothing. The view that middle-class women have even less power or clout than working-class women is an often rehearsed view. Virginia Woolf was explicit about it in *Three Guineas*, *op. cit.*, when she wrote. 'If the working women of the country were to say "If you go to war, we will refuse to make munitions or to help in the production of goods," the difficulty of war-making would be seriously increased. But if all the daughters of educated men were to down tools tomorrow nothing essential either to the life or to the war-making of the community would be embarrassed. Our class is the weakest class in the state. We have no weapon with which to enforce our will.' (p. 16)

42 Michel Foucault, *The History of Sexuality. Volume One. An Introduction*, translated by Robert Hurley, Penguin, 1981, p. 93.

43 *Ibid.*, p. 100.

44 Edward W. Said, 'Travelling Theory' in *Raritan*, Winter 1982, p. 66.

45 Lorna Tracy, *Amateur Passions. Love Stories?*, Virago, 1981.

46 *Ibid.*, p. 120.

47 Virginia Woolf, *A Room of One's Own, op. cit.*, p. 24.

48 Inga-Stina Ewbank, for instance, in her 'Ibsen and the Language of women' in Mary Jacobus (ed.), *op. cit.*, writes 'women have to be bilingual in a male society' (p. 128), and Angela Carter (*op. cit.*, p. 232) writes, 'often women develop two distinct forms of speech, just as people who come from areas with dialectical peculiarities do. When we go home, that is, to mother, we fall into the primordial usage of all women everywhere, even if we don't like her very much. Women active in the "man's world" of public activity unconsciously accept male speech patterns except in moments of absence of mind, when they can lose their jobs.'

49 Adrienne Rich, *Of Woman Born, op. cit.*, p. 279.

50 Maxine Hong Kingston, *The Woman Warrior*, Picador, 1981, p. 183.

51 *Ibid.*, p. 13.

52 *Ibid.*, p. 21.

53 *Ibid.*, p. 49.

54 *Ibid.*, p. 166.

55 Maxine Hong Kingston, *China Men*, Picador, 1981, p. 296.

56 *Ibid.*, p. 245.

57 *Ibid.*, p. 92.

58 *Ibid.*, p. 214.

59 *Ibid.*, p. 301.

60 Julia Kristeva, 'Oscillation between Power and Denial' in Elaine Marks and Isabelle de Courtivron (eds), *op. cit.*, p. 166.

61 Flora Tristan, *The London Journal. 1842. The Aristocracy and the Working Class of England*, translated and introduced by Jean Hawkes, Virago, 1982, p. 244.

62 Naomi Mitchison, 'Organised Crime' in *Guardian*, 6 June 1984.

63 Martin Amis, 'The Utopian Woman'. An article about Gloria Steinem in *Observer Magazine*, 15 April 1984.

64 In the *Times Educational Supplement*, 15 June 1984.

The Writers and their Works

Since I have used various editions of the novels of Jane Austen, the Brontës and George Eliot, and because I assume that the same will be true for most readers, I have referred in my notes to chapter rather than page numbers. I include below the dates of first publication (in brackets) and an edition which is currently available of other writers' work.

Daisy and Angela Ashford
  Love and Marriage. Three Stories (1920). Oxford University Press
Jane Austen
  Sense and Sensibility (1811).
  Pride and Prejudice (1813).
  Mansfield Park (1814) Penguin
  Emma (1815).
  Northanger Abbey (1818. Posthumous).
  Persuasion (1818. Posthumous).

Anne Brontë
  Agnes Grey (1847).
  The Tenant of Wildfell Hall (1848).

Charlotte Brontë
  Jane Eyre (1847).
  Shirley (1849).
  Villette (1853).
  The Professor (1857. Posthumous).

Emily Brontë
  Wuthering Heights (1847).

Angela Carter
  The Passion of New Eve (1977). Virago

Kate Chopin
  The Awakening (1899). The Women's Press

Colette
  The Pure and the Impure (1941). Penguin

Maria Edgeworth
Castle Rackrent (1800). Oxford University Press
Helen (1833)

George Eliot
Adam Bede (1859).
The Mill on the Floss (1860).
Silas Marner (1861).
Felix Holt (1866).
Middlemarch (1871-2).
Daniel Deronda (1876).

Rosa Guy
A Measure of Time (1983). Virago

Maxine Hong Kingston
The Woman Warrior (1975). Picador
China Men (1977). Picador

Alexandra Kollontai
Love of Worker Bees (1923). Virago
A Great Love (1923). Virago

Rosamond Lehmann
Dusty Answer (1927). Penguin
Invitation to the Waltz (1932). Virago
The Weather in the Streets (1936). Virago
The Echoing Grove (1953). Penguin

Doris Lessing
Martha Quest (1952). Granada
The Golden Notebook (1962). Granada

Paule Marshall
Brown Girl, Brownstones (1959). Virago
Praisesong for the Widow (1982). Virago

Harriet Martineau
Deerbrook (1839). Virago

Toni Morrison
The Bluest Eye (1970). Granada
Sula (1973). Granada
Song of Solomon (1977). Granada

Tillie Olsen
Tell Me A Riddle (1962). Virago
Yonnondio: From the Thirties (1974). Virago

Jean Rhys
  Good Morning, Midnight (1939). Penguin
  Wide Sargasso Sea (1966). Penguin

Dorothy Richardson
  Pointed Roofs (1915)
  Backwater (1916)
  Honeycomb (1917)
  The Tunnel (1919)
  Interim (1919)
  Deadlock (1921)
  Revolving Lights (1923)
  The Trap (1925)
  Oberland (1927)
  Dawn's Left Hand (1931)
  Clear Horizon (1935)
  Dimple Hill (1938)
  March Moonlight (1967. Posthumous). All these novels are available as
  Pilgrimage, vols 1–4, Virago.

Olive Schreiner
  From Man to Man (1926). Virago

Murasaki Shikibu
  The Tale of Genji (c. 1015). Penguin

Christina Stead
  The Man who Loved Children (1940). Penguin
  For Love Alone (1945). Virago
  Letty Fox: Her Luck (1946). Virago
  Cotters' England (1966). Virago
  Miss Herbert (The Suburban Wife) (1976). Virago

Lorna Tracy
  Amateur Passions. Love Stories? (1981). Virago

Alice Walker
  You Can't Keep a Good Woman Down (1981). The Women's Press
  The Color Purple (1983). The Women's Press

Rebecca West
  The Judge (1922). Virago

Virginia Woolf
  To the Lighthouse (1927). Penguin

Selected Bibliography

Elizabeth Abel, 'Editor's Introduction' in *Critical Inquiry*, Winter 1981.

Anna Akhmatova, *White Flock*, in Russian and English, translated and selected by Geoffrey Thurley, Oasis Books, 1978.

Sally Alexander and Barbara Taylor, 'In Defence of "Patriarchy" ' in Mary Evans (ed.), *The Woman Question*, Fontana, 1982.

Judith Arcana, *Every Mother's Son*, The Women's Press, 1983.

Shirley Ardener (ed.), *Defining Females. The Nature of Women in Society*, Croom Helm in association with the Oxford University Women's Studies Committee, 1978.

Rosemary Ashton, 'Two Velvet Peaches', an article on George Eliot's treatment of sex in the *London Review of Books*, Vol. 5, No. 3, 17 Feb–2 March 1983.

George Eliot, Oxford University Press, 1983.

Jane Austen, *Selected Letters 1796–1817*, selected and edited by R. W. Chapman, Oxford University Press, 1955.

Michèle Barrett, *Women's Oppression Today. Problems in Marxist Feminist Analysis*, Verso, 1980.

Patricia Beer, *Reader, I Married Him*, Macmillan, 1974.

Elena Gianini Belotti, *Little Girls*, Writers and Readers, 1975.

Catherine Belsey, 'Re-reading the Great Tradition' in P. Widdowson (ed.), *'Re-reading English'*, Methuen, 1982.

Walter Benjamin, *Illuminations*, Fontana, 1977.

John Berger, *Ways of Seeing*, BBC and Penguin, 1972.

C. R. Blake, *Dorothy Richardson*, University of Michigan Press, 1960.

Wayne Booth, *The Rhetoric of Fiction*, University of Chicago Press, 1983, 2nd edn.

'Freedom of Interpretation: Bakhtin and the Challenge of Feminist Criticism' in *Critical Inquiry* 9, Sept 1982.

Johanna Brenner and Maria Ramas, 'Rethinking Women's Oppression' in *New Left Review* 144, Mar/April 1984.

Shirley Brice Heath, *Ways with Words*, Cambridge University Press, 1983.

Vincent Brome, 'A Last Meeting with Dorothy Richardson' in *London Magazine*, 6 June 1959.

Steve Burniston, Frank Mort and Christine Weedon, 'Psychoanalysis and the Cultural Acquisition of Sexuality and Subjectivity' in Women's Studies Group (see below).

Marilyn Butler, *Jane Austen and the War of Ideas*, Clarendon Press, 1975.
Romantics, Rebels and Reactionaries: English Literature and its Background. 1760–1830, Oxford University Press, 1981.

Antonia Byatt, Introduction to George Eliot's *The Mill on the Floss*, Penguin, 1979.

Jenni Calder, *Women and Marriage in Victorian Fiction*, Thames & Hudson, 1976.

The Cambridge Women's Studies Group, *Women in Society: Interdisciplinary Essays*, Virago, 1981.

Angela Carter, 'The Language of Sisterhood' in Leonard Michaels and Christopher Ricks (eds), *The State of the Language*, University of California Press, 1980.
The Sadeian Woman, Virago, 1979.

Nancy Chodorow, *The Reproduction of Mothering. Psychoanalysis and the Sociology of Gender*, University of California Press, 1978.
'Mothering, Male Dominance and Capitalism' in Z. R. Eisenstein (ed.), (see below).

Helène Cixous, 'The Laugh of the Medusa' in E. Marks and I. de Courtivron (eds), (see below).

The Combahee River Collective, 'A Black Feminist Statement' in Z. R. Eisenstein (ed.), (see below).

Rosalind Coward, *Patriarchal Precedents. Sexuality and Social Relations*, Routledge & Kegan Paul, 1983.
Female Desire, Women's Sexuality Today, Paladin, 1984.

Jonathan Culler, *Structuralist Poetics*, Routledge & Kegan Paul, 1975.
Saussure, Fontana, 1976.
The Pursuit of Signs, Routledge & Kegan Paul, 1981.
On Deconstruction. Theory and Criticism after Structuralism, Routledge & Kegan Paul, 1983.

C. N. Davidson and E. M. Broner (eds), *The Lost Tradition. Mothers and Daughters in Literature*, Frederick Ungar Publishing Co., 1980.

Christine Delphy, *Close to Home. A materialist analysis of women's oppression*, translated and edited by Diana Leonard, Hutchinson in association with the Explorations in Feminism Collective, 1984.

Margaret Drabble, Introduction to Charlotte Brontë's *Villette*, Everyman, 1983.

Terry Eagleton, *Literary Theory. An Introduction*, Basil Blackwell, 1983.
Zillah R. Eisenstein (ed.), *Capitalist Patriarchy and the Case for Socialist Feminism*, Monthly Review Press, 1979.
Mary Ellman, *Thinking About Women*, Virago, 1979.
Friedrich Engels, *The Origin of the Family, Private Property and the State*, edited with an introduction by E. B. Leacock, Lawrence & Wishart, 1972.
Mary Evans (ed.), *The Woman Question. Readings on the Subordination of Women*, Fontana, 1982.
Inga-Stina Ewbank, 'Ibsen and the Language of Women' in Mary Jacobus (ed.), (see below).

Leslie Fiedler, Introduction to C. R. Blake's *Dorothy Richardson* (see above).
Eva Figes, *Patriarchal Attitudes*, Panther, 1972.
   Sex and Subterfuge. Women Writers to 1850, Macmillan, 1982.
Shulamith Firestone, *The Dialectic of Sex*, Paladin, 1972.
Viviane Forrester, 'What Women's Eyes See' in E. Marks and I. de Courtivron (eds), (see below).
E. M. Forster, *Aspects of the Novel*, Penguin, 1974.
Michel Foucault, *The History of Sexuality. Volume One. An Introduction*, translated by Robert Hurley, Penguin, 1981.
Sigmund Freud, 'The Oedipus Complex' in *General Introduction to Psychoanalysis*, translated by Joan Riviere, George Allen & Unwin, 1963.
   On Sexuality in *The Pelican Freud Library*, Vol. 7. Penguin, 1983.
Gloria G. Fromm, *Dorothy Richardson*, University of Illinois Press, 1977.

Elizabeth Gaskell, *The Life of Charlotte Brontë*, Penguin, 1975.
Xavière Gauthier, 'Is There Such a Thing as Women's Writing?' in E. Marks and I. de Courtivron (eds), (see below).
G. Genette, *Narrative Discourse*, Basil Blackwell, 1980.
Winifred Gérin, *Emily Brontë*, Oxford University Press, 1971.
Sandra M. Gilbert and Susan Gubar, *The Madwoman in the Attic: The Woman Writer and the Nineteenth-Century Literary Imagination*, Yale University Press, 1979.
Marion Glastonbury, 'The Best Kept Secret – How working-class women live and what they know' in *Women's Studies International Quarterly*, Vol. 2, 1979.
   'What Books tell Girls: A Memoir of Early Reading' in Jane Miller (ed.),

Eccentric Propositions. Essays on Literature and the Curriculum, Routledge & Kegan Paul, 1984.

John Goode, 'Woman and the Literary Text' in Juliet Mitchell and Ann Oakley (see below).

Geoffrey Gorer, 'The Myth in Jane Austen' in Wilbur Scott (ed.), *Five Approaches of Literary Criticism*, Collier Books, 1962.

Robert Graves, *The Greek Myths* (2 vols), Penguin, 1977.

Germaine Greer, *The Female Eunuch*, Granada, 1981.

Caren Greenberg, 'Reading Reading: Echo's Abduction of Language' in Sally McGonnell-Ginet, Ruth Borker and Nelly Furman (eds), (see below).

Susan Griffin, *Woman and Nature. The Roaring Inside Her*, The Women's Press, 1984.

Susan Gubar: '"The Blank Page" and the Issues of Female Creativity' in *Critical Inquiry*, Winter 1981.

Gordon S. Haight, *George Eliot: a Biography*, Oxford University Press, 1968.

Gordon S. Haight (ed.), *A Century of George Eliot Criticism*, Methuen, 1965.

C. Hamilton, *Marriage as a Trade*, The Women's Press, 1981.

Gillian E. Hanscombe, *The Art of Life. Dorothy Richardson and the Development of Feminist Consciousness*, Peter Owen, 1982.

D. W. Harding, 'Regulated Hatred: An Aspect of the Work of Jane Austen' in *Scrutiny*, Vol. VIII, No. 4, March 1940.

Introduction to Jane Austen's *Persuasion*, Penguin, 1965.

Elizabeth Hardwick, *Seduction and Betrayal. Women and Literature*, Random House, 1974.

Rachel Harrison, '*Shirley*: Relations of Reproduction and the Ideology of Romance' in Women's Studies Group (see below).

Frigga Haug, 'Morals Also Have Two Genders' in *New Left Review*, No. 143, Jan–Feb 1984.

Jeremy Hawthorn, *Multiple Personality and the Disintegration of Literary Character. From Oliver Goldsmith to Sylvia Plath*, Edward Arnold, 1983.

C. G. Heilbrun and M. R. Higonnet (eds), *The Representation of Women in Fiction*, Selected Papers from the English Institute, 1981, New Series No. 7, The Johns Hopkins University Press, 1983.

Erich Heller, *Kafka*, Fontana Modern Masters, 1974.

Claudine Herrmann, 'Women in Space and Time' in E. Marks and I. de Courtivron (eds), (see below).

Luce Irigaray, 'This Sex Which Is Not One' and 'When the Goods Get Together' in E. Marks and I. de Courtivron (eds), (see below).

Wolfgang Iser, *The Implied Reader*, Johns Hopkins University Press, 1974.
The Act of Reading, Routledge & Kegan Paul, 1978.
Mary Jacobus (ed.), *Women Writing and Writing about Women*, Croom Helm in association with Oxford University Women's Studies Committee, 1979.
'The Question of Language: Men of Maxims and *The Mill on the Floss*' in *Critical Inquiry*, Winter 1981.
Henry James, *Daniel Deronda: A Conversation* in F. R. Leavis, *The Great Tradition*, Chatto & Windus, 1948.
Selma James, *The Ladies and the Mammies. Jane Austen and Jean Rhys*, Falling Wall Press, 1983.
James Joll, *Gramsci*, Fontana Modern Masters, 1977.

Cora Kaplan, 'Radical Feminism and Literature: Rethinking Millett's *Sexual Politics*' in Mary Evans (ed.), (see above).
Introduction to Elizabeth Barrett Browning's *Aurora Leigh with other poems*, The Women's Press, 1978.
Frank Kermode: *The Sense of an Ending*, Oxford University Press, 1966.
The Genesis of Secrecy, Harvard University Press, 1979.
G. S. Kirk, *The Nature of Greek Myths*, Penguin, 1983.
Annette Kolodny, 'Turning the Lens on "The Panther Captivity": A Feminist Exercise in Practical Criticism' in *Critical Inquiry*, Winter 1981.
Julia Kristeva, *Desire in Language. A Semiotic Approach to Literature and Art*, Basil Blackwell, 1980.
'Oscillation between Power and Denial' in E. Marks and I. de Courtivron (eds), (see below).
'The Ruin of a Poetics' in *Twentieth-Century Studies*, No. 7/8.

Suzanne Langer, *Feeling and Form*, Routledge & Kegan Paul, 1953.
Marghanita Laski, *Jane Austen and her World*, Thames & Hudson, 1969.
Peter Laslett, *The World We Have Lost*, Methuen, 1979.
Family Life and Illicit Love in Earlier Generations, Cambridge University Press, 1977.
Jane Lazarre, *On Loving Men*, Virago, 1981.
F. R. Leavis, *The Great Tradition*, Chatto & Windus, 1948.
Claude Lévi-Strauss, 'The Structural Study of Myth' in A. K. Pugh, V. J. Lee and J. Swann (eds), *Language and Language Use*, Heinemann Educational Books, 1980.
G. H. Lewes, '*Shirley: a Tale*. By CURRER BELL, Author of "Jane Eyre". Smith, Elder, and Co. 1849' in *Edinburgh Review* No. CLXXXIII, January 1850.

Sally McConnell-Ginet, Ruth Borker and Nelly Furman (eds), *Women and Language in Literature and Society*, Praeger, 1980.

J. McCrindle and S. Rowbotham, *Dutiful Daughters: Women talk about their lives*, Allen Lane, 1977.

Katherine Mansfield, *Journal of Katherine Mansfield 1904–1922*, edited by John Middleton Murry, Constable, 1984.

Elaine Marks and Isabelle de Courtivron (eds), *New French Feminisms*, Schocken Books, 1981.

Harriet Martineau, *Autobiography* (2 vols), Introduction by Gaby Weiner, Virago, 1983.

John Stuart Mill, *Autobiography*, edited by Jack Stillinger, Oxford University Press, 1971.

John Stuart Mill and Harriet Taylor Mill, *The Subjection of Women* and *Enfranchisement of Women*, Introduction by Kate Soper, Virago, 1983.

Jane Miller, *Many Voices. Bilingualism, Culture and Education*, Routledge & Kegan Paul, 1983.

Jean Baker Miller, *Toward a New Psychology of Women*, Penguin, 1978.

Karl Miller, *Cockburn's Millenium*, Duckworth, 1975.

Doubles, Oxford University Press, 1985.

Kate Millett, *Sexual Politics*, Virago, 1977.

Juliet Mitchell, *Women's Estate*, Penguin, 1971.

Psychoanalysis and Feminism, Penguin, 1975.

Juliet Mitchell and Ann Oakley (eds), *The Rights and Wrongs of Women*, Penguin, 1976.

Juliet Mitchell and Jacqueline Rose (eds), *Feminine Sexuality, Jacques Lacan and the Ecole Freudienne*, Macmillan, 1982.

Rosalind Mitchison, 'The Numbers Game', a review of Peter Laslett's *Family Life and Illicit Love in Earlier Generations* (Cambridge University Press, 1977) and Lawrence Stone's *The Family, Sex and Marriage in England 1500–1800* (Weidenfeld & Nicolson, 1977) in the *New Review*, Vol. 4, No. 47, Feb. 1978.

Ellen Moers, *Literary Women*, The Women's Press, 1978.

Toril Moi, 'Representation of Patriarchy: Sexuality and Epistemology in Freud's Dora' in *Feminist Review*, No. 9, Autumn 1981.

F. W. H. Myers, *Essays Modern*, Macmillan, 1897.

Judith L. Newton, Mary P. Ryan and Judith R. Walkowitz (eds), *Sex and Class in Women's History*, History Workshop Series, Routledge & Kegan Paul, 1983.

Ann Oakley, *Sex, Gender and Society*, Temple Smith, 1972.
The Sociology of Housework, Martin Robertson, 1974.
Judith Okely, 'Privileged, Schooled and Finished: Boarding Education for Girls' in Shirley Ardener (ed.), (see above).
Tillie Olsen, *Silences*, Virago, 1980.
The Open University, *The Changing Experience of Women*, Basil Blackwell, 1984.
Ursula Owen (ed.), *Fathers. Reflections by Daughters*, Virago, 1983.

Ivy Pinchbeck, *Women Workers and the Industrial Revolution 1750–1850*, Virago, 1981.
Cathy Porter, *Alexandra Kollontai. A Biography*, Virago, 1980.
John Cowper Powys, *Dorothy Richardson*, Village Press, 1974.

Adrienne Rich, *Of Woman Born. Motherhood as Experience and Institution*, Virago, 1977.
The Dream of a Common Language. Poems 1974–1977, W. W. Norton, 1978.
On Lies, Secrets, and Silence. Selected Prose 1966–1978, Virago, 1980.
Joan Riviere, 'Hate, Greed and Aggression' in Melanie Klein and Joan Riviere, *Love, Hate and Reparation, Two Lectures*, Hogarth Press, 1937.
Jacqueline Rose, *The Case of Peter Pan or The Impossibility of Children's Fiction*, Macmillan, 1984.
Sheila Rowbotham, *Woman's Consciousness, Man's World*, Penguin, 1976.
Dreams and Dilemmas. Collected Writings, Virago, 1983.
Joanna Russ, *How to Suppress Women's Writing*, The Women's Press, 1984.

Lorna Sage, *Doris Lessing*, Methuen, 1983.
Edward W. Said, 'Travelling Theory' in *Raritan*, Winter 1982.
'Secular Criticism' in *Raritan*, Winter 1983.
Eve Kosofsky Sedgwick, 'Homophobia, Misogyny, and Capital: The Example of *Our Mutual Friend*' in *Raritan*, Winter 1983.
Marjorie Shostak, *Nisa. The Life and Words of a !Kung Woman*, Vintage, 1983.
Elaine Showalter, *A Literature of Their Own. British Women Novelists from Brontë to Lessing*, Virago (revised edn), 1982.
'Feminist Criticism in the Wilderness' in *Critical Inquiry*, Winter 1981.
'Towards a Feminist Poetics' in Mary Jacobus (ed.), (see above).
Sophocles, *The Theban Plays*, translated by E. F. Watling, Penguin, 1961.
Electra and other Plays, translated by E. F. Watling, Penguin, 1971.
P. M. Spacks, *The Female Imagination*, George Allen & Unwin, 1976.
Gayatri, C. Spivak, 'Unmaking and Making in *To the Lighthouse*' in Sally McConnell-Ginet, Ruth Borker and Nelly Furman (eds), (see above).

Leslie Stephen, *George Eliot*, Macmillan, 1902.
Sir Leslie Stephen's Mausoleum Book, edited and introduced by Alan Bell, Clarendon Press, 1977.
Lawrence Stone, *The Family, Sex and Marriage in England 1500–1800*, Penguin (abridged edn), 1979.
Patricia Stubbs, *Women and Fiction*, Methuen, 1979.
John Sturrock (ed.), *Structuralism and Since. From Lévi-Strauss to Derrida*, Oxford University Press, 1979.
Susan R. Suleiman and Inge Crosman (eds.), *The Reader in the Text. Essays on Audience and Interpretation*, Princeton University Press, 1980.

Tony Tanner, *Adultery in the Novel. Contract and Transgression*, Johns Hopkins University Press, 1979.
Robert Taubman, 'Doris Lessing and Nadine Gordimer' in *The New Pelican Guide to English Literature. Vol. 8. The Present*, edited by Boris Ford, Penguin, 1983.
Barbara Taylor, *Eve and the New Jerusalem. Socialism and Feminism in the Nineteenth Century*, Virago, 1983.
Sebastiano Timpanaro, *On Materialism*, New Left Books, 1975.
G. M. Trevelyan, *Illustrated English Social History*, Vol. 4, Penguin, 1968.
Flora Tristan, *The London Journal of Flora Tristan. 1842. The Aristocracy and the Working Class of England*, translated and introduced by Jean Hawkes, Virago, 1982.

Martha Vicinus (ed.), *A Widening Sphere. Changing Roles of Victorian Women*, Methuen, 1980.
L. S. Vygotsky, *Mind in Society. The Development of Higher Psychological Processes*, Harvard University Press, 1978.

Alice Walker, *In Search of Our Mothers' Gardens, Womanist Prose*, The Women's Press, 1984.
Michele Wallace, *Black Macho and the Myth of the Superwoman*, John Calder, 1979.
Micheline Wandor (ed.), *On Gender and Writing*, Pandora Press, 1983.
Rebecca West, *St. Augustine*, Peter Davies, 1933.
The Essential Rebecca West, introduced by Samuel Hynes, Penguin, 1983.
Raymond Williams, *The Country and the City*, Penguin, 1974.
Marxism and Literature, Oxford University Press, 1977.
Women's Studies Group, *Women Take Issue. Aspects of Women's Subordination*, Hutchinson and Centre for Contemporary Cultural Studies (University of Birmingham), 1978.

Virginia Woolf, *A Room of One's Own*, Granada, 1977.
   Three Guineas, Penguin, 1978.
   A Writer's Diary, edited by Leonard Woolf, Triad Granada, 1983.
   The Common Reader, First Series, The Hogarth Press, 1984.

Anthea Zeman, *Presumptuous Girls. Women and their World in the Serious Woman's Novel*, Weidenfeld & Nicolson, 1977.

Index

Adam, 189, 190
Adam Bede, see Eliot, George
Adelphi, 281n
Aeschylus, 105
Agamemnon, 105, 108
Agnes Grey, see Brontë, Anne
Akhmatova, Anna, 162, 279n
A la Recherche du Temps Perdu, see
  Proust, Marcel
Alexander, Sally, 286n
Amateur Passions, see Tracy, Lorna
Amis, Martin, 289n
Arcana, Judith, 115, 274n, 276n
Ardener, Edwin, 195, 283n
Ardener, Shirley, 158, 160, 278n,
  279n, 283n
Armand, Inessa, 136
Arnold, Matthew, 100
Ashford, Angela, 278n
Ashford, Daisy, 134, 278n
Ashton, Rosemary, 122, 277n
Austen, Jane, 4, 5, 6, 14, 16, 17, 20,
  32–45, 46–76, 87, 103,
  144–147, 149, 159, 163, 191,
  231, 233, 234, 250, 256, 265n,
  266n, 267n, 268n, 269n, 270n,
  276n, 278n. *Emma*, 36, 37, 40,
  42, 43, 49–51, 53, 54, 58, 61,
  64–66, 68–71, 73, 81, 113, 234,
  268n, 269n, 270n, 271n, 276n.

Mansfield Park, 50–58, 64,
  66–68, 71, 73, 74, 159, 269n,
  270n. *Northanger Abbey*, 14,
  33–35, 42, 44, 50, 54–56, 62,
  67, 71, 74, 268n, 270n.
  Persuasion, 41, 48–50, 53, 54, 58,
  62, 63, 65, 67, 68, 74, 269n,
  270n. *Pride and Prejudice*, 36,
  42–44, 47, 50–54, 61, 62, 64,
  66–68, 71, 74, 268n, 269n,
  270n, 271n. *Sense and Sensibility*,
  49, 50, 53, 54, 61, 63, 67, 68, 74,
  103, 147, 159, 269n, 270n.
  Letters, 14, 20, 44, 62, 66,
  144–146, 265n, 267n, 268n,
  270n, 278n
Austen, J. Edward, 265n
Austen-Leigh, J. E., 265n

Bakhtin, M., 26, 177, 267n, 282n
Barrett, Michèle, 286n
Bayley, John, 283n
Bell, Alan, 195, 283n
Bell, Currer, *see* Brontë, Charlotte
Berger, John, 91, 272n
Blake, C. R., 185, 281n, 283n
The Bluest Eye, see Morrison, Toni
Blythe, Ronald, 16, 266n
Booth, Wayne, 26, 267n
Brenner, Johanna, 286n, 288n

Brod, Max, 265n
Brome, Vincent, 280n, 282n
Brontë, Anne, 5, 6, 16, 77, 79, 82,
    87, 142, 143, 163. *Agnes Grey*,
    77, 79. *The Tenant of Wildfell
    Hall*, 16, 79
Brontë, Branwell, 79–84, 142
Brontë, Charlotte, 5, 6, 15, 16, 27,
    28, 32, 36, 39, 72, 75–103, 142,
    143, 148–151, 159, 163, 268n,
    271n, 272n, 273n, 274n, 278n,
    284n. *Jane Eyre*, 80, 81, 83, 85,
    166, 210, 271n, 284n. *The
    Professor*, 15, 84, 85, 98, 151,
    271n, 278n. *Shirley*, 77–79, 85,
    86, 148–151, 159, 271n, 274n,
    278n, 279n. *Villette*, 15, 27, 28,
    36, 77, 78, 85–101, 103, 104,
    147, 166, 268n, 271n, 272n,
    273n
Brontë, Emily, 5, 6, 77, 79, 81–83,
    86, 87, 142, 143, 163, 271n.
    Wuthering Heights, 77, 79, 81, 82,
    98. Emily's dog 'Keeper', 81, 82
Brontë, Patrick, 77, 79
Brown Girl, Brownstones, see
    Marshall, Paule
Bryher, 170, 281n
Butler, Marilyn, 43, 47, 58, 70,
    268n, 269n, 270n
Byatt, Antonia, 141, 278n

Carlyle, Jane, 195, 197
Carlyle, Thomas, 195, 197, 283n
Carter, Angela, 8, 25, 133, 160,
    161, 249, 250, 265n, 267n, 277n,
    279n, 288n, 289n
Castle Rackrent, see Edgeworth,
    Maria

Chamberlain, Joseph, 117
Chapman, R. W., 265n
China Men, see Kingston, Maxine
    Hong
Chodorow, Nancy, 114, 115, 276n
Chopin, Kate, 248, 276n
Cinderella, 53, 61
Clear Horizon, see Richardson,
    Dorothy
Cleopatra, 90–93, 96
Close-Up, 170, 281n
Clytemnestra, 105, 108, 109, 111,
    116, 118
Colette, 280n, 281n
The Color Purple, see Walker, Alice
The Combahee River Collective,
    236, 286n
Conrad, Joseph, 13, 167, 168, 226
'The Convalescent', *see* John, Gwen
Così Fan Tutte, 86
Cotters' England, see Stead,
    Christina
Cowper Powys, John, 183, 184, 282n
Critical Inquiry, 265n, 266n, 267n,
    268n
Culler, Jonathan, 267n

Daniel Deronda, see Eliot, George
Dawn's Left Hand, see Richardson,
    Dorothy
Deadlock, see Richardson, Dorothy
Deerbrook, see Martineau, Harriet
Delphy, Christine, 271n, 286n,
    288n
Desai, Anita, 226
Dickens, Charles, 74, 281n
Dimple Hill, see Richardson,
    Dorothy
Douglas, James, 276n

Drabble, Margaret, 273n
Dusty Answer, see Lehmann,
    Rosamond
Dybenko, P., 138

Eagleton, Terry, 26, 267n
The Echoing Grove, see Lehmann,
    Rosamond
Edgeworth, Maria, 3, 15, 47, 50,
    70, 73, 149
Edinburgh Review, 148, 274n, 278n
Electra, 108
Eliot, George, 5, 6, 16, 20–26, 30,
    32, 39, 40, 43, 48, 79, 96, 103,
    104, 115, 121–133, 139–141,
    143, 148, 149, 152–159, 163,
    184, 222, 223, 267n, 273n, 274n,
    276n, 277n, 278n. *Adam Bede*,
    26, 104, 121, 159. *Daniel
    Deronda*, 16, 20–24, 43, 115,
    122–123, 129–133, 141, 148,
    152–155, 267n, 273n, 277n,
    278n, 279n. *Felix Holt*, 104, 115,
    121–129, 274n, 277n.
    Middlemarch, 16, 23, 30, 43,
    139–141, 154, 156, 166, 268n,
    278n. *The Mill on the Floss*, 6, 23,
    79, 121, 122, 132, 141, 155–157,
    159, 197, 268n, 278n. *Silas
    Marner*, 23
Eliot, T. S., 2
Emerson, R. W., 7, 265n
Enfranchisement of Women, see Mill,
    Harriet Taylor
Engels, F., 251
Eve, 116, 189
Ewbank, Inga-Stina, 289n

Felix Holt, see Eliot, George

Fiedler, Leslie, 185, 187, 190, 191,
    193, 283n
Flaubert, G., 113
For Love Alone, see Stead, Christina
Forrester, Viviane, 28, 268n
Forster, E. M., 176, 282n
Foucault, Michel, 252–254, 288n
Freud, Sigmund, 106–111, 115,
    116, 120, 231, 269n, 274n, 275n
Fromm, Gloria, 182, 184, 185,
    282n, 283n
From Man to Man, see Schreiner,
    Olive

Gaskell, Elizabeth, 32, 81, 83, 98,
    99, 142, 268n, 271n, 272n, 273n,
    278n
Gauthier, Xavière, 282n
Genesis, 189
Genette, G., 283n
Gérin, Winifred, 82, 271n, 279n
Gilbert, Sandra, 20, 29, 266n, 267n
Gissing, George, 167
Gliddon, Anne, 157
Goethe, J. W., 170
The Golden Notebook, see Lessing,
    Doris
Gordimer, Nadine, 285n
Good Morning, Midnight, see Rhys,
    Jean
Gorer, Geoffrey, 48, 49, 70, 269n
Graves, Robert, 105, 274n
A Great Love, see Kollontai,
    Alexandra
The Great Tradition, see Leavis,
    F. R.
Greenberg, Caren, 110, 276n
Greg, Margaretta, 72
Griffin, Susan, 273n

Gubar, Susan, 20, 29, 266n, 267n
Guy, Rosa, 287n

Hamlet, 101
Hanscombe, Gillian E., 179, 186, 187, 282n, 283n
Harding, D. W., 45, 53, 59, 71, 265n, 269n, 270n
Hardwick, Elizabeth, 197, 284n
Hardy, Thomas, 113
Harrison, Rachel, 159, 279n
Haug, Frigga, 42, 268n
Hawthorn, Jeremy, 87, 89, 272n
Helen, see Edgeworth, Maria
Heller, Erich, 265n
Herrmann, Claudine, 163, 280n
Honeycomb, see Richardson, Dorothy
Hynes, Samuel, 116, 276n
In Search of our Mothers' Gardens, see Walker, Alice
Interim, see Richardson, Dorothy
Invitation to the Waltz, see Lehmann, Rosamond

Jacobus, Mary, 27, 28, 267n, 268n, 275n, 289n
James, Henry, 40, 152, 167, 168, 278n, 281n
James, Selma, 269n
James, William, 167
Jane Eyre, see Brontë, Charlotte
Jocasta, 49, 105–111, 114–116, 119, 120, 125, 131, 133, 269n, 276n
John, Gwen, 163, 164, 280n
Joyce, James, 167, 170, 281n
The Judge, see West, Rebecca

Kafka, Franz, 12, 226, 265n

Kermode, Frank, 176, 282n
Kingston, Maxine Hong, 7, 226, 257–260, 289n
Klein, Melanie, 267n, 279n
Knight, Fanny, 144–146
Kollontai, Alexandra, 135–139, 278n
Kolodny, Annette, 266n
Kristeva, Julia, 176, 177, 259, 267n, 276n, 282n, 289n
Krupskaya, Nadezhda, 136

Lacan, Jacques, 27, 177, 282n
Laius, 106–109, 114
Langer, Suzanne, 268n
Laski, Marghanita, 73, 270n, 271n
Laslett, Peter, 47, 269n, 270n
Lawrence, D. H., 167
Lazarre, Jane, 115, 276n
Lear, King, 14, 125
Leavis, F. R., 22–26, 40, 155, 156, 267n, 268n, 277n, 278n, 279n
The Left Bank, see Rhys, Jean
Lehmann, Rosamond, 199, 203–209, 223, 284n
Lenin, 135, 138
Leonard, Diana, 286n
Lessing, Doris, 31, 199, 209, 214, 220–226, 234, 285n
Letty Fox: Her Love, see Stead, Christina
Lévi-Strauss, Claude, 106, 274n
Lewes, George H., 16, 26, 75, 100, 103, 148–153, 157, 271n, 274n, 278n, 279n
The Life of Charlotte Brontë, see Gaskell, Elizabeth
A Literature of Their Own, see Showalter, Elaine

Little Review, 280n
Locke, John, 59, 140
London Magazine, 280n
London Review of Books, 283n
Love and Marriage, see Ashford,
  Daisy and Angela

McEwen, Christian, 281n
McQuilland, L. J., 276n
The Madwoman in the Attic, see
  Gilbert, Sandra and Gubar,
  Susan
Mailer, Norman, 193, 283n
The Man Who Loved Children, see
  Stead, Christina
Mansfield, Katherine, 31, 157, 279n
March Moonlight, see Richardson,
  Dorothy
Marcus, Jane, 276n, 277n
Marshall, Paule, 236–241, 249,
  286n, 287n
Martha Quest, see Lessing, Doris
Martineau, Harriet, 32, 85, 89, 94,
  101, 233, 272n, 274n
Martineau, James, 101
Marx, Karl, 225, 231, 232, 251,
  275n, 286n
The Mausoleum Book, see Stephen,
  Leslie
Melly, Diana, 284n
Meredith, George, 134
Merope, 107
Middlemarch, see Eliot, George
Middleton Murry, John, 157, 279n
Mill, Harriet Taylor, 46, 195, 196,
  269n
Mill, John Stuart, 20, 26, 45, 95,
  96, 195–197, 267n, 269n, 272n,
  283n

The Mill on the Floss, see Eliot,
  George
Miller, Jane, 266n, 267n, 285n
Miller, Karl, 272n
Millett, Kate, 87, 89, 98, 272n,
  273n
Miss Herbert (The Suburban Wife), see
  Stead, Christina
Mitchell, Juliet, 231, 250, 275n,
  286n, 288n
Mitchison, Naomi, 289n
Mitchison, Rosalind, 60, 270n
Mitford, Miss, 149
Moers, Ellen, 74, 271n, 278n
More, Hannah, 74
Morrison, Toni, 227–231, 233,
  235, 241, 248–250, 252, 285n,
  286n, 287n, 288n
Murasaki, Shikibu, 15, 266n
Myers, F. W. H., 16, 154, 266n,
  279n

National Black Feminist
  Organization, 236, 286n
Nesbit, E., 269n
New Left Review, 268n, 286n
New Review, 270n
New Statesman, 285n
Northanger Abbey, see Austen, Jane
Nussey, Ellen, 83, 84

Odle, Alan, 182
Oedipus, 15, 49, 70, 105–110, 114,
  122, 126, 129, 269n, 274n, 275n,
  277n
'The Oedipus Complex', *see* Freud,
  Sigmund
Oedipus Rex, see Sophocles
Okely, Judith, 142, 143, 278n

Olsen, Tillie, 115, 245–249, 251, 276n, 287n, 288n
Ophelia, 101
Orestes, 108
Owen, Ursula, 269n, 270n

Penelope, 143, 151
Phèdre, 116
Pilgrimage, see Richardson, Dorothy
Pinchbeck, Ivy, 72, 74, 270n, 271n
Polybus, 107
Porter, Cathy, 278n
Portrait of a Lady, see James, Henry
Praisesong for the Widow, see Marshall, Paule
The Professor, see Brontë, Charlotte
Proust, Marcel, 12, 111, 113, 167, 187, 283n

Rachel, 94, 95
Racine, Jean, 116
Raglan, Lord, 269n
Ramas, Maria, 286n, 288n
Raritan, 268n, 288n
Read, Lady, 74
Revolving Lights, see Richardson, Dorothy
Rhys, Jean, 31, 199, 203, 209–214, 234, 269n, 284n
Rich, Adrienne, 9, 33, 81, 115, 116, 257, 265n, 268n, 271n, 274n, 276n, 289n
Richardson, Dorothy, 6, 8, 11, 13, 163–193, 203, 221, 223, 265n, 280n, 281n, 282n, 283n, 285n
Riviere, Joan, 25, 267n, 274n, 279n
Roberts, Michèle, 52, 269n
A Room of One's Own, see Woolf, Virginia

Rosenberg, John, 184, 283n
Rowbotham, Sheila, 231, 286n
Rubens, P. Paul, 92
Rushdie, Salman, 226
Russ, Joanna, 266n, 267n

Sade, Marquis de, 160, 279n
Said, Edward W., 30, 31, 254, 268n, 288n
Sage, Lorna, 220, 226, 285n
St. Augustine, see West, Rebecca
Schiller, J. C. F. von, 182
Schreiner, Olive, 38
Scott, Walter, 14, 265n, 266n
Shakespeare, William, 32, 143
Shirley, see Brontë, Charlotte
Shostak, Marjorie, 279n
Showalter, Elaine, 13, 26, 27, 186, 265n, 266n, 267n, 275n, 283n
Silences, see Olsen, Tillie
Sinclair, May, 167, 280n
Song of Solomon, see Morrison, Toni
Sophocles, 106–110, 116, 133, 274n, 275n, 276n, 277n
Southey, Robert, 77, 78, 100, 271n
Spock, Dr Benjamin, 111
Stalin, J., 138, 278n
Stead, Christina, 31, 199, 203, 209, 214–220, 222, 234, 284n, 285n
Steedman, Carolyn, 277n, 278n
Stephen, Julia, 195–198
Stephen, Leslie, 100, 141, 152–156, 195–198, 202, 278n, 279n, 283n
Stevenson, Robert Louis, 152, 279n
Stone, Lawrence, 59, 60, 270n
The Subjection of Women, see Mill, John Stuart

Sula, see Morrison, Toni

The Tale of Genji, see Murasaki,
    Shikibu
Tanner, Tony, 275n, 276n
Taubman, Mary, 280n
Taubman, Robert, 285n
Taylor, Barbara, 286n
Taylor, James, 39, 268n
Tell Me a Riddle, see Olsen, Tillie
The Tenant of Wildfell Hall, see
    Brontë, Anne
Thackeray, William, 78, 84, 89, 90,
    134, 271n
Thatcher, Margaret, 190
Thomas à Kempis, 155
Tolstoy, Leo, 113, 134, 179
Tracy, Lorna, 255, 288n
The Trap, see Richardson, Dorothy
Trevelyan, G. M., 73, 271n
Trilling, Lionel, 113, 131, 193,
    276n, 283n
Tristan, Flora, 260, 289n
Trollope, Anthony, 266n
Trotsky, Leon, 138, 278n
The Tunnel, see Richardson,
    Dorothy
Turgenev, Ivan, 179
Typhoon, see Conrad, Joseph

Ulysses, 14, 143
Vashti, 94–96, 100
Villette, see Brontë, Charlotte

Wallace, Michele, 286n
Walker, Alice, 227, 241–245, 248,
    249, 274n, 285n, 286n, 287n,
    288n
The Weather in the Streets, see
    Lehmann, Rosamond
Wells, H. G., 164, 179, 277n
West, Anthony, 277n
West, Rebecca, 6, 115–122,
    124–127, 276n, 277n
Wide Sargasso Sea, see Rhys, Jean
Wollstonecraft, Mary, 27, 143
The Woman Warrior, see Kingston,
    Maxine Hong
Woolf, Leonard, 198
Woolf, Virginia, 9, 13, 32, 82, 100,
    156, 157, 184–186, 188, 193,
    197–203, 208, 223, 226, 248,
    249, 255, 265n, 268n, 271n,
    274n, 279n, 283n, 284n, 285n,
    288n
Wright, Richard, 227
Wyndham, Francis, 209, 210, 212,
    213, 284n

Yonge, Charlotte, 269n
Yonnondio, see Olsen, Tillie
*You Can't Keep a Good Woman
    Down, see* Walker, Alice

Zeman, Anthea, 35, 36, 58, 266n,
    268n, 270n